Dancefilm

Dancefilm

Choreography and the Moving Image

ERIN BRANNIGAN

OXFORD

UNIVERSITY PRESS

New York

OXFORD
UNIVERSITY PRESS

Oxford University Press, Inc., publishes works that further
Oxford University's objective of excellence
in research, scholarship, and education.

Oxford   New York
Auckland   Cape Town   Dar es Salaam   Hong Kong   Karachi
Kuala Lumpur   Madrid   Melbourne   Mexico City   Nairobi
New Delhi   Shanghai   Taipei   Toronto

With offices in
Argentina   Austria   Brazil   Chile   Czech Republic   France   Greece
Guatemala   Hungary   Italy   Japan   Poland   Portugal   Singapore
South Korea   Switzerland   Thailand   Turkey   Ukraine   Vietnam

Published by Oxford University Press, Inc.
198 Madison Avenue, New York, New York 10016
www.oup.com

Library of Congress Cataloging-in-Publication Data
Brannigan, Erin.
   Dancefilm : choreography and the moving image / Erin Brannigan.
      p. cm.
Includes bibliographical references and index.
ISBN 978-0-19-536723-2; ISBN 978-0-19-536724-9 (pbk.)
   1. Dance in motion pictures, television, etc.
   2. Choreography.   I. Title.   II. Title: Dance film.
   GV1779.B73 2010
   792.8'2   [22] 2009044232

Recorded video examples (marked in text with ⏵) are available online at www.oup.com/us/dancefilm.
Access with username Music5 and password Book1745.
For more information on Oxford Web Music, visit www.oxfordwebmusic.com.

Printed in the United States of America
on acid-free paper

For Mum and Dad, Maura and Peter Brannigan

Preface

A field of activity involving dance and the moving image, which has been referred to as videodance, screen dance, and cinedance (among other things), provided the initial inspiration for this book. I will use the term *screen dance* to refer to these predominantly short films and videos made by collaborative director/choreographer teams, such as director David Hinton's work with DV8 Physical Theatre and Clara van Gool's work with Jordi Cortès Molina, or choreographers who have also taken on the role of director as in the case of Amy Greenfield, Anna de Manincor, Philippe Decouflé, Wim Vandekeybus, and Miranda Pennell. Over the past few decades, such work has become a significant activity for major dance companies, independent choreographers, and certain film directors. It has been funded and broadcast by television stations such as the U.K.'s BBC and NPS in the Netherlands, and has caused a network of dedicated screen dance festivals to emerge across the world.[1] Most recently, this field of activity has been expanded by artists, curators, and funding bodies, reconnecting dance with a tradition of technologically mediated performance and reception begun by Loïe Fuller and interfacing with contemporary visual arts practices in new media.

In *Dancefilm: Choreography and the Moving Image*, I consider strategically selected single-screen examples from this recent body of work that has been identified, contextualized, and promoted through curated programmes and competitions, within the much broader history of screen practices, which I will call *dancefilm*. Dancefilm is understood as a modality that appears across various types of films including the musical and experimental shorts and is characterized by a *filmic performance* dominated by choreographic strategies or effects. My starting point then became specific works from across this expanded field of dancefilm that exemplify particular common approaches or themes: an interest in gesture or the close-up, in the corporeal facility of the dancing "star" or the transference of movement across people and things. Rather than plotting a comprehensive history of dancefilm or creating a canon of key works, my aim in this book is to reexamine and repropose the parameters of dancefilm through the questions raised by these specific approaches to the form. How is the concept and practice of choreography reconfigured for the screen? What filmmaking techniques are appropriate for the production of screen choreographies?

---

[1] In 2002, a meeting between screen dance festival directors at Monaco Dance Forum listed twenty annual and biannual festivals dedicated to screen dance in countries as diverse as Argentina, Canada, Russia, and Australia. Monaco Dance Forum 2002 hosted the largest festival, IMZ Dance Screen. Since then new festivals have developed in countries such as Israel, Hungary, Hong Kong, and Indonesia, expanding the number of festivals to around forty.

Can we determine where the dance ends and the dancefilm begins? What kinds of film structures or forms are best suited to dancefilm?

In using the term *dancefilm* I do not mean to negate work made using video or digital technologies, but to include these newer formats in a term that recognizes a continuity between the earliest screen practices and the most current. This is in response to some writing on *screen dance* that uses terms such as *dance video* to suggest that recent work constitutes an entirely new and autonomous genre.[2] *Dancefilm: Choreography and the Moving Image* reveals how dancefilm practices found in early cinema, the historic avant-garde, and Hollywood's classical era resonate with recent dancefilm examples and are significant regarding broader cinematic innovations. This strategy is supported by concepts from cinema studies that have been essential in developing new interdisciplinary terminology, and the term *dancefilm* reflects this approach.[3]

Fundamental to this book is an understanding of *filmic performance* as a comprehensive term incorporating all aspects of cinematic production, so that the choreographic quality of the dancefilm can be considered in relation to both the profilmic and filmic elements. For if the *profilmic* refers to the events as they occur in real time at the moment of filming, and *filmic* to the elements of the final screen version, both are equally important when dealing with the parameters of both dance and film in dancefilm. Laleen Jayamanne's definition provides my working model of the term:

> In film the lighting, editing, camera distance, and movement are equally potent "performers," so that one could talk of *filmic performance* as including all these technical elements. These elements can transform the phenomenal body to such an extent that one could say that the body that cinema materialises did not exist prior to the invention of film.[4]

Jayamanne provides a model of filmic performance that is particularly useful for analyzing dancefilm, leading from a discussion of hybridity to one of transformation. The dance that is realized in dancefilm did not exist prior to the invention of film and needs to be considered entirely in terms of its cinematic manifestation.

In the films under discussion in this book, the cinematic process is written through by a variety of choreographic operations. This, I will argue, is a crucial defining feature of dancefilm and is important in understanding the key element of *movement* that links the two forms of dance and film. Choreography and cinema share an intense interest in moving bodies and their relation to space and time. Both could be considered *moving arts*, interrogating the nature and quality of movement and producing new varieties of movement through their work with the body, theater design, mise en scène, objects, camera, edit, and postproduction effects. Dance and film meet in *a cinema of movement* where a dancerly or choreographic approach to filmmaking emphasizes exceptional movement on various levels of filmic

---

[2] For example, Douglas Rosenberg writes of a "transition from film (cine-dance) to video (video dance) in the late 1960s" ("Video Space: A Site for Choreography," *Leonardo* 33, 4 [2000]: 275).

[3] It could also be argued that the original and extreme differences between the image quality of film and video have been reduced through improvements in video technology and that the common practice of transferring from film to video before postproduction has further complicated the aesthetic distinction between the two formats.

[4] Laleen Jayamanne quoted in Lesley Stern, "As Long As This Life Lasts," *PHOTOFILE* (Winter 1987): 18. (My emphasis.)

production. The variety of movements featured in dancefilm are produced through the cinematic process and can be of any nature: the movement of a body part, crowd, object or graphic detail, and may be animated by outside forces such as natural elements or technological manipulation. It is these movements that create the *cine-choreographies* that constitute filmic performance in dancefilm. The lack of distinction between filmic and choreographic elements suggested here places "straight" documentations of dance performances beyond the parameters of my project. Rather, my aim is to identify and describe work that constitutes new choreographic practices specifically for the screen.

Acknowledgments

First and foremost I would like to thank Jodi Brooks for her support over the duration of this twelve-year project. Without her advice and guidance I could not have completed this book. I would also like to thank others who have offered valuable feedback throughout: Ross Harley, Elizabeth Dempster, Philipa Rothfield, Lisa Trahair, Richard Smith, Jonathan Bollen, Tara Forrest, Julie-Anne Long, Martin del Amo, Lesley Stern, Ramsay Burt, George Kouvaros, Andrew Humphries, and Amanda Card. And thank you to Norman Hirschy at Oxford University Press who has been so patient and helpful.

For their assistance during my research I would like to acknowledge the Nederlands Filmmuseum (Amsterdam), Theater Instituut Nederlands (Amsterdam), Cinématèque de la Danse (Paris), Centre de ressources musique et danse (Paris), Videotheque du Paris (Paris), New York Public Library (New York), Deutsches Tanzarchiv (Cologne), The Kitchen Library (New York), Dance Films Association (New York), The Video Place (London), and Surrey University (Surrey). Thanks also to those kind friends who showed me true hospitality during my travels: Donatella Saccani and Marilena Riccio, Joanne Manning, Sebastian Schneiders, Klaus and Goodren in Cologne, the Gallois family in Paris, Kathy Mattick and Chris Miller, and the Westbury family in London. Individuals who have offered research information and assistance include Christiane Hartter, Françoise Vanhems, Nicolas Villodre, Nico de Klerk, Giovanni Lista, Ellen Bromberg, Sherril Dodds, Deirdre Towers, Douglas Rosenberg, Maryvonne Neptune, Michèle Prélonge, David Hinton, Wendy Houstoun, Margie Medlin, Gina Czarnecki, Michelle Mahrer, Mahalya Middlemist, Claudia Rosiny, and Elisa Vaccarino. Thanks also to my support gang at the University of New South Wales: Briony Trezise, Sean Pryor, Clare Grant, and Meg Mumford. And thanks to Andrew Lancaster and Glenn Thompson for technical advice and support and Lisa Ffrench for pretending to be interested in my daily word count.

A special thanks to my family for their support over the duration of this project, especially my husband Joseph Westbury who has had a gut full of dancefilm, my parents Maura and Peter Brannigan, and my brother Sean who have also helped so much with the two children who arrived during this project—our daughter Sunny and son Billy.

I would also like to acknowledge support from the Faculty of Arts and Social Sciences, University of New South Wales (Publishing Subvention) and the Australian Academy of the Humanities Publication Subsidies Scheme.

Contents

About the Companion Web Site

www.oup.com/us/dancefilm

Oxford University Press has created a password-protected Web site to accompany *Dancefilm: Choreography and the Moving Image*.

Film examples and excerpts are signaled throughout the text with the symbol ⦿. Visiting the Web site at these points in the text you can watch high-resolution clips that are analyzed in the book, supporting the reader's journey through the text.

On the Web site you will also find links to other clips and excerpts discussed in the book that are available online, some on the artists' Web sites where further information including distribution details are available.

You may access the Web site with username Music5 and password Book1745.

VIDEO 2.1
Hands (1995, d. Adam Roberts)
Film courtesy of Adam Roberts and Concord Media. For more information on Adam Roberts and for distribution details, visit www.adamroberts.eu. For information on Concord Media visit www.concordmedia.co.uk. Hands features on Forward Motion: www.britishcouncil.org/forwardmotion

VIDEO 2.2
Monoloog van Fumiyo Ikeda op het einde van Ottone, Ottone (1989, d. Anne Teresa De Keersmaeker and Walter Verdin)
Film courtesy of Walter Verdin. For distribution details visit www.rosas.be and www.walterverdin.com

VIDEO 2.4
Element (1973, d. Amy Greenfield)
Film courtesy of Amy Greenfield. For distribution details (for educational only), visit www.canyoncinema.com (USA) or www.cjcinema.org and www.cjcatalogue.org (Europe).

VIDEO 2.5
Transport (1971, d. Amy Greenfield)
Film courtesy of Amy Greenfield. For distribution details visit www.canyoncinema.com (USA) or www.cjcinema.org and www.cjcatalogue.org (Europe).

VIDEO 2.6
Resonance (1991, d. Stephen Cummins and Simon Hunt)
Clip copyright Stephen Cummins and Australian Film Commission, courtesy of Frameline. For distribution details visit www.frameline.org

VIDEO 2.7
Vivarium (1993, d. Mahalya Middlemist)
Film courtesy of Mahalya Middlemist. Performance and choreography by Sue-ellen Kohler. For more information on Mahalya Middlemist and distribution details, visit www.vivariummedia.net

VIDEO 3.1
boy (1995, d. Peter Anderson and Rosemary Lee)
Clip courtesy of the Arts Council of England. boy features on Forward Motion: www.britishcouncil.org/forwardmotion. For more information on Rosemary Lee's work visit www.rescen.net & www.artsadmin.co.uk

VIDEO 3.2
Magnetic North (2005, d. Miranda Pennell)
Clip courtesy of Miranda Pennell. For more information and distribution details visit www.mirandapennell.com

VIDEO 4.4
Touched (1994, d. David Hinton)
Clip courtesy of the Arts Council of England. Touched features on Forward Motion: www.britishcouncil.org/forwardmotion. For more information on Wendy Houstoun visit www.wendyhoustoun.com

VIDEO 5.2
Infected (2001, Gina Czarnecki)
Film clip courtesy FORMA Arts & Media Ltd. Supported by Arts Council England. For distributor details visit www.forma.org.uk

VIDEO 5.3
Scrub Solo Series (1999–2001, d. Antonin De Bemels)
Clip courtesy of Antonin De Bemels. Distribution: info@videographe.qc.ca (Videographe, Montreal, Canada) and info@nimk.nl (Netherlands Media Art Institute). For information on Antonin De Bemels visit www.antonindb.be

VIDEO 7.2
da nero a nero. Tempo per pensare (1999, d. Anna de Manincor)
Clip courtesy of Anna de Manincor. For more distribution details and information on Anna de Manincor visit: www.zimmerfrei.co.it

Dancefilm

Introduction

Between Dance and Film

*...the affinity between the dance and the movies seems unquestionable....
[D]ifficulties arise, however, when the camera abandons its role as the mere
recorder of movement and begins to assert its own personality.*

Walter Sorell[1]

The nature of dance performance has been irrevocably altered by the cinema. There are many examples of choreographic practices that have resulted from contact with the cinematic process.[2] New, intimate dances located on corporeal surfaces and specific bodily sites have become the subject of films shot primarily in close-up. The gestural language of dramatic screen performance has been informed by, and informs, choreographic practice to produce moments of gestural dance. Various forms of editing such as jump cuts and matches-on-action have enabled new forms of dance as choreographic continuity is spread across bodies and locations, or non-figural dance is produced from inanimate objects. Challenging dances that elude perception in performance are presented to the camera to be both revealed and manipulated through the use of experimental film techniques. Show dancing has been "restaged" on city streets in film musicals that choreograph the shift from everyday activities to corporeal extremes. Such films, which are the subject of this book, indicate the extent to which choreography has impacted upon the screen arts. They stage dance as one performative element within the cinematic field, often turning the films themselves into dances.

Alongside forms of *cine-choreography* in dancefilm there is another aspect to the influence that cinema has had upon the choreographic arts: film *in* dance. As U.K.-based choreographer Wendy Houstoun states, "once you've done film work it's very hard to go back to rough and ready theatre—you start manipulating it until it's nearly like a film."[3] This has resulted in *cinematic* approaches to the composition and

---

[1] Walter Sorell, *The Dance Through the Ages* (London: Thames and Hudson, 1967), 291.

[2] My discussion here does not include the use of film or video as a component of stage productions. The earliest use of this kind of multimedia stage design is Rolf de Maré's *Relâche* for Ballets Suédois in 1924, which featured René Clair and Francis Picabia's film classic *Entr'acte* (1924). This was followed by Ballets Russes's *Ode* in 1928 (Lynn Garafola, "Dance, Film, and the Ballets Russes," *Dance Research* 16, 1 [1998]: 17). On this early history of multimedia performance, see also Felicia McCarren's chapter, "Ballets without Bodies," in *Dancing Machines: Choreographies of the Age of Mechanical Reproduction* (California: Stanford University Press, 2003, 99–127). A more recent history of this stage practice is outlined by Jochen Schmidt as including works by Trisha Brown (*A String* 1966), Hans Van Manen (*Live* 1979), Pina Bausch (*Waltzes* 1982), Jerome Robbins (*I'm Old Fashioned* 1983), and William Forsythe (*Slingerland* 1990) (Jochen Schmidt, "Exploitation or Symbiosis," *Ballett International* 1 [1991]: 97).

[3] Unpublished interview with the author, February, 1999.

staging of dance that demonstrates the long and multifaceted history of hybrid approaches to dance and film.

The influence of film on *popular* dance goes as far back as the earliest years of cinema. Marshall and Jean Stearns describe an example of "cultural feedback" in dance in the early twentieth century involving film. An African dance called the Giouba was transported to America, where it was known as the Juba. The Patting Juba involved a rhythmic slapping of hands on the body and was the influence behind the crossing and uncrossing of hands on knees in the Charleston. Performed by Joan Crawford in the film *Our Dancing Daughters* (1928, d. Hunt Stromberg), the step fed back into popular mainstream dance.[4] Stearns and Stearns also describe how the Makwaya people of Northern Rhodesia began mimicking the tap dancers they had seen in Hollywood films in the 1940s, bringing the form full-circle from its African origins.[5] There are also accounts of "slow-motion" dancing in African American revues of the jazz age, including Tommy Woods's performance in the Broadway show *Shuffle Along*.[6]

The influence of cinema was also apparent on the classical stage of the early twentieth century. Lynn Garafola's account of the parallel development of cinema and the Ballets Russes includes an encounter between the company and the Futurists during their stay in Rome around 1917.[7] The Futurists were producing many films at the time and this influenced company choreographer Léonard Massine, resulting in a collaboration with Giacomo Balla, *Feu d'artifice*. This performance involved "a light show played on a setting of geometrical solids," which Garafola says "most closely approximated film."[8] Jean Cocteau and Bronislava Nijinska also used cinematic effects such as slow-motion action, freezes, and silent film characters in their ballets, including *Le Train Bleu* (1924), and Garafola lists many other ballets from the first few decades of the twentieth century that utilized "film as a setting and a mimetic device."[9] Garafola and Jane Pritchard also suggest that Ballets Russes choreographer Michel Fokine was influenced by the new, more subdued acting style of the silent cinema in his revolutionary opposition to balletic pantomime, aiming to "replace gestures of the hands by [a] mimetic of the whole body."[10]

Cinematic effects are increasingly evident in contemporary dancework, facilitated by ever more sophisticated theater technology. These effects include editing a series of jumps with a strobe to create the illusion of flight, framing stage space through lighting to mimic a close-up, or creating a piece as a series of discrete "scenes" separated by a black-out. One of the most significant choreographers to have been influenced by cinema in creating her live work is Pina Bausch. German dance critic Jochen Schmidt has stated that, "German dance theatre found a new form" derived from painting and film—collage and montage—and concludes, "the works of Pina Bausch are much closer to an Eisenstein movie than to classical or

[4] Marshall and Jean Stearns, *Jazz Dance: The Story of American Vernacular Dance* (New York: Da Capo Press, 1994), 29.
[5] Ibid, 16.
[6] Constance Valis Hill, *Brotherhood in Rhythm: The Jazz Tap Dancing of the Nicholas Brothers* (New York: Oxford University Press, 2000), 26.
[7] Garafola (1998), 12–14.
[8] Ibid, 13. According to Garafola, the Futurists produced four films in 1916 (12–13).
[9] Ibid, 16–17.
[10] Ibid, 4–5, and Jane Pritchard, "Movement on the Silent Screen," *Dance Theatre Journal* 12, 3 (1996): 29.

narrative ballet."[11] Ana Sanchez-Colberg describes Bausch's revolutionary stagework that introduced methods as early as 1976 that "have by now become staple choreographic devices." Sanchez-Colberg lists them as "montage, cross-fades, fade-outs, and foreground/background contrast...translated into the stage space." These devices in turn "allowed for a game with time and space which challenged the linear, syntactical approach favoured by most theatrical dance."[12] Composers are also now often used as "sound engineers" to create soundtracks for performance, and action is being sped up and intensified to compete with cinematic possibilities.

In Bob Morris's 1989 article on New York's younger generation of postmodern choreographers and their engagement with filmic aesthetics, he writes of two generations of dance practitioners who have drawn inspiration from the screen:

> For the most part it was film's formal, graphic, even spiritual quality that intrigued choreographers through the Sixties and Seventies. Representing a New York cross section of the most recent activity in the field, postmodern choreographers [Yoshiko] Chumo, [Stephen] Petronio, and [Fred] Holland have shifted with the rest of the avant-garde toward the narrative, humorous, splashy, and emotional.[13]

Morris refers here to an earlier interest within the New York avant-garde dance scene in the formal qualities of film, citing the work of Merce Cunningham, Twyla Tharp, and the choreographers associated with the Judson Church.[14] Writing in 1989, Morris found that this interest had combined with generic and narrative references in the work of the next generation of choreographers—a generation for whom the cinema has figured as prominently in their artistic development as the stage.

Morris's observations remain relevant at the end of the twentieth century and into the twenty-first. William Forsythe has used film as an influence on his process, having his dancers improvise to sequences from *Alien* (1979, d. Ridley Scott) and *Aliens* (1986, d. James Cameron) in his stage work *Alie/na(c)tion* (1992), translating the two-dimensional images into "a physical reading."[15] Ian Bramley writes that, in London, choreographers Mark Murphy and Matthew Bourne have "sourced their artistic vision in examples from the big screen....Bourne...happily cites Fred Astaire as a hero and the screen musical as an abiding influence....Murphy's lore comes from...a darker canon that includes Scorcese, Coppola, Hartley, Kubrik, and 'particularly David Lynch.'"[16] The global shift outlined here, as a generation of choreographers draw on their familiarity with film culture, evidences an increasing openness on the part of dance practitioners to cinema as a cultural, structural, and aesthetic influence and a key reference point.

[11] Jochen Schmidt quoted in Ann Daly, "Tanztheater: The Thrill of the Lynch Mob or the Rage of a Woman?" *Critical Gestures: Writings on Dance and Culture* (Middletown, Connecticut: Wesleyan University Press, 2002), 12.

[12] Ana Sanchez-Colberg, "Reflections on Meaning and Making in Pina Bausch's *The Lament of the Empress*," in *Parallel Lines: Media Representations of Dance*, ed. Stephanie Jordan and Dave Allen (London: John Libbey and Co., 1993), 219–20.

[13] Bob Morris, "35mm Motions," *Film Comment* 25, 2 (1989): 47.

[14] Idem.

[15] Roslyn Sulcas, "Forsythe and Film: Habits of Seeing," in *Envisioning Dance on Film and Video*, ed. Judy Mitoma (New York and London: Routledge, 2002), 99. See also Bill T. Jones on cinematic staging in "Dancing and Cameras," in Mitoma 2002, 102.

[16] Ian Bramley, "Return of the Narrative," *Dance Theatre Journal* 14, 4 (1999): 26.

This brief account of some of the ways that cinema has influenced the development of choreography in the twentieth and twenty-first centuries contrasts with much of the current writing on dancefilm.[17] While practitioners have embraced and explored the potential of the points of contact between dance and film, critics and theorists have struggled to reconcile the two forms in their analysis of the same, and it is this gap in critical theory that has shaped my approach to this project. The lack of development in discourse on dancefilm could be seen as the result of a stand off, a no man's land that is reflective of current structures of institutionalized thought.

Dance writing on dancefilm has generally entered the discussion with an overwhelming bias toward the profilmic choreographic content and the primary condition of live performance, in the tradition of Walter Sorell's opening quote from 1967. There is also a general lack of engagement with film theory even though this field of critical inquiry has covered many of the recurring issues in relation to screen performance more broadly. Film theory offers approaches to the moving body and the moving image that are particularly valuable for developing discussions of dancefilm in relation to screen performance, cinematic presence and gestural articulation, categories of cinematic movement, framing and editing, spectatorship, and the historical film avant garde.

This resistance is perhaps symptomatic of the "collaboration anxiety" filtering throughout the process of dancefilm (sometimes including production), which here takes the form of a reluctance on the part of dance writers to take on film culture, which makes up half of the creative equation.[18] This body of writing does, however, foreground two pivotal issues. First, this work indicates the increasing significance of film and video within the broader culture of dance, tracing its development and

---

[17] Six books have been published in the last sixteen years on the subject of screen dance: Jordan and Allen, 1993; Elisa Vaccarino, *La Musa dello schermo freddo* (Genova: Kosta and Nolan, 1996); Claudia Rosiny, *Videotanz: Panorama einer intermedialen Kunstforum* (Zurich: Chronos Verlag, 1999a); Sherril Dodds, *Dance On Screen: Genres and Media from Hollywood to Experimental Art* (Houndmills, Basingstoke, Hampshire: Palgrave, 2001); Mitoma, 2002; and Katrina McPherson, *Making Video Dance* (London and New York: Routledge, 2006). Conference papers have been published: Opensource {Videodance} Symposium, eds. Simon Fildes and Katrina McPherson (Nairnshire, Scotland: Goat Media, 2007); Opensource {Videodance} Symposium 2007, eds. Simon Fildes and Katrina McPherson (Nairnshire, Scotland: Goat Media, 2009); and others such as Screendance Proceedings (American Dance Festival, Duke University, Durham USA, 2006 and 2008) and moves08: movement on screen are available online at www.dvpg.net and www.movementon-screen.org.uk respectively. While questions around naming and categorizing dancefilm persist, new topics for discussion have included the challenge to gravity that certain dancefilms represent, the idea that the form has reached a limit or point of exhaustion and the role of curation in defining the form. And there are numerous articles in publications such as Dance Theatre Journal, Dance Research Journal, Ballett International, and Writings on Dance by writers such as Virginia Brooks, Harro Eisele, Vera Maletic, Sarah Rubidge, Annie Bozzini, and Jane Pritchard that have progressed debates on dancefilm. Most recently, Erin Manning has included diverse examples of dancefilm into her interdisciplinary approach to "a new philosophy of movement" in *Relationscapes: Movement, Art, Philosophy* (Cambridge, Massachusetts, 2009). Manning's project shares with my own an interest in dance, certain theorists (Bergson, Deleuze) and concepts (affect, gesture, potential), however this publication has been too recent to incorporate into my project here.

[18] There are some exceptions to this generalization regarding dance writing on dancefilm and the absence of film theory. Amy Greenfield refers to Hugo Munsterberg's 1916 publication The Film: A Psychological Study (New York: Dover Publications, 1970) in her essay, "Filmdance: Space, Time and Energy," in the Filmdance Festival program (New York: The Experimental Intermedia Foundation, 1983), 1–6; Virginia Brooks writes: "Some theories on how we attend to film suggest that an interaction between the dynamic content and the substantive content of a shot determines the best duration for that shot to remain on the screen" ("Movement in Fixed Space and Time," Ballett International 3 [1993b]: 26). Both Helen Simondson and Douglas Rosenberg quote the same passage from Walter Benjamin's "The Work of Art in the Age of Mechanical Reproduction" and both refer to his notion of "aura" to support a progression in the dancefilm debate from a privileging of the profilmic event (Helen Simondson, "Stranger in a Strange Land," in Is Technology the Future? Greenmill 1995, ed. Hilary Trotter [Canberra: Australian Dance Council, 1996], 148, and Douglas Rosenberg, "Video Space: A Site for Choreography," *Leonardo* 33, 4 [2000]: 280). Sherril Dodds also refers to this Benjamin essay (2001, 151) and compares the dancefilm work of Billy Cowie and Liz Aggiss to German Expressionist cinema in "Screen Divas: A Filmic Expression of the Grotesque Aesthetic," in *Anarchic Dance*, ed. Liz Aggiss and Billy Cowie with Ian Bramley (London: Routledge, 2006), 127–41.

growing popularity. Second, the writing reflects the historical function of these films and videos in documenting and advocating a relatively marginalized performing art. But the preservation and advocacy functions of dance on film need to be distinguished from the analysis of a discrete art form. The generic boundaries are crystal clear for Dave Allen, who confidently states:

> A clear distinction needs to be made here between those programmes which seek to re-present existing dance on the screen in order to make the work more widely available…and other works in which directors, choreographers, and dancers attempt to address themselves to the nature of the medium and create *dance* film video specifically to be screened.[19]

Allen's essay draws dancefilm's various influences together: early cinema, the musical, avant-garde cinema, advertising, popular dance, music video, and even feature film opening sequences. Following Allen, developments in dancefilm from across the twentieth century are referred to throughout *Dancefilm: Choreography and the Moving Image* to substantiate the proposition that issues of collaboration, hybridity, and transformation have been addressed and processed in production, outstripping the surrounding critical debates.

While dance studies has often kept its distance from debates in film theory, film theory has also avoided dialogue with issues in dance studies.[20] In writings on the film musical, which come mostly from film studies, for example, there is a marked absence of dance theory.[21] And discussions of "cine-dance" in important publications in 1967 and 1983, with contributions from Shirley Clarke, Jonas Mekas, and Amy Greenfield, fail to give a clear account of the choreographic contribution to dancefilm.[22] As Roger Copeland argues, the earlier publication formulates an abstract concept of dance to support the experimental practices of the artists represented, but then he, in turn, gets caught up in definitions and terminology, only touching on promising examples for analysis.[23]

Dance theory offers understandings of the moving body and its ability to produce and express meaning that are particularly useful for addressing both popular film genres and other categories of dancefilm. In *Dancefilm: Choreography and the Moving Image* I draw on the early dance commentaries of the French Symbolists, dance historians on the form and structure of classical ballet and the artistic practice of the first "modern" dancers, French dance theory on the production of original movement in

[19] Dave Allen, "Screening Dance," in Jordan and Allen 1993, 26.

[20] One recent exception is Karen Pearlman's *Cutting Rhythms: Shaping the Film Edit*, (Amsterdam: Focal Press, 2009), a guide to editing applying a choreographic understanding of rhythm to the craft.

[21] One exception is Adrienne L. McLean whose analysis of Judy Garland's on-screen performance draws on dance theory. McLean describes the tension enacted between Garland's actual physicality, what dance theorist Susan Leigh Foster calls the "meat-and-bones," and the body disciplines associated with Hollywood studio system ideals, including dance techniques associated with the "show dancing" featured in musicals ("Feeling and the Filmed Body: Judy Garland and the Kinesics of Suffering," *Film Quarterly* 55, 3 [2002], 2–15). McLean has followed this interdisciplinary approach in her monographs: Being Rita Hayworth: Labor, Identity, and Hollywood Stardom (New Brunswick: Rutgers University Press, 2005) and *Dying Swans and Madmen: Ballet, the Body and Narrative Cinema* (New Brunswick: Rutgers University Press, 2008).

[22] The "Cine-dance" issue of Dance Perspectives 30 (1967) and Filmdance Festival program (New York: The Experimental Intermedia Foundation, 1983).

[23] Roger Copeland, "The Limitations of Cine-dance," Filmdance Festival program (New York: The Experimental Intermedia Foundation, 1983), 7–11. What Copeland does provide in his essay is an exciting map of potential films for discussion including work by: René Clair, Ralph Steiner, Charles Eames, Emile Cohl, Leni Riefenstahl, Jean Vigo, Max Ophuls, and Jean Renoir. (This type of list is matched only by Peter Wollen and Vicky Allan in "A-Z of Cinema: D-Dance," Sight and Sound 6, 9 [1996]: 28–31.)

contemporary dance, various approaches to the relation between dance and everyday movement, commentaries on social dance forms, and the writings of Yvonne Rainer and others on the aesthetics of postmodern dance.[24] To read the choreographic in film it seems essential to draw on the knowledges developed in dance studies.

The terms for analysis of dancefilm set up in dance writing have often restricted discussion to a comparison between live and filmed dance, between documentation and filming dance created for the camera, and general observations regarding the place of contemporary work within the history of dancefilm practice. What is required are new definitions of the parameters of the form in keeping with the radical practices found across the generic breadth and historical depth of the field, and new terms for the dancefilm operations found in such work. *Dancefilm: Choreography and the Moving Image* is the first book to chart this theoretical territory by mobilizing ideas from both dance and film studies, along with philosophy, cultural theory, and artists' accounts of their own practice, in order to develop a more rigorous and productive approach to analyzing dancefilm.

The interdisciplinary status of contemporary dance-based short films and videos, and the issues raised by this condition, provides a chance to look at a hybrid practice that can be traced both back in time, as well as outward to a variety of cross-cultural activities. I find points of contact between the concurrent birth of modern dance and cinema and a new understanding of the conditions of movement, between an historical moment in avant-garde dance in the second-half of the twentieth century and an exploration into registering dance on film, and between the popularity of the dance musical during Hollywood's golden years and recent screen dance practices. Considering my project in this way allows me to move from Bob Fosse's corporeally charged leading ladies to Maya Deren's radical incorporation of dance into her experimental film practice in the 1940s and 1950s, from Chris Cunningham's video for Björk's *All is Full of Love* (1999), to Trisha Brown's work with filmmaker Babette Mangolte. What have emerged are pivotal ways in which dance and film work on each other and how the resulting film or video works on the spectator, results that draw together seemingly disparate forms of dancefilm.

0.1 Locating the Dance in Dancefilm

> *Film moves, it is ephemeral.*
>
> Lesley Stern and George Kouvaros[25]

Critical debate around the relations between dance and film has frequently stalled over the question of *presence*: the condition of dance as elusive, corporeal, immediate expression. As Susan Leigh Foster and colleagues write in the introduction to

[24] I will make no attempt to overview the various approaches to dance theory represented in the field, but suggest Susan Leigh Foster's "Dance Theory?" (in *Teaching Dance Studies*, ed. Judith Chazin-Bennahum [New York: Routledge, 2005], 19–33) as a concise overview.

[25] Lesley Stern and George Kouvaros, "Introduction," in *Falling for You: Essays on Cinema and Performance*, ed. Lesley Stern and George Kouvaros (Sydney: Power Publications, 1999), 19.

Corporealities, "much like the body, dancing has been celebrated for its evanescence and for the speechlessness it produces as a response in those who witness it."[26] Or, as Clement Crisp more bluntly puts it, dance is "an art where impermanence is endemic."[27] Writing about and recording dance are complex activities in an economy where elusiveness has defined all aspects of the form. Dancefilm, for example, has often been seen as locking down and undermining the singular, affective experience of any given dance performance. Daniel Nagrin writes, "both in film and video…the rigid, rectangular window too often robs dance of dynamic nuance, spatial relevance, and the sweating, exultant immanence of the living dancer."[28] Nagrin's comments articulate an anxiety regarding the loss of qualities such as spontaneity, indeterminacy, immediacy, kinetic force, and presence when dance appears on and for the screen.

To resolve an opposition between the presence and kinaesthetic affect of bodies performing live and bodies on screen articulated here by Nagrin, I will recast the issues involved for the following discussion of dancefilm. For instance, what models of cinematic presence have been developed in film studies and how do they relate to ideas of liveness in dance studies? What can notions of cinematic presence offer to a discussion of corporeal presence in dancefilm and what new ideas about the dancing body are involved? And what of the affective impact of screen dance performance? Addressing these questions can lead us toward a cine-choreographic model of the dancing body liberated from theatrical concepts of liveness.

The question of corporeal presence plays a substantial role in both the theater-film and dance-film discussions. Comparisons of live and filmed performance were explored earlier in the century within film theory by writers such as Walter Benjamin, André Bazin, and Béla Balázs.[29] For example, Benjamin wrote in 1936: "The camera that presents the performance of the film actor to the public need not respect the performance as an integral whole.…It comprises certain factors of movement which are in reality those of the camera, not to mention special camera angles, close-ups etc."[30] In 1951, Jack Cole, choreographer for Gene Kelly, Marilyn Monroe, and Gwen Verdon, among others, compares physical presence on screen to live presence regarding dance:

> The difficulty of obtaining presence on the screen is enormous. Movement always seems to be under glass.…The camera obliterates all stress and strain and all kinetic drama is lost.[31]

---

[26] Susan Leigh Foster, Mark Franko, Lena Hammergren, Randy Martin, Sally Ness, Peggy Phelan, Nancy Ruyter, Marta Savigliano, and Linda Tomko, "Introduction," in *Corporealities: Dancing Knowledge, Culture and Power*, ed. Susan Leigh Foster (London and New York: Routledge, 1996a), xi.

[27] Clement Crisp, "Past Glories Recaptured," *Financial Times*, December 16, 1989.

[28] Daniel Nagrin, "Nine Points on Making Your Own Dance Video," *Dance Theatre Journal* 6, 1 (1988): 33.

[29] For discussions on the relation between theater performance and screen performance see: Walter Benjamin, "The Work of Art in the Age of Mechanical Reproduction," in *Illuminations*, ed. Hannah Arendt, trans. Harry Zohn (Suffolk: Fontana/Collins, 1982), 211–44; André Bazin, "Theater and Cinema, Parts One and Two," in *What is Cinema? Volume 1*, trans. Hugh Gray, 76–124 (Berkeley: University of California Press, 1967); and Béla Balázs, *Theory of the Film: Character and Growth of a New Art*, trans. Edith Bone, Chapters 2 and 3 (New York: Arno Press, 1972). See also Philip Auslander for more recent debates around "liveness" and "mediatization" of the peforming body (*Liveness: Performance in a Mediatized Culture*, [London: Routledge, 1999]).

[30] Benjamin (1982), 222.

[31] Jack Cole quoted in Arthur Todd, "From Chaplin to Kelly: The Dance on Film," *Theatre Arts* XXXV, 8 (1951): 91.

Kelly himself states, "What you do miss in motion pictures is, mainly, the kinetic force."[32] Nagrin, Cole, and Kelly's statements bear some relation to concerns addressed in early film theory by Benjamin, Bazin, and Balázs, who all deal with the question of theatrical presence and screen performance in different ways. In the case of dancefilm, the stakes regarding corporeal presence are higher given the focus on bodily articulations. There is usually a lack of spoken text and other cinematic elements such as character development that channels our attention toward physical action and the way it manifests on the screen. Theorization of the presence of cinematic bodies can be mobilized to consider a dancerly corporeality that exists only in dancefilm.

Gilles Deleuze points to Bazin's two-part article, "Theater and Cinema," as the first significant model of cinematic corporeal presence.[33] Bazin agrees with critics of "filmed theater" who find that cinema lacks "the physical presence of the actor" and writes, "There is no answer to this argument."[34] Bazin, however, redefines the kind of presence at issue, arguing that cinema appears to challenge the dominant concept of presence prior to the arrival of photography. Photography introduced a method whose "automatic genesis" distinguished it from all prior modes of reproduction, producing a "tracing" or "impression" of the original object.[35] The cinema takes this one-step further: "It takes a moulding of the object as it exists in time and, furthermore, makes an imprint of the duration of the object." In the face of such technologies, Bazin found that the theater had begun to qualify its use of the term "presence" by adding "in flesh and blood," suggesting to Bazin that the terms for the discussion of corporeal presence in performance had been irrevocably altered by the arrival of cinema.[36]

Deleuze takes up Bazin's line of thought in the second of his film books, *Cinema 2: The Time-Image*. Citing Bazin's ideas regarding a cinematographic type of bodily presence, Deleuze goes on to describe what he sees as cinema's alternative objective to that of theater:

> ... it spreads an "experimental night" or a white space over us; it works with "dancing seeds" and a "luminous dust"; it affects the visible with a fundamental disturbance, and the world with a suspension, which contradicts all natural perception.[37]

Deleuze is at his most poetic here, attempting to account for the alternative sense of corporeal presence cinema offers to the spectator. He goes on to describe cinema as carrying out a "genesis" of bodies: a "'beginning of visible which is not yet a figure, which is not yet an action,'"[38] "a proceeding, a process of constitution of bodies from the neutral image."[39] Deleuze is describing cinematic spectatorship as a disturbance

---

[32] Gene Kelly quoted in Beth Genné, "Dancin' in the Rain: Gene Kelly's Musical Films," in Mitoma 2002, 75.

[33] Bazin (1967), 76–124. Referenced by Gilles Deleuze in *Cinema 2: The Time-Image*, trans. Hugh Tomlinson and Robert Galeta, (Minneapolis: University of Minnesota Press, 1989), 201.

[34] Bazin (1967), 95.

[35] Ibid, 96.

[36] Ibid, 97.

[37] Deleuze (1989), 201.

[38] Idem. Here he is quoting Jean Louis Schefer in *L'homme ordinaire du cinema* (Paris: Cahiers du cinema, Gallimard, 1980).

[39] Ibid, 201–2. Here Deleuze is referring specifically to the films of Philippe Garrel and Robert Bresson but is also speaking about the issue of cinematic presence more generally.

or contradiction of the conditions of everyday perception: a reworking of the visible that approaches a kind of birth from dancing, "luminous dust." The figural presence that emerges is constituted through the cinematic process and exists only in the world that brought it forth, just as the dancing in dancefilm exists only for the screen.

In Stephen Heath's discussion of "different conditions of presence" in cinema, he constructs a classification of how "people" figure on screen, distinguishing between agent, character, person, and image, the latter pertaining to "the person, the body, in its conversion into the luminous sense of its film presence, its cinema."[40] Cinematic presence is thus something over and above narrative function, fictional personality, and the extra-cinematic profile of the performer—a definition pertinent to the conditions of much dancefilm. This idea of presence results from the conversion of the performer through the cinematic apparatus—light, movement, photographic registration—onto the screen as image. The theme of *filmic genesis* or creation continues here; we leave the "actual" body and the terms relevant to such bodies behind when we consider the screened body and our experience of its "presence." When Heath writes, "Cinema is the machine of a certain presence, the institution of certain conditions of the body," he is, along with Bazin and Deleuze, pointing toward the genesis of figures that create new experiential and perceptual conditions for the actualization of a sense of presence.[41]

In discussing dancefilm, the various understandings of corporeal screen presence put forth by Bazin, Deleuze, Heath, and others provide a counter to an attachment to the profilmic performance and a privileging of "live" presence. The on-screen presence of the performing body is the product of a filmic genesis, existing only "for the film, its cinema."[42] It is a body created through the cinematic machinations of light, dust, and duration and the expanded filmic performance as defined by Laleen Jayamanne and including editing and camera distance/movement. The filmic genesis of the dancefilm body can be distinguished from other cinematic bodies through the specificities of its production. This production is described in this book as involving a variety of cine-choreographic operations where we see choreographic elements written through by the cinematic apparatus. The conversion of the body into a dancefilm component involves the genesis of something that is "not yet a figure" but much more than a figure, proceeding from the cinematic elements and movements that make up the filmic performance: something that "is not yet action" but exceeds action as we know and understand it, disturbing our perception of human locomotion. New definitions of both choreography and film are required in the following discussion of a corporeal screen presence informed by the discipline of dance. Taking up where most writing on dancefilm stops, the recognition of a distinct manifestation of dance in dancefilm, and an interrogation of the terms of this discrete form, can then be pursued.

If corporeal presence in dancefilm offers a new model of the dancing body, what of the affective impact of screen dance performance? Much has been written about

---

[40] Stephen Heath, *Questions of Cinema* (London: Macmillan Press, 1981), 178–81.
[41] Ibid, 191.
[42] Idem.

the kinetic impact of live dance performance on the spectator. In 1946, dance critic John Martin wrote of "the inherent contagion of bodily movement, which makes the onlooker feel sympathetically in his own musculature the exertions he sees in somebody else's musculature."[43] In 1976, Sorell describes "kinaesthetic or emotional perception" as "the inexpressible dialogue occurring between dancers and between dancers and the audience; the experienced sensation over and above what can be reiterated in words."[44]

In her article, "Performing Sexuality, The Scintillations of Movement," dancer, dance writer, and philosopher Philipa Rothfield draws a distinction between the kinaesthetic experience of live dance and video recordings of dance, describing an oppositional relation with the former involving "participation" and the latter "observation."[45] Rothfield suggests that, "one can have a kinaesthetic experience by being in a relation of proximity to movement."[46] She draws on Merleau-Ponty's notion of "syncretic sociability," an "indistinction between me and the other," which is experienced in childhood and which, Rothfield argues, is revisited during certain dance performances as "a return to a primitive state of inter-corporeality."[47] She elaborates on this in relation to video documentation:

> This is why and where video is very different from the corporeality of the performance. The video tends to invite observation rather than participation, whereas performance allows for feeling, proximity, and corporeal relationship.... Being in the same room as someone dancing bristles with corporeal interrelations.... The body of the camera and the flesh of the film replace the viscera of performance.[48]

Rothfield's example is Australian choreographer Shelley Lasica's *Behaviour* (1994–1995), a solo that was originally performed in various tight spaces with the audience awkwardly backed to the four walls, completing the performance space. In the Hi-8 video of the same work by Margie Medlin made in 1995, the effect of proximity to movement that Rothfield describes in relation to live dancing is actualized through the screen medium. In Medlin's video, doubling occurs on several levels: the space of the room by the mobile and active frame, the proximity of the audience by the close-up, the sound of the body in space by the soundtrack of swooshes and slaps. Lasica's "connection and incorporation of the audience" now extends to the video viewer who not only identifies with the "real" audience, but has another direct

[43] John Martin, "Dance As a Means of Communication," in *What is Dance?*, ed. Roger Copeland and Marshall Cohen (Oxford: Oxford University Press, 1983), 22.

[44] Walter Sorell quoted in *Dance Words*, ed. Valerie Preston-Dunlop (Switzerland: Harwood Academic Publishers, 1995), 553. Mary M. Smyth attempts a more scientific approach to the subject in "Kinaesthetic Communication in Dance," *Dance Research Journal* 16, 2 (1984): 19–22. For more recent writing on kinaesthetic spectatorship see Carrie Lambert's brief historical summary in "On Being Moved: Rainer and the Aesthetics of Empathy," *Yvonne Rainer: Radical Juxtapositions 1961–2002*, ed. Sid Sachs (Philadelphia: The University of the Arts, 2003), 45–6; Susan Leigh Foster's excellent account of the historical origins of "kinetic empathy" in writings by Abbé de Condillac, Bernard Lamy, and Jean-Baptiste Du Bos among others in "Choreographing Empathy," *Topoi* 24 (2005): 81–91; and *The Senses in Performance*, ed. Andre Lepecki and Sally Banes (New York: Routledge, 2007). Events such as the Kinaesthetic Empathy: Concepts and Contexts conference (The University of Manchester, 22–23 April 2010) suggest growing interest in this area of critical inquiry.

[45] Philipa Rothfield, "Performing Sexuality, The Scintillations of Movement," in *Performing Sexualities*, ed. Michelle Boulous Walker (Brisbane: Institute of Modern Art, 1994), 62.

[46] Ibid, footnote 2, 57.

[47] Ibid, 63.

[48] Ibid, 62.

relationship with Lasica's screen performance through proximity to the moving image. The "participation" Rothfield finds lacking in video recordings of dance is, in this case, replaced with a different spectatorial experience that is no less engaged or affected but of a different order. Rather than a false binary setting live dance against filmed dance, participation against observation, the affective order of the two art forms must be considered as distinct and particular to each.

Ideas about a kinaesthetic contagion induced by live dance articulated by Martin, Sorell, and Rothfield, among others, are related to similar discussions in film theory on affectivity in the cinema. The notion of affect in film and its physical impact on the viewer has been addressed by film theorists such as Steven Shaviro, Gilles Deleuze, Laura Marks, and Vivian Sobchack.[49] Through a focus on the physical activities of actors, many new writings on screen performance inevitably conclude with what Ross Gibson calls "a somatic response" on the part of the audience.[50] Just as cinema instituted new categories of "presence," so too did the emergent technology create new corporeal experiences for the viewer.

The film theory mentioned here, with its focus on physical screen performance, often involves a descriptive approach to writing and analysis. A comparison can be drawn with the revolution in dance criticism in the United States brought about by writers such as Marcia Siegel, Deborah Jowitt, Arlene Croce, and Nancy Goldner. What characterizes the work of these female dance critics is an unapologetic subjectivity, detailed "re-creative" descriptions of both the distinguishing aesthetic *and* the impact of performed choreographies, a lack of recourse to extra-textual information, and an unrepressed enthusiasm for their subject.[51] For such writers, analysis begins with the work itself and any conclusions regarding meaning, value, historical significance, and so on are drawn through a close description of *form*.

In the introduction to a collection of essays on screen performance, *Falling for You*, Lesley Stern and George Kouvaros bring together questions of cinematic presence, affect, and problems with language. They write of an aim to convey "a sensory effect registering somehow in your body... to discover how the semantic and somatic are linked."[52] They ask:

> ...where are the models for understanding the ways in which the human bodies are moved within the cinematic frame, the ways in which those bodily motions may move viewers?... How to convey, in language, not merely the "scene" that is being analysed but its affect?[53]

---

[49] See: Steven Shaviro, *The Cinematic Body* (Minneapolis and London: University of Minnesota Press, 1993); Deleuze's two cinema books, *Cinema 1: The Movement-Image*, trans. Hugh Tomlinson and Barbara Habberjam (Minneapolis: University of Minnesota Press, 1986) and Deleuze 1989; Laura Marks, *The Skin of the Film: Intercultural Cinema, Embodiment and the Senses* (Durham, NC: Duke University Press: 2000) and *Touch: Sensuous Theory and Multisensory Media* (Minneapolis and London: University of Minnesota Press, 2002); and Vivian Sobchack, *Carnal Thought: Embodiment and Moving Image Culture* (Berkeley: University of California Press, 2004). For a summary of writings on cinema and the sensate body see Sobchack, "What My Fingers Knew: The Cinesthetic Subject. Or Vision in the Flesh," *Senses of Cinema*, www.sensesofcinema.com/contents/00/5/fingers.html.

[50] Ross Gibson, "Acting and Breathing," in Stern and Kouvaros 1999, 46.

[51] Diana Theodores, *First We Take Manhattan: Four American Women and the New York School of Dance Criticism* (Amsterdam: Harwood Academic Publishers, 1996), 1–9. For a critique of this tendency in dance criticism see Roger Copeland, "Dance Criticism and the Descriptive Bias," *Dance Theatre Journal* 10, 3 (1993): 26–32.

[52] Stern and Kouvaros (1999), 2.

[53] Ibid, 9.

Questioning the "place of description," Stern and Kouvaros call for a focus on the activity of evoking "that lost object" of filmic performance, lost in the time and space in which it occurred.[54] As the opening quote above states, "film moves…it *is* ephemeral." Just as live performance slips through our fingers as we write, so too does the cinematic experience challenge language to keep up with its "moves." The descriptions of dancefilm that follow seek not only to conjure the image and its movements for the reader, but to give some sense of the *gestural exchange* occurring between the gestures on the screen—physical and otherwise—and the responding gestures of the viewer, the somatic response to these cine-choreographies.

0.2 Screen Choreography

> It is my earnest hope that dance-film will be rapidly developed and that, in the interest of such a development, a new era of collaboration between dancers and film-makers will open up—one in which both would pool their creative energies and talents towards an integrated art expression.
>
> Maya Deren[55]

Dance and film are both vast fields of commercial, creative, and critical activity. Some very basic principles relating to each can serve as a starting point for exploring the variety of practices and outcomes that the interdisciplinary activity of dancefilm can produce. Many of the ideas about choreography and dance that inform the following discussion of cine-choreography have been drawn from across twentieth-century theater dance. While I will be referencing a broad range of dance practices including social, popular, and ritual dance, it is theater dance—a form distinguished from classical ballet and coming to prominence in the twentieth century—that has a special role to play. Contemporary theater dance has carried out rigorous movement research and generated a considerable body of literature on the nature of dance and choreography. From the French Symbolists' ideas regarding dance through early models of modern dance to recent theories of postmodern dance, dance is established as an exceptional mode of corporeal activity that can be described as "oppositional."

For the Symbolists, dance is a type of eloquence that exceeds the parameters of language. It derives from everyday movement but finally opposes the familiar and recognizable, creating an autonomous, expressive force. For early modern dancers such as Loïe Fuller and Isadora Duncan, the emphasis was on creating a form independent of the other arts through the creation of new types of movement. The model of dance informing the films of mid-twentieth–century filmmaker Maya Deren can be affiliated with contemporary dance practices and looked to stylization, abstraction, and depersonalization to distance movements from the utilitarian,

---

[54] Ibid, 7.

[55] Maya Deren quoted in *The Legend of Maya Deren: A Documentary Biography and Collected Works, Volume 1 Part Two: Chambers (1942–47)*, ed. VèVè A. Clark, Millicent Hodson, and Catrina Neiman (New York: Anthology Film Archives, 1988), 266.

everyday, and cliché. And dance artists of the later twentieth century, such as Yvonne Rainer and Trisha Brown, turned their attention to even more radical methodologies that dramatically altered the phrasing and quality of movement, purposefully opposing habit, recognition, and familiarity. Across the history of theater dance, an interest in interrogating ideas about theatrical representation and developing new and challenging types of human movement resulted in corporeal activities that radically depart from any other human actions depicted on screen.

Jean-François Lyotard provides a cinematic model that complements the definition of dance as an "oppositional" corporeal activity and provides a framework for working through the tendencies of dance and corporeal movement in relation to film, tendencies that have aligned dance with avant-garde film practices throughout cinema history. In his 1978 essay, "Acinema," Lyotard describes a cinematic economy where "a crowd...of elements in motion, a throng of possible moving bodies which are candidates for inscription on film," must be brought into line by "a real oppression of orders":

> This oppression consists of the enforcement of a nihilism of movements. No movement, arising from any field, is given to the eye-ear of the spectator for what it is: a simple *sterile difference* in an audio-visual field.[56]

Lyotard is describing a model of cinema where an "order" operates under "the law of value." If "cinematography is the inscription of movement," then in this model all movements conspire to an ordering notion of "production." This order is opposed to a cinema of "heterogeny" where "sterile motion" exists for its own sake.[57] In such an order the gestures of the performers operate under the ruling economy that controls all cinematic motion including camera movement, film speed, editing, and so on. *Utility* becomes the key term and any potential for action beyond what is expedient is suppressed.

If we put the models of dance and film outlined above *together*, we can see how the movements of dance—which tend toward unproductivity, originality, and exploration—have the potential to railroad the cinema of productivity described by Lyotard. Heterogeneity and homogeneity. Art and industry.[58] Of course neither of these ideals actually exists. As two trajectories working toward their opposites, they collide at various points along their paths. The tendency of dance toward unrestrained, hyperbolic motility and unexplained stasis, and film's tendency to order, restrain, frame, and cut, work upon each other in dancefilm to produce limitless variations and experiments that test the limits of cinematic production. Filmic performance will become a key element in analyzing where specific dancefilm works fall within the kind of "map" suggested here.

Lyotard goes on to explore the forms of filmmaking that stray from the rules of production. He brings the avant-garde or underground cinema into the discussion, distinguishing "two poles," "immobility and excessive movement," and calls the

---

[56] Jean-François Lyotard, "Acinema," *Wide Angle* 2, 3 (1978): 53.
[57] Idem.
[58] Lyotard refers to "an industry, the cinema" in relation to "the representational and narrative form of the commercial cinema" (Ibid, 55).

cinema that occupies one or the other of these poles "Acinema."[59] Lyotard's two poles of Acinema lead us to consider how dance exploits these two extremes of movement, triggering a larger shift in a film toward acknowledging "simple *sterile differences*" freed from signification or function, creating a cinema of "heterogeny." Static or still moments within dancefilm must be considered with the same weight and attention as those moments of hyperbolic motion. The slowing down or suspension of recognizable movements is a common means of breaking a gesture away from utility, developing a physical action into something dance-like through manipulating its progression through space and time.

As we shall see throughout *Dancefilm: Choreography and the Moving Image*, and corresponding with Lyotard's description of Acinema, dance as subject matter and inspiration has a strong relationship with film's historic avant-garde; it informs the work of filmmakers such as Fernand Léger, Man Ray, and René Clair, singular revolutionaries such as Maya Deren, and the New York-based collectives of the sixties and seventies, which included filmmakers such as Amy Greenfield and Shirley Clark. If dance as a performance activity induces heterogeneous tendencies in film, the effect on narrative film structures such as the classic Hollywood musical makes for a special case study; Acinematic tendencies are introduced to the form through its privileging of the dance star and their corporeal performance.

Dancefilm: Choreography and the Moving Image begins with the birth of both modern dance and the cinema at the end of the nineteenth century. Theories of modernity have tended to focus on the effects of the technologies of industry, leisure, and entertainment upon the broader urban milieu with some reference to the conditions for the human body, which is generally figured as under duress. My discussion aims to refigure the role of the dancer as a cultural influence that was translating the forces of technology, along with new notions of the moving body and movement itself in society, medicine, science, and philosophy, into an influential artistic force. Chapter 3 looks at the operations of gesture in dancefilm and the production of *gestural cinema* both historical and current. In the early years of cinema in Hollywood, many actors were originally dancers or were sent to study with the early modern dance duet, Ruth St. Denis and Ted Shawn, at the Denishawn School in Los Angeles. The focus on physical performance in the silent film era brought dance and acting into an intimate relationship and produced a gestural *mediality* that can be traced through to contemporary dancefilm. This chapter highlights the function of the profilmic performance that makes up one element within the filmic performance of dancefilm.

As already stated, *Dancefilm: Choreography and the Moving Image* also traces the significant role of avant-garde cinema in dancefilm history, arguing that it is the very nature of dance as a physical mode, a mode outstripping the everyday body, that challenges cinema to "match its moves." In examples from across the cinematic avant-garde right up to the present, dance tests the limits of technological reproduction leading cinema to invent new ways to meet its demands. Chapters 2, 3, 4 and 5 focus on specific strategies taken by featured artists such as Maya Deren,

---

[59] Ibid, 54.

Man Ray, Pina Bausch, Chris Cunningham, David Hinton, Jean Renoir, Gina Czarnecki, and Babette Mangolte. These include a reconsideration of the role of the close-up beyond the face where the body reveals its microchoreographies in Chapter 2, and the development of new models of film form by artists such as Deren, Bausch, and Mangolte to accommodate somatic expression rather than story and dialogue in Chapters 3, 4 and 5.

Here and elsewhere, the book provides some background on the work and writings of major female artists who produced aesthetic and conceptual opportunities for cinema, but it also telescopes out to the global community of experimental filmmakers and contemporary dance artists who have produced dancefilms. In Chapter 3, the analysis of silent film actor Lillian Gish highlights corporeal performance in a period that is traditionally discussed in relation to other male film personnel such as directors and cinematographers. And in my discussion of the musical, I primarily focus on female dance stars because, although dance is, more often than not, associated with women, the two major stars of the classic Hollywood era of the screen musical are Fred Astaire and Gene Kelly. Their position as men, along with their undeniable talent as dancers and choreographers, enabled them to register artistic input in the films they appeared in.[60] Approaches to the female musical star and chorus within film studies have generally taken a negative view of their portrayal and function.[61] Most film musical studies that focus on dance have looked at male choreographers, directors, and dancers in relation to the film industry's links with Broadway, the role of choreographers in the filmmaking process, and the influence of musical stars regarding dance styles and film aesthetics. This book attempts to redress such tendencies by focusing on the contributions female dancers, choreographers, and filmmakers have made to the development of dance, film, and dancefilm.

Foregrounding the points where dance and film meet leads to an analysis of the moment where the everyday body moves into dance in the film musical. While the musical number is traditionally seen as an interruption within the fiction film narrative, the musical star is refigured in Chapter 6 as the unifying element, holding together shaky plotlines and outrageous scenarios with pure corporeal force. Through the body of the dancer, the movements of everyday life and dance spill into and across each other, challenging the centrality of the linear drive in these classical fiction films. So here as elsewhere, *Dancefilm: Choreography and the Moving Image* brings together avant-garde and popular dancefilm traditions by identifying strategies common to both.

The final chapter looks at the unifying tendencies across the breadth of dancefilm practice and the relationship between dancefilm and the spectator. It is based on

---

[60] Eleanor Powell was one female exception who choreographed her own material with the ensemble work handled by dance directors such as Dave Gould or Bobby Connolly.

[61] See for example: Maureen Turim, "Gentlemen Consume Blondes," in *Issues in Feminist Film Criticism*, ed. Patricia Erens (Bloomington: Indiana University Press, 1993), 101–11; Lucy Fischer's chapter on the musical in *Shot/Countershot: Film Tradition and Women's Cinema* (Princeton, New Jersey: Princeton University Press, 1989), 132–71; and Nadine Wills, "'110 per cent Woman': The Crotch Shot in the Hollywood Musical," *Screen* 42, 2 (2001): 121–41. An important exception is McLean 2004 where she takes direct issue with such feminist readings of the female musical star. McLean draws attention to Rita Hayworth's skills and ability as an actress and dancer to counter the dominant readings of her screen performances.

Jean-François Lyotard's essay, "Gesture and Commentary," which deals with the operations of the work of art as "gesture" and the challenge it presents to philosophical discourse.[62] Lyotard offers a particularly performative model of the gesture of the work of art that has a clear affinity with the conditions of dancefilm. I use Lyotard's gestural model of aesthetic production and reception to develop a conceptual framework for reading dancefilm, allowing me to move on from questions regarding the specificities of cine-choreographic orders to pursue a means by which the general characteristics, operations, and processes of the form can be considered across a broad variety of examples.

[62] Jean-François Lyotard, "Gesture and Commentary," *Iyyun, The Jerusalem Philosophical Quarterly* 42, 1 (1993): 37–48.

1

Modern Movement, Dance, and the Birth of Cinema

It is no coincidence that as modern dance began, the cinematograph was invented and that as the first swirls of Loïe Fuller's veils occurred, the Lumière brothers cranked their camera for the first time. Méliès would surely not contradict me, he, who chose his actresses among the dancers of the Chatelet, and whose every situation, every movement of the characters is, as if by magic, naturally choreographed.

Patrick Bensard[1]

In this passage, Patrick Bensard brings together the figure of Loïe Fuller, the birth of modern dance, and the work of early filmmakers such as the Lumière brothers and Georges Méliès, to conjure a creative, urban milieu where magic, cinema, dancers, and dance-like actions happily and productively co-exist. Besides Méliès's use of chorus dancers and the possible collaboration between Fuller and the Lumière brothers in Paris, one could cite further examples to support the proposition of a fundamental collaborative practice between dance and film in cinema's early years.[2] There are of course numerous short dancefilms amongst the earliest moving pictures, made between 1894 and 1910, featuring solo dancers mainly from vaudeville and burlesque including *Karina* (1902, American Mutoscope and Biograph Co.), *Betsy Ross Dance* (1903, American Mutoscope and Biograph Co.), and *Little Lillian Toe Dancer* (1903, American Mutoscope and Biograph Co.). Dance was also included in the earliest narrative feature films such as Ruth St. Denis's work in *Intolerance* (1916, d. D. W. Griffiths).

The appearance of the new theater art of modern dance alongside technological advancements in the field of photographic reproduction at the beginning of the twentieth century has been linked to other fields that were undergoing parallel

---

[1] *Impressions Danse Catalogue*, ed. Michèle Bargues and Anne Coutinot (Paris: Georges Pompidou Centre, 1988), 11. Patrick Bensard has been the Director of the Cinémathèque de la danse in Paris since 1982, a one-of-a-kind collection of dancefilms initially connected to the French Cinémathèque and now operating as an independent organization.

[2] Giovanni Lista—who has researched the "imitation" films in France, written *Loïe Fuller: Danseuse de la Belle Époque* (Paris: Stock Somogy editions d'Art, 1994; which has a revised edition Paris: Hermann Danse, 2007), and produced the film *Loïe Fuller et ses imitatrices* (1994) with the Cinémathèque de la danse in Paris—believes that to date no films featuring Fuller in performance have been found (correspondence with Lista, July 2009). In her autobiography, *Fifteen Years of a Dancer's Life* (New York: Dance Horizons, 1913), Fuller makes no reference to being filmed. And for a rare film studies perspective on the confluence of dance and film in early cinema see Laurent Guido, "Rhythmic Bodies/Movies: Dance as Attraction in Early Film Culture," in *The Cinema of Attractions Reloaded*, ed. Wanda Strauven (Amsterdam: Amsterdam University Press, 2007), 140–56. Guido gives an account of writings by experimental French filmmakers Marcel L'Herbier, Louis Delluc, René Clair, and Germaine Dulac on the significance of Fuller's stage and screen work for the development of cinema (148).

periods of intense innovation and reinvigoration. Interfaces between the emergence of modern dance and cinema, electricity, photographic motion studies, new psychiatric and medical practices, theories of evolution, and an emerging body consciousness in fin de siècle culture have been charted by theorists such as Clare De Morinni, Sally Sommer, Dee Reynolds, Felicia McCarren, Rhonda Garelick, Ann Cooper Albright, and Jane Goodall.[3] Central to these discussions is the figure of Loïe Fuller, or "La Loïe" as her fans knew her, perhaps supporting Garelick's observation that she has hypnotized contemporary writers who project onto her "blank screen" their particular critical desires.[4] If this is true, we have learned nothing from our counterparts who saw her perform live. Loïe Fuller appears in writings of this historical period as the figure who *embodied* so many influential ideas, including one of particular significance to dance and dancefilm—the changing perception of the body in motion and its function regarding the production of meaning.

Fuller began her performance career as an actress, received international acclaim for her "serpentine dances," and went on to direct her own screen work.[5] The only surviving reel of her work is a segment from *Le Lys de la Vie*, a narrative film that features a show within a show with classically costumed figures dancing by the sea, a banquet, royal intrigue, and romance with René Clair featured as a prince on horseback. This odd snippet of silent film evokes a time when it was possible for choreographers working in the new field of modern theater dance, and filmmakers working with the new technology of the cinematograph, to cross-over with ease in collaborations and experiments. While others such as Albright have given attention to Fuller's "development in her later career of a cinematic vision, both in her large scale company works and in her forays

[3] See Clare De Morinni, "Loie Fuller: The Fairy of Light," *Dance Index* 1, 3 (1942): 40–51; Sally Sommer, "Loïe Fuller," *The Drama Review* 19, 1 (1975): 53–67; Dee Reynolds, "The Dancer as Woman: Loïe Fuller and Stéphane Mallarmé," in *Impressions of French Modernity*, 155–72 (Manchester: Manchester University Press, 1998); Jane Goodall, *Performance and Evolution in the Age of Darwin: Out of the Natural Order* (London: Routledge, 2002); Felicia McCarren, "The 'Symptomatic Act' Circa 1900: Hysteria, Hypnosis, Electricity, Dance," *Critical Inquiry* 21 (Summer 1995a): 748–74; Felicia McCarren, "Stéphane Mallarmé, Loïe Fuller, and the Theater of Femininity," in *Bodies of the Text*, ed. Ellen W. Goellner and Jacqueline Shea Murphy (New Brunswick: Rutgers University Press, 1995b), 217–30; Felicia McCarren, *Dance Pathologies: Performance, Poetics, Medicine* (California: Stanford University Press, 1998); and Felicia McCarren, *Dancing Machines: Choreographies of the Age of Mechanical Reproduction* (California: Stanford University Press, 2003). The two recent monographs on Fuller focus on very different aspects of her work. Ann Cooper Albright's, *Traces of Light: Absence and Presence in the Work of Loïe Fuller* (Middletown, Connecticut: Wesleyan University Press, 2007), elaborates primarily on Fuller's physical practice as a revision of image-based readings of her work, but also her stage craft and the issues of expression, gender representation, nationality, visual rhythm, dance spectatorship, and her connections with the Art Nouveau movement. And in *Electric Salome: Loie Fuller's Performance of Modernism* (Princeton: Princeton University Press, 2007), Rhonda K. Garelick gathers her writing around themes such as doubleness, (sexual) disavowal, modernism, colonialism, and expression and argues convincingly for continuity between Fuller's art and the aesthetics of Romantic Ballet, and for recognition of her role as a revolutionary theater maker regarding scenography and abstraction.

[4] Garelick (2007), 15.

[5] Sommer writes that Fuller made her first experimental film in 1904 and made "at least 3 more," with only the excerpt from *Le Lys de la Vie* (1921) surviving (Sommer 1975, 53). The making of *Le Lys de la Vie* is detailed by Giovanni Lista (Lista 2007, 530–39), and the first book published in English on Fuller, Richard Nelson Current and Marcia Ewing Current's *Loie Fuller: Goddess of Light* (Boston: Northeastern University Press, 1997, 271–83). A second unfinished film, *Visions de rêves*, is also described by both Lista and Current and Current through reference to Fuller's correspondence at the time. Lista makes reference to a third film, *Les Encretitudes du docteur Coppélius* (1927), which no longer exists (Lista 2007, 645). A final film was made posthumously by Gab Sorère and George Busby, *La féerie des ballets fantastiques de Loïe Fuller* (1934), which includes excerpts of her later stage works based on shadow play.

into film,"[6] I will focus on her signature stage performances regarding two major aspects of significance to the emergence and development of dancefilm. First, the reclaiming of the body as a major and radical site for producing and expressing meaning, and the body's engagement with the new technologies of twentieth-century modernity.

This chapter explores how dance both informs and performs the poetics of the French Symbolists and philosophies of Henri Bergson in order to refigure the role of dance within the intercultural milieu at the beginning of the twentieth century. In contemporary cultural theory, cinema is seen as the major phenomena translating effects of twentieth-century modernity, and modern dance has been overlooked as a potent cultural force. Accounts of late nineteenth-century/early twentieth-century modernity have tended to focus on the effects of the technologies of industry, leisure, and entertainment upon the broader urban milieu with some reference to the conditions for the human body, which is generally figured as under duress.[7] I am arguing for the importance of the dancer as a cultural influence that was translating the forces of technology—along with new notions of the moving body and movement itself in society, medicine, science, and philosophy—into an influential artistic force that would ultimately exceed the possibilities of early cinema.

In the opening chapters of Gilles Deleuze's influential cinema books, he introduces the idea that fin de siècle dance shares with cinema the role of manifesting a new understanding of motion particular to the twentieth century. Deleuze applies Henri Bergson's theory of "modern movement," which describes the dissolution of the pose into the "endless flow" of life experience, to the concurrently emerging technology of the cinema. Bergson's work provides the basis for Deleuze's model of the development of the art form throughout his cinema books.[8] The centrality of Bergson's ideas to Deleuze's theory of the cinema points to his broader significance for the theorization of modernity. For Anson Rabinbach, it was in Bergson's theories that the "crisis of space and time," brought about by the industrial and scientific revolution, "found cogent philosophical expression."[9] Deleuze not only provides a way into Bergson's ideas and their relevance for the cinema, but he draws dance into the discussion using it as an historical example *and* analogy. These connections serve as my starting point for exploring a conceptualization of movement in the work of fin de siècle movement practitioners that corresponds with Bergson's model and resonates across dancefilm practice.

---

[6] Albright (2007), 182. Albright argues for Fuller's influence on the historic avant garde in cinema through her contact with Clair and the writings of Germaine Dulac, and she draws a connection to the film work of Sally Potter (199–201). Albright also traces Fuller's influence through to current work involving virtual dance, which can be considered part of the larger field of screen dance, citing in particular *Ghostcatching* (1999) by Bill T. Jones with Paul Kaiser and Shelley Eshkar (201–5).

[7] Exceptional here is the work of McCarren, particularly *Dancing Machines*, in her account of "twentieth-century intellectual and cultural history both inspired by and inspiring dance" (McCarren 2005, 7). And also Andrew Hewitt's important book, *Social Choreography* (Durham: Duke University Press, 2005), which argues persuasively for fin de siècle dance "not simply as a privileged figure for social order but as the enactment of a social order that is both reflected in and shaped by aesthetic concerns" (2).

[8] Gilles Deleuze, *Cinema 1: The Movement-Image*, trans. Hugh Tomlinson and Barbara Habberjam (Minneapolis: University of Minnesota Press, 1986), and *Cinema 2: The Time-Image*, trans. Hugh Tomlinson and Robert Galeta (Minneapolis: University of Minnesota Press, 1989).

[9] Anson Rabinbach, *The Human Motor: Energy, Fatigue, and the Origins of Modernity* (Berkeley: University of California Press, 1990), 84.

The literary revolution of the Symbolists' new poetics, which drew its inspiration from dance, is important here for two reasons. First, the writings of the Symbolists illustrate the significance of dance within the historic-cultural milieu under discussion, thus restoring the field of dance to a stage often dominated by the appearance of the motion picture apparatus. Second, the kind of corporeality that the "new poetics" of the French Symbolists propose affords a model of dance that connects with modern movement and the dissolution of the pose more generally. They understood dance as an activity of transformation and fluidity that eludes definition and exemplifies the notion of movement-as-flux.

From my discussion of contemporary literature and philosophy, I turn to particular fin de siècle movement practices that inspired the Symbolists and illustrate Bergson's ideas regarding modern movement. In the seminal choreographic system of American Delsartism, American dance historian Nancy Lee Chalfa Ruyter pinpoints the transition from physical culture as a private and amateur activity, to movement as an artistic, choreographic, and public practice existing outside established institutions such as the ballet. This transition, as outlined by Ruyter, also entails a shift in the choreographic conceptualization of movement that parallels Bergson's theses of movement; Delsartism represents a moment of conversion within fin de siècle body practices from the order of the pose to the principle of uninterrupted flow. From this point, the central figures of Isadora Duncan and Loïe Fuller, traditionally set in opposition to each other in the history of Western theater dance, can be brought together via Bergson's model of "modern movement." It will be shown that early modern dance did not simply anticipate cinema in terms of how dance was realizing the dissolution of the pose. Fuller's combination of continuous movement with popular entertainment technologies produced a "moving image" that calls for a rechoreographing of the history of the moving image.

1.1 Dance and the Symbolists' New Poetic

> . . . the female dancer will eventually return to the cultural and even intellectual
> center stage with a vengeance. Described as a poet and metaphysician in her
> own right, she appears in nineteenth century Paris as the true muse of poets and
> philosophers.
>
> Felicia McCarren[10]

In Frank Kermode's article, "Poet and Dancer before Diaghilev," he describes the Parisian theatrical scene at the end of the nineteenth century.[11] It was populated by music-hall dancers Yvette Guilbert, Marie Lloyd, Jane Avril, and other physical performers such as Little Tich, the actress Eleanora Duse, and Isadora Duncan, and visual artists such as theater designer Gordon Craig and Toulouse-Lautrec. At the center of this world are Loïe Fuller and Stéphane Mallarmé. For Kermode it is in the

[10] McCarren (1998), 2.
[11] Frank Kermode, "Poet and Dancer before Diaghilev," in *What is Dance? Readings in Theory and Criticism*, ed. Roger Copeland and Marshall Cohen (Oxford: Oxford Universal Press, 1983), 145–60.

dance writing of Mallarmé that art and literature combine to most clearly illustrate the artistic and intellectual current of this period. Mallarmé found in Fuller's art a perfect subject for his aesthetic ideals and, consequently, through his writing Fuller takes her place in history as a pivotal artist who preempted the more widely recognized radicals of early modern dance—Isadora Duncan and Serge Diaghilev's Ballet Russes.[12]

Fuller's dancing involved manipulating a circle of silk panels worn from the neck attached to rods that extended her arms to enable a dramatic flow and dance of fabric. She then added different coloured lighting effects to create what would have been a remarkable theatrical display. As indicated in various artistic representations of Fuller, the material extends and surrounds the dancer, creating a motile, fluid figure that obscures and dissolves the dancing body. The resulting spectacle is a figure in constant transformation—an unstable signifier sourced in, yet moving beyond, the efforts and intentions of the dancer. This dancing figure was a remarkable departure from both the ballerina and the showgirl in terms of her physical dimensions and kinetic range.

According to Kermode, Mallarmé's writing on Fuller departs from the dance writing of Charles Baudelaire and Théophile Gautier, which focused on the dancer's "human and palpable element," and, in doing so, constituted "a shift in the whole climate of poetry."[13] But he admits that "not even Mallarmé could start a renaissance single-handed," and in exploring "whatever it was that predisposed everybody to get excited...about dancers" during this time, reels off scores of other writers throughout his essay who turned their attention to dance and dancers, including Georges Rodenbach, T. S. Eliot, Arthur Symons, W. B. Yeats, Roger Marx, Emanuel Levinson, Paul Valéry, and Albert Thibaudet.[14] Dance had become an influential and inspirational cultural force. But what was that "climate shift," and why was dance such a powerful force in relation to it?

In their introduction to *André Levinson on Dance*, Joan Acocella and Lynn Garafola put their finger on it:

> ...literary symbolism, enemy of realism, had established in certain quarters a new idea of art: art not seen as representation but as vision.... [T]his antirealist aesthetic influenced artistic perception in general and created a soil in which abstract dance, when it began its new growth in the West in the early twentieth century, could flourish....Dance received from the symbolists a special blessing: endorsement by their most respected thinker, Stéphane Mallarmé.[15]

---

[12] Kermode, for example, uses Mallarmé's writing on Fuller to forcefully argue that Fuller, not Duncan or Diaghilev, can "take us to the root of the matter" regarding the "renaissance" that put dance center stage at the beginning of the twentieth century (Kermode 1983, 145–46). He describes Fuller as "the woman who seemed to be doing almost single-handed what Diaghilev was later to achieve only with the help of great painters, musicians, and dancers" (151).

[13] Ibid, 157.

[14] Ibid, 145–60. Kermode's list of names here backs up Amy Koritz's argument that the significance of dance within literature during this period was not limited to France but extended to England (*Gendering Bodies/Performing Art: Dance and Literature in Early Twentieth-Century British Culture* [Ann Arbor: The University of Michigan Press, 1995], 15). Terri Mester's *Movement and Modernism: Yeats, Eliot, Lawrence, Williams and Early-Twentieth Century Dance* (Fayetteville: The University of Arkansas Press, 1997) also sets out to revise the position of dance as a major literary influence during this period.

[15] Joan Acocella and Lynn Garafola, "Introduction," in *André Levinson on Dance: Writings from Paris in the Twenties*, ed. Joan Acocella and Lynn Garafola (Anover and London: Wesleyan University Press, 1991), 2.

The description here of the Symbolists' "antirealist" and nonrepresentational aesthetic and the compatibility with "abstract dance"—a term well-suited to Fuller's art and applied to theater dance throughout the twentieth century—makes clear the common ground that the literary and choreographic works shared. At the same time that Fuller had created an abstract, moving figure through costume and lighting effects, the French Symbolists were led by Mallarmé in a search for "poetic purity." This was an antinaturalist, speculative, and abstract form of literature clearly distinguished from reportage, narrative, instructional, and descriptive text.[16] It is dance that provides the model for this new poetics, which, as we shall see, is also compatible with the emerging and radical understanding of modern movement.

McCarren, like Kermode, is also explicit about the interrelations between the nature of dance and this new form of literature:

> The nineteenth-century French dance writing…imagines dance embodying a literary "idea": bypassing words and moving freely; translating the abstract into the human physique.…[Théophile Gautier, Mallarmé, and Louis-Ferdinand Céline] ultimately identify themselves writing with the dancer dancing. All three conceive of the literary "idea" as figured by dance and attempt to emulate the way dance works in their writing.[17]

The figure of the dancer that McCarren evokes in this passage as a direct inspiration for these writers draws us to the heart of the issue here: the productivity of a dancerly model for these poets as a means of establishing a new poetics, a productivity that surfaced in defiance of the oppositions between language and dance, mind and body, which have been in place since Descartes. Dance was thus drawn into the most progressive debates about literature and art as an exemplary form that could "translate the abstract" through embodiment.

Paul Valéry—perhaps with a fresh perspective on the inspiration dance had provided for his mentor, Mallarmé—is clear in his writing when it comes to the function of dance as both inspiration *and* model for his own art. He expresses this sentiment in his essay, "Dance and the Soul"—a fictional dialogue set at a banquet where a dancer named Athiktè becomes the object of discussion. Socrates says of Phaedrus's response to Athiktè: "So then, your lips envy the volubility of these amazing feet! You would like to feel their wings on your words, and adorn your speech with figures as lively as their leaps."[18] Phaedrus's response to Athiktè's dance is clearly not just one of admiration, but of unrepressed envy and a desire to emulate the corporeal expressivity that his words cannot match. This is the plight of the Symbolist poet confronted with the new abstract dances of artists like Fuller and Duncan; if words could not match their "volubility," something very productive resulted from their attempts.[19]

In another of his essays—an introductory lecture to a performance by flamenco artist Mme Argentina—Valéry makes a clear comparison between dance as an

---

[16] A. G. Lehmann, *The Symbolist Aesthetic in France 1885–1895* (Oxford: Basil Blackwell, 1950), 64.

[17] McCarren (1998), 11. McCarren's understanding of *ideal* here is derived from Plato and Georg Wilhelm Friedrich Hegel (224, footnote 11).

[18] Paul Valéry, "Dance and the Soul," in *Selected Writings* (New York: New Directions, 1950), 191.

[19] See Koritz for a discussion of the influence of Isadora Duncan on the English symbolist movement (1995, 59–73).

activity operating independently of exterior forces, objects, and systems, and the type of poetics he aspires to. He describes dance as "an action that *derives* from ordinary, useful action, but *breaks away* from it, and finally *opposes* it" so that "all action which does not tend toward utility and which on the other hand can be trained, perfected, developed, may be subsumed under this simplified notion of the dance."[20] Valéry's theory that dance harnesses the human impetus for motor activity beyond the utilitarian, that it accommodates the fact we possess "more vigour, more suppleness, more articular and muscular possibilities" than we need, and that it gives release and form to the "frantic motor expenditure" that we are capable of, provides a model of dance both grounded in the actualities of the everyday body but also operating as an alternative born of excess.[21] This broad model of dance can accommodate the potential for new categories of movement that are in line with both the contemporary kinetics of modernity and the variety of dancefilms produced since the earliest experiments with the form. For this reason, throughout this book I will revisit Valéry's notion of dance as an alternative to language processes and structures of knowledge, a model of somatic intelligence and corporeal signification that challenges many of the paradigms relating to filmmaking, yet having an affinity with its very essence—movement.

Valéry continues his description of how the dancer's art is a discrete world unrelated to the exigencies of everyday life:

> …acts have no outward aim; there is no object to grasp, to attain, to repulse or run away from, no object which puts a precise end to an action and gives movements first an outward direction and co-ordination, then a clear and definite conclusion.[22]

Valéry goes on to say that, while this description can be applied to all the arts, dance is "*a poetry that encompasses the action of living creatures in its entirety.*"[23] The lack of a beginning and an end to actions in Valéry's description of dance here suggests an absence of ideal poses or forms, which coincides with the dissolution of the pose that cinema was implicated in. Here is human movement that literally embodied the quality of continual flow described by Henri Bergson.

1.2 Henri Bergson's Movement Theory and the New Dance Aesthetic

> …art, ballet and mime became actions capable of responding to accidents of the environment; that is, to the distribution of the points of a space, or of the moments of an event. All this served the same end as the cinema.
>
> Gilles Deleuze[24]

---

[20] Paul Valéry, "Philosophy of the Dance," in *The Collected Works of Paul Valéry, Volume 13*, ed. Jackson Mathews, trans. Ralph Manheim (London: Routledge and Kegan Paul, 1964), 207.

[21] Ibid, 198. See McCarren (2003) for a discussion of Valéry's ideas about dance as "non-productive or non-signifying" in relation to the ubiquitous machine aesthetics at the beginning of the twentieth century (146–51).

[22] Ibid, 205.

[23] Ibid, 210.

[24] Deleuze (1986), 7.

In a conversation on his cinematic model, Gilles Deleuze says, "It's an interesting coincidence that cinema appeared at the very time philosophy was trying to think motion."[25] In his book, *Cinema 1: The Movement-Image*, Deleuze employs the theories of Henri Bergson to arrive at a relationship between Bergson's new philosophy of movement, modern dance, and the emerging art form of the cinema.[26]

Deleuze begins *Cinema 1* with the three theses of movement from Bergson's *Creative Evolution*.[27] The first two of these theses are relevant here because they focus on describing the conditions of movement itself, while the third thesis looks at the relation of movement to the duration or the whole. Deleuze explains that the first thesis establishes movement as distinct from the space covered. That is, the space covered can be divided up infinitely into "immobile sections," but you cannot reconstitute movement merely by reproducing the positions in space (immobile sections). You will only produce "false movement" by adding "the abstract idea of a succession, of a time which is mechanical, homogeneous, universal." Thus, "immobile sections + abstract time" = "false movement."[28] In *Creative Evolution*, Bergson explains this idea in relation to human existence. What we recognize as mental states are actually part of the flow of experience, the "uninterrupted change" that our lives are made up of:

> But it is expedient to disregard this uninterrupted change, and to notice it only when it becomes sufficient to impress a new attitude on the body, a new direction on the attention.[29]

These mental states that we recognize and isolate only when they sufficiently impress themselves upon us both psychically and physically can be equated to the immobile sections of the above formula. So our "psychical life" becomes a series of discontinuous "separate steps," new attitudes or directions cut out of the "endless flow" of life requiring "an artificial bond" (or "false movement"). Bergson compares this to a bead necklace, the mental states constituting the beads and the thread the "formless ego" onto which the states are threaded.[30] Bergson concludes that, "never can these

[25] Gilles Deleuze, *Negotiations: 1972–1990* (New York: Columbia University Press, 1995), 57.

[26] The connections I make here among dance, cinema, and the philosophical writing of Henri Bergson were first outlined in "'La Loïe' as Pre-Cinematic Performance—Descriptive Continuity of Movement," *Senses of Cinema* 28 (Sept-Oct 2003), (www.sensesofcinema.com/contents/03/28/la_loie.html). Tom Gunning also brings these elements together in his discussion of Fuller's art as resolving tensions found within other art forms regarding the ideal of an "art of motion" ("Loïe Fuller and the Art of Motion," in *Camera Obscura, Camera Lucida*, ed. Richard Allen and Malcolm Turvey [Amsterdam: Amsterdam University Press, 2003], 75–89). McCarren also connects Bergson's theories to the dancing of Fuller and Duncan via Jules Marey's motion studies, and to dance and cinema via Deleuze (McCarren 2003, 51–63). It should be noted that a precedent exists regarding the connection between Bergson's theories and fin de siècle dance. In Deirdre Pridden's account of Stéphane Mallarmé and Paul Valéry's writings on dance in her book, *The Art of Dance in French Literature*, (London: Adam & Charles Black, 1952), she comments on a Bergsonian quality in the writing of both French poets. Pridden finds concepts of duration, fluidity, movement, transition, and uninterrupted flow in these fin de siècle writers, and thus indirectly draws out the relation between the emerging art of modern dance and Bergson's philosophy. Indirectly because, while Pridden applies most of Mallarmé and Valéry's writing to classical ballet, she does point out that, "Mallarmé experienced a sudden revelation in the person of Loïe Fuller" (74).

[27] Henri Bergson, *Creative Evolution*, trans. Arthur Mitchell (New York: Dover Publications, 1998). (First published in translation in 1911, Deleuze refers to a 1954 edition in Deleuze, 1986.)

[28] Deleuze 1986, 1.

[29] Bergson 1998, 2.

[30] Ibid, 3. Bergson's example here of "mental states" signals the earlier theories of William James, which are outlined in Kern (1983). Kern argues convincingly that James's ideas, including his coining of the phrase "stream of thought," "anticipate" Bergson's theories regarding the spatialization of time (24).

solids strung upon a solid make up that duration which flows," and suggests that this reconstituted reality or "static equivalent" would "lend itself better to the require-ments of logic and language."[31]

Deleuze explains how Bergson thus identifies "two very different illusions" of movement in his second thesis—the "ancient" and the "modern." The *ancient* model is the embodiment of Forms or Ideas (the beads) that are "eternal and immobile"—an "ideal synthesis" that results in "the regulated transition from one form to another, that is, an order of *poses* or privileged instants, as in a dance."[32] Deleuze's introduction here of an analogy with dance needs to be considered. What is being described is a movement through poses or privileged moments that, in Bergson's words, "express the quintessence, all the rest of this period being filled by the transition, of no interest in itself, from one form to another form."[33]

What type of dancing would this be? The most obvious candidates are classical ballet and the court dances from which the form emerged. Susan Leigh Foster traces the emergence of theatrical dance or ballet as an art form independent of the opera across three versions of the Pygmalion story at the Paris Opéra in 1734, 1789, and 1847.[34] The dance forms on which ballet was originally based—the minuet, passe-pied, rigaudon, allemande, and sarabande—consisted of small steps and beats of the feet with an emphasis on posture and pose; Foster describes them as "noble lines traced by the dancer's body in space."[35] The period from the mid-eighteenth century to the mid-nineteenth century also marked the emergence of the genre of "the danced story," a form whose influence on theater dance Foster equates to the impact of the novel on literature. Foster explains how the narrative form shaped the cho-reographic content:

> In order to accommodate the story ballet's need to substitute gestures for words, chore-ographers drew from the rich vocabulary of pantomimed expressions of the hands and face.... Considerable choreographic ingenuity was needed to soften the transitions between the didactic indications of thoughts and feelings and the elegant execution of ideal forms.[36]

This dancing consisted of "didactic" gestures and "ideal forms," with transitions simply marking the movement between privileged moments that formed part of the story. Ballet also exemplifies the "traditional phrasing" described years later by Yvonne Rainer as consisting of "maximal output or 'attack' at the beginning of a phrase, followed by abatement or recovery at the end, with energy often arrested somewhere in the middle." Such phrasing creates units of movement that mimic the larger theatrical structure; they have a beginning, a climax, and an end. These are

---

[31] Ibid, 4.

[32] Deleuze (1986), 4.

[33] Bergson quoted in Idem.

[34] Susan Leigh Foster, *Choreography and Narrative: Ballet's Staging of Story and Desire* (Bloomington and Indianapolis: Indiana University Press, 1996b), 7.

[35] Ibid, 17.

[36] Ibid, 8. The type of dancing developed for the narrative ballet would dominate theatrical dance up to the late nineteenth century and its pantomimic tendencies would launch the reactive twentieth-century pursuit of "original gestures."

dances with privileged instants, or as Rainer puts it, moments of "registration," that take precedence over the transitional moments.[37]

What is certain is that the dance Deleuze is referring to here is very different to the forms of dancing he aligns with Bergson's *modern* conception of movement. Deleuze writes that this concept of movement "has consisted in relating movement not to privileged instants, but to any-instant-whatever," taking into account the "endless flow" of life.[38] Deleuze uses the example of Eadweard Muybridge's "equidistant snapshots," a method he places within the prehistory of cinema just prior to the transference of such images to the cinematic apparatus, to explain how all the images in the sequence of, for example, a horse's gallop, "relate the . . . whole of the canter to any-point-whatever."[39]

Bergson's work offers an understanding of the conditions of motion and a new kinaesthetic force exemplified by constant flux. Of the various art forms developing at the same time as this new idea of movement, Deleuze cites "dance, ballet, and mime" as some of the most relevant fields of innovation, where dancers were "abandoning figures and poses to release values which were not posed, not measured, which related movements to any-instant-whatever."[40] It is this quality in early modern dance that so inspired the writings of the French Symbolists. In this passage, Deleuze could be referring to the art of Isadora Duncan, which was marked by its constant and consistent flow and was revolutionary in its informality and softness of form, or to the art of Loïe Fuller, whose dancing was an exemplary model of transformation through flux and rhythmic continuity. Deleuze writes:

> When one relates movement to any-moment-whatevers, one must be capable of thinking the production of the new, that is, of the remarkable and the singular, at any one of these moments: this is a complete conversion of philosophy. . . . Can we deny that the arts must also go through this conversion . . . ?[41]

That the arts were effected, and affected, by Bergson's ideas cannot in fact be denied, and the impact of this modern conception of motion can be traced through twentieth-century theater dance right up to the present.

Of course, Deleuze also applies his reading of Bergson's movement theses to the emergence of cinema as a new art form at the beginning of the twentieth century. Deleuze believes cinema is the "last descendent" of the scientific lineage traced by Bergson through modern astronomy, physics, geometry, and calculus.[42] What Bergson found in the wake of the modern scientific revolution at the end of the nineteenth century was that "everywhere the mechanical succession of instants replaced the dialectical order of poses."[43] According to Deleuze, like the following examples of early modern dance, the

[37] Yvonne Rainer, "A Quasi Survey of Some 'Minimalist' Tendencies in the Quantitively Minimal Dance Activity Midst the Plethora, or an Analysis of *Trio A*," in Copeland and Cohen 1983, 327–28.

[38] Deleuze (1986), 4.

[39] Ibid, 5.

[40] Ibid, 6.

[41] Deleuze (1986), 7.

[42] Ibid, 4. It should be noted that while Deleuze uses Bergson's movement theories to create his taxonomy of cinematic images in his two cinema books, he also critiques Bergson's own application of those same theories to the cinematic apparatus. See the first chapter of *Cinema 1* for Deleuze's critique of Bergson on the cinema.

[43] Ibid, 4.

technology of the cinema "does not give us a figure described in a unique moment," that is a pose, "but the continuity of the movement which describes the figure."[44]

The compatibility of both early modern dance and the cinema with Bergson's theories challenges the centrality of cinema in relation to the kinetics of modernity. Genevieve Stebbins's seminal physical performance model of American Delsartism can be considered the very first manifestation of *modern movement* as a nascent dance theater practice. Consequently, Duncan, via Delsartism, produced a dance style that is thoroughly sympathetic with the theory of modern movement outlined here, while Fuller fully illustrates its application to dance.

It is important to iterate that the two models of movement drawn from Bergson—the "ancient," which is aligned with traditional dance styles such as classical ballet, and the "modern," which is collocated with new dance practices—provide a binary framework for thinking through changes in aesthetic practice related to dance and photographic reproduction. In this instance, ballet can be figured as a movement lexicon in which the pose dominates, while modern dance, particularly in the form of La Loïe, represents an aesthetic commitment to the principle of flux. These two ideals function as poles or extremes rather than as a total ontological distinction. Dance, of course, embraces every variation that includes and falls between the two poles—the infinite diversity of motion. I am dealing with a particular historical moment in the development of dance practice, the specific qualities emerging in this new body of work, the affinity of such qualities with Bergson's ideas about movement and the type of movement associated with the concurrently developing cinematic apparatus.

1.3 Modern Movement and the Dissolution of the Pose in Fin de Siècle Dance

> [The poses] *flow gracefully onwards from the simple to the complex. They are a natural evolution of beauty produced by the changing curve of the spiral line from head to toe, commencing with a simple attitude, and continuing with a slow, rhythmic motion of every portion of the body, until it stands before you as the most perfect representation of art.*
>
> (Unidentified reviewer)[45]

This quotation is from an 1893 review of a performance by Genevieve Stebbins, an artist revealed by Ruyter as one of the most successful exponents of American Delsartism and an overlooked pioneer of American modern dance.[46] This description could stand to represent an historical moment between the "ancient" and "modern" forms of movement identified by Bergson. While there is mention of the

[44] Ibid, 5.

[45] Unidentified reviewer cited in Nancy Lee Chalfa Ruyter, *The Cultivation of Mind and Body in Nineteenth Century American Delsartism* (Connecticut: Greenwood Press, 1999), 117.

[46] An earlier dance historian who linked Stebbins to the birth of modern dance in America was Olga Maynard (*American Modern Dancer: The Pioneers*, [Boston, Toronto: Little, Brown and Company, 1965]) and contemporary with Ruyter's 1979 publication, *Reformers and Visionaries: The Americanization of the Art of Dance* (New York: Dance Horizons, 1979), was Elizabeth Kendall's *Where She Danced* (New York: Alfred A. Knopf, 1979).

sort of privileged moments so integral to Bergson's "ancient" theory of movement—that is, the immobile "perfect representation of art"—there is also room for attention to the transitional moments—the evolving, changing curve of the spine that instigates transformations in every part of the physical whole. From the transition being "of no interest in itself,"[47] Stebbins's Delsartism gave form to the "any-instant-whatevers" while remaining true to the ideal forms of the past, placing her seminal form of modern dance in direct relation to the transition toward "modern" movement.

François Delsarte's system of expression had its heyday in mid-nineteenth-century France and was the result of research into the details of expression of both character and emotion "in each minute part of the face and body."[48] I will return to Delsarte's theories for my discussion of gesture, silent cinema, and gestural dancefilm in a later chapter, but my interest here is in American Delsartism, which, while related to Delsarte's work, was a distinct type of body culture and of particular relevance to the shift from pose to flow. Delsartism crossed the Atlantic in the late nineteenth century. Verbal aspects gave way to the physical, and the system was taken up first by professional performers, then middle-class women who could afford amateur artistic pursuits. It finally moved back into the professional sphere in America with the emergence of artists such as Isadora Duncan from within the circuit of training and performance.[49] In her book, *The Cultivation of Body and Mind in Nineteenth Century American Delsartism*, Ruyter stresses the connection between the French system, its American adaptations, and the rise of early modern dance.

In an instructional passage from Stebbins's 1902 publication, *Delsarte System of Expression*, Ruyter points out that she "focuses on the transitions—the movement into a pose and between poses—rather than on the poses themselves." The key aspects of the transitional movement are identified as: "simultaneous movement of all parts of the body"; a slow and subtle quality to the movement itself; the movements must "unfold from within to without"; and the gradation of movement must be smooth. This movement should conform to what she termed "the Laws of Sequence (or Succession)."[50] It is this attention to, and formal consideration of, the in-between moments or "any-instants-whatever" that exist outside the perfected static forms, and the dissolving of those forms into a continual flow of movement, that makes Stebbins's art resonate with the ideas of motion described above that apply to modern dance and the cinema.

If Genevieve Stebbins's American Delsartism represents a transitional phase in both the understanding of movement and the expressive and artistic potential of the body at the beginning of the twentieth century, Loïe Fuller and Isadora Duncan represent a wave of female soloists who established a new theatrical context for dance, and whose work

---

[47] Bergson quoted in Deleuze (1986), 4.

[48] Ruyter (1999), 76.

[49] For more on Duncan and Delsartism see Ruyter (1979) and (1999), where the writer lists the Delsartean elements of Duncan's practice comprehensively. Amy Koritz notes that contemporary English reviewers saw the influence of Delsarte on Duncan (Koritz 1995, 48). And Deborah Jowitt writes: "The rising young salon artist Miss Isadora Duncan, interviewed in 1898 by the *New York Herald Sun*, made it clear that she admired Delsarte...and that she had absorbed his message about the connection between movement and mental attitude....It would have been hard for a bright, serious young person with theatrical aspirations growing up in America in the 1880s and 1890s *not* to have been influenced by Delsarte" (Deborah Jowitt, *Time and the Dancing Image* [Berkeley: University of California Press, 1988], 78–79).

[50] Ruyter 1999, 118.

engaged with the influential new ideas about the body and movement that were shaping contemporary literature, philosophy, and new technologies for (re)producing motion.

In considering these two particular artists in relation to the concurrent philosophical developments regarding the nature of movement, I am challenging the tendency within dance history to place Fuller and Duncan at the vanguard of opposing streams of choreographic innovation. It is generally believed that Duncan's innovations were in distinguishing her art from existing dance traditions, such as the ballet and burlesque, and turning to choreographic innovation inspired by nature, the feminine form, and individual expression precipitated by a theme or piece of music.[51] Fuller, on the other hand, is mostly associated with both the sensationalist performances of the popular stage and the technological innovations that were finding their audience there.

Fuller has inspired many connections between her art and the history of twentieth-century dance.[52] Helen Thomas stresses that "it is often overlooked that much of the value accorded to Duncan's dance had its roots in Fuller's work," pointing in particular to her success in Europe, her elevation of a popular dance act to the status of "art," and her role as "the first American woman to put her hallmark on nonacademic dance."[53] But Thomas also suggests that it was not Fuller's dancing skills that earned her a place in dance history (she had fewer than six lessons in her life), but her use of electric light. Sommer outlines how Fuller's dance departed from the skirt dances and nautch dances popular at the time that emphasized the display of the female form and the skill of the dancer in performing popular dance steps:

> First [Fuller] increased the size of the skirt until it became "draperies." This allowed a radical shift in emphasis to take place and changed the performance matrix.... [T]he skirt itself became the central focus as the most important and the most essential mobile image.... By carefully choosing and arranging twelve coloured lights of great intensity, she further abstracted and enlarged the image, creating a new dance.[54]

The "new dance" that Fuller created was written though by the technologies she employed. Fuller's creative process continued with increasingly complicated staging arrangements. Her lighting produced effects that had never been seen before—sideways from the wings where electricians were perched on step-ladders of varying heights, above in the flies, and "shining upwards through glass plates in the boards."[55] Sommer, whose seminal research in the 1970s uncovered many details regarding Fuller's stagecraft, also quotes from a New York newspaper describing the backstage preparations carried out between acts. The report reveals that a black curtain and "jet black carpet"

---

[51] This reductive historicizing of Duncan was challenged by dance theorists and historians in the late 1980s and 1990s, most significantly by Mark Franko in *Dancing Modernism/Performing Politics* (Bloomington: Indiana University Press, 1995), and Ann Daly, *Done into Dance: Isadora Duncan in America* (Bloomington: Indiana University Press, 1995).

[52] In Francis Sparshott's *A Measured Pace: Toward a Philosophical Understanding of the Arts of Dance* (Toronto: University of Toronto Press, 1995), he includes a lengthy footnote outlining the debate regarding Fuller's status as a "dancer" (507, footnote 27). For the most recent contributions to this discussion see Garelick (2007) and Albright (2007), who both champion Fuller as a legitimate modern dance pioneer.

[53] Helen Thomas, *Dance Modernity and Culture* (London and New York: Routledge, 1995), 54. Thomas later elaborates on this claim, stating that Fuller "preceded Duncan in using the works of the great classical composers... in dancing solo and in training a group of dancers in her style." She also pre-dates Duncan in "abandoning the corset" (60).

[54] Sommer (1975), 58.

[55] Ibid, 58.

with a square cut out for the glass plate were installed to intensify the lighting effects, creating the blackened theater that would soon become standard in cinemas.[56] Lighting design and experimentation were a passion for Fuller, and Mallarmé gives an indication of how intrinsic the use of technology was to the character of Fuller's innovations in referring to her performance as "an industrial accomplishment."[57] Fuller thus developed a performance mode that produced a "moving image" independent of text-based models, grounded in the body and technology.

A description of Fuller by Duncan—who travelled with Fuller to Berlin prior to her own successful tours to Europe—gives a sense of the effect of this combination of movement and technology:

> Before our very eyes she turned to many-coloured, shining orchids, to a wavering, flowing sea-flower, and at length to a spiral-like lily, all the magic of Merlin, the sorcery of light, colour, flowing form.... She transformed herself into a thousand colourful images before the eyes of her audience. Unbelievable. Not to be repeated or described.[58]

This was a dance of transformation through motion; her flowing, spiralling, wavering, turning movements fired audiences' imaginations and inspired multiple readings of the morphing shapes she created. This art, which was marked by an unstable signifier and a quality of constant flux, was "not to be repeated or described," a dance of continual invention that bypassed poses and postures, emulating the ephemeral "flow of life."[59]

The very nature of Fuller's art shared the characteristics of the modern conception of movement that Bergson describes. As if taking Stebbins's moderate and regulated attention to transition to an extreme, Fuller's dance was all "in-betweenness," a display of constant transformation and motion, the definition of Deleuze's modern motility; she "does not give us a figure described in a unique moment, but the continuity of the movement which describes the figure."[60] The emphasis on ceaseless motion in her performance (which was actually necessary to maintain the effect as a momentary lapse in impetus would cause the fabric to either drop or tangle) resulted in a display of the "uninterrupted change" of Bergson's modern movement. The "any-instants-whatever" were there in the "duration which flows" and were almost impossible to fix in a still image, *belonging entirely to that flow*. Photographs of Fuller illustrate the difficulty of registering her movement in a still image, so that she is often posing with her skirts held aloft or, when in motion, becomes a blurred and imperceptible shape (see fig. 1.1).

While Fuller's art is firmly aligned with the technological changes at the beginning of the twentieth century, Duncan's modern dance is more commonly pitched against these changes as a reactionary return to the organic and the natural. If Duncan's art

---

[56] Ibid, 61. Ted Merwin writes, "it took ten minutes and many hands just to darken an auditorium. [Fuller's] 'Fire dance' alone required fourteen technicians" (Ted Merwin, "Loïe Fuller's Influence on F. T. Marinetti's Futurist Dance," *Dance Chronicle* 21, 1 [1998]: 88).

[57] McCarren (1995a), 758.

[58] Isadora Duncan, *My Life* (London: Victor Gollanz, 1928), 104. It should be noted that Fuller refers to Duncan as "my protégée" in her autobiography and was embarrassed by Duncan's near nudity after organizing a performance for her in Vienna. Fuller never actually mentions Duncan's name in her account of their relations and falling out, but it could not be clearer who she is referring to (Fuller 1913, 223–31).

[59] Albright discusses the transition from pose to sequential movement in Fuller's work, stressing the progression from center to periphery and back, which she aligns with Hillel Shwartz's recent theorizing of a "new kinaesthetics" at the turn of the century (Albright 2008, 28–30).

[60] Deleuze (1986), 5.

Figure 1.1 *Loie Fuller as blurred figure in room* (anonymous). Jerome Robbins Dance Division, New York Public Library for the Performing Arts, Astor, Lenox and Tilden Foundations.

grew out of the Delsarte tradition, and that tradition can be discussed in relation to the modern conception of movement, what was Duncan's position in relation to that same concept of motion?

In Mark Franko's book, *Dancing Modernism/Performing Politics*, he writes that "historically, movement as a modernist object is tied to 1920s experiments with labour efficiency," and that it was "the technological aesthetic in opposition to which

Duncan founded modern dance."[61] But Bergson's influential movement theories had much broader resonance than the motions of the new machines of labour, being applicable to the performing and screen arts. Duncan's modernity is signalled by her connections with contemporary dress reforms, the new body consciousness represented by physical activities such as Delsartism, but, moreover, the quality of her dancing that was marked, as I have stated, by constant flow.

In the reconstruction of Duncan's early dances such as *The Blue Danube* (1902), *Water Study* (1900), and *Momente Musicale* (1907), the emphasis is on uninterrupted, continuous, and self-propelled motion, with patterns being traced out through repetition and a near absence of static postures or poses.[62] Duncan herself describes her choreographic process:

> I also dreamed of finding a first movement from which would be born a series of movements without my volition, but as the unconscious reaction of the primary movement.[63]

This type of movement, described as a corporeal "stream of consciousness," lends itself so readily to the model of "any-instants-whatever" and can thus be read in direct relation to Bergson's concept of modern motility. If, as Elizabeth Dempster has suggested, the first generation of modern dancers produced an "affective" force rather than a "pictorial" quality, Duncan has a special place in the shift from dance styles bound to pictorial modes of choreography and perception to dance as a force exemplifying the movement of modernity.[64] And this stands despite Duncan's rejection of modern theater technologies; she preferred a plain velvet curtain and no special lighting effects for her performances, in direct opposition to Fuller's keen investment in technological innovations.

While dance histories have placed Fuller and Duncan in opposing artistic corners, the dissolution of the pose in modern movement brings the two artists into the same field of motion—for Duncan via Delsartism and the idea of an involuntary stream of movement, and for Fuller via her use of technology and costume. Both dancers can now be seen as part of a movement revolution that brought together high art and popular culture, modern dance and cinema, against the backdrop of developments in the field of philosophy.

1.4 Re-choreographing History

> *Thanks to [Fuller], the dance has once more become the "poem without words"*
> *of Simonides. . . . [A]bove all one is grateful to her for giving substance to that*
> *ideal spectacle of which Mallarmé once dreamed—a mute spectacle, which*
> *escaped the limits of space and time alike . . .*
>
> Roger Marx[65]

---

[61] Franko (1995), xi & 7.

[62] These reconstructions are featured in the documentary, *Movement from the Soul* (1990, d. Dayna Goldfine and Daniel Geller), and are danced by pupils of Duncan's adopted children, Irma and Lisa Duncan, two of the Isadorables (Duncan's troupe of regular chorus dancers).

[63] Duncan (1928), 86.

[64] Elizabeth Dempster, "Women Writing the Body: Let's Watch a Little How She Dances," in *The Routledge Dance Studies Reader*, ed. Alexandra Carter (London: Routledge, 1998), 224.

[65] Roger Marx quoted in Kermode (1983), 154.

In concluding this chapter, I consider Fuller's art independently of the techno-aesthetic lineage that places cinema at the pinnacle of fin de siècle technological developments toward producing a moving image. From long-exposure photographs that demanded stillness across time, through popular entertainments such as the pan-orama, diorama, phantasmagoria, and magic lantern, to Jules Marey's chronophotog-raphies that represented movement at equidistant moments, the invention of the cinematograph has lead to the labelling of all that came before it *proto-cinematic*.

In performance, Fuller produced an abstracted, disembodied image by combining body movement, light, and color, a mixture that prefigured both the invention of color film and the experiments of the historical cinematic avant-garde. As Sommer states, rather than a moving image on a static screen, Fuller's dancing body "animated" the lights and projections, implicating her moving form in the overall effect of tech-nically contrived phantoms. Fuller herself became a "moving image."[66] While tech-nology played a role in the perceived movement quality in Fuller's performance—that is, her realization of Bergson's modern movement linking her to precinematic phe-nomena—it also played a direct role in two aspects of her performance that exceeded the effects of the body as it appeared in early, or "primitive," cinema: the destabili-zation of the moving figure as signifier, shifting performance away from text-based models and stereotyped representations of women; and dissolving the material parameters of the moving body into the fabric of the image itself allowing room to indulge in movement-for-movement's-sake.

In her essay, "The 'Symptomatic Act' Circa 1900: Hysteria, Hypnosis, Electricity, Dance," Felicia McCarren places Fuller's art at the end of the chronological development of motion studies and directly prior to the revolutionary technology of the cinema, right amongst the technological developments that realized Bergson's theories. In an aside to her central argument around the convergence of fin de siècle pathology and performance, McCarren describes the art of Loïe Fuller as a precine-matic performance employing the new technology of electricity, along with elabo-rate costumes, to create an effect both preempting the possibilities of cinema and providing a perfect subject for some of the earliest records of dance on screen. McCarren writes:

> Given the cinematic effect of Fuller's sequential movement, it is not surprising that Fuller and her imitators were the subjects of early films by Edison and others and define as well as demonstrate the passage from sequential photography by Marey and Muybridge to the uninterrupted flow of movement on film.[67]

McCarren thus summarizes Fuller's significance regarding the progression from the technological and aesthetic dominance of photography and the pose, to the repre-sentation of "sequential movement" associated with the cinema. But perhaps there is another way of thinking about Fuller's position within the techno-aesthetic

---

[66] Sommer (1975), 54.
[67] McCarren (1995a), footnote 18, 757. As I have stated elsewhere, it is contentious as to whether any films of Fuller did or do exist. McCarren continues this line of thought in *Dancing Machines*: "...Loïe Fuller's dance was also one of many entertainments that anticipated cinema, staging elements that the cinematograph would bring together...Fuller's serial movements...provoked a kind of looking that can be analogized to the persistence of vision that makes cinematic projection...appear to present uninterrupted motion" (McCarren 2003, 50).

genealogy dominated by the spectre of the cinematic apparatus. In many ways, the art of Loïe Fuller exceeded the possibilities of early cinema, a nascent form that would take some decades to reach an advanced technological and aesthetic level particularly regarding the way in which the moving body was figured.[68]

There are two ground-breaking elements of Fuller's art that effectively rewrite her position within such a chronology, suggesting that her work actually preceded and extended effects only approximated by early cinema. First, there is the radical redefinition of the role of the body as the site of signification and meaning production in Fuller's dancing, which exceeds the achievements of early cinema, a revolution recognized in the writings of the Symbolists. Although Fuller's serpentine dances began as representations of recognizable objects such as flowers and butterflies, she moved on to representing elements such as fire and snow and finally "fantastic imaginative scenes" such as the Aurora Borealis.[69]

This was nonmimetic dance, departing from the character-based performances of narrative ballets and the generic dance steps of burlesque and vaudeville, both of which depended upon engaging or alluring personalities and role-playing. Moving beyond the limitations of the body as a determined and discrete figure and becoming a transformative site, Fuller's dancing body was a radical intervention within a history of female performance based around characterization, titillation, idealization, and voyeurism. The tendency of her work to thwart singular readings is what appealed to the French Symbolists; Fuller's dance was regarded as a "poem without words," which Roger Marx describes in the quotation that opens this section as "a mute spectacle, which escaped the limits of space and time alike." The transformative capacity of this dancing body and its ability to create its own spatio-temporal reality operates well beyond representations of the human form in early cinema where, for example, dancers (almost entirely female) performed against black or painted backdrops, dressed to accentuate small waists and shapely legs, kicking, spinning, and performing tricks pulled from the standard repertoire of popular stage choreography. The frame is mostly static, operating as a double of the proscenium frame.

Second, Fuller's redrawing of the physical parameters of a technologically transformed body regarding its relation to the performance space also exceeds the use of the moving body in early cinema. It was through the stage technology of costume and lighting, along with the choreographed movements, that Fuller produced dancing that became disassociated from "the representation of single images," realizing an independent and abstracted "moving image." This also involved a disassociation from the body of the performer so that the performer and the performed conflate into one entity brought into being through texture, movement, light, and color. Here, the dancer disappears into a play between recognition and abstraction where the only continuity is motion itself. As Fuller herself explains, "I can express

---

[68] Gunning would disagree with me here. He argues, via the writings of Germaine Dulac, that the earliest actuality films contain elements of the art of motion that he finds exemplified in the work of Fuller and adds that early trick films exhibit "the syntax of Fuller's constant metamorphoses out of a matrix of movement" (Gunning 2003, 85).

[69] Sommer (1975), 64. Sommer writes, "Throughout this evolution, her images became more and more abstract, until unencumbered and unattached to any form."

this force which is indefinable but certain in its impact. I have motion…motion and not language is truthful."[70] This fusion of a motile corporeality with technology transforms the figure's capacity to produce meaning, and the figure's ability to influence the space-time configuration within which it exists. This type of cinematic body would not appear until the first avant-garde cinematic experiments of early innovators such as Man Ray, Jean Renoir, René Clair, and Dudley Murphy, whose 1929 film, *Black and Tan*, will be discussed in detail. Fuller's influence on avant-garde film and theater makers has been well-documented, but what I am focusing on here is her profound legacy regarding the choreographic in cinema. *Black and Tan* provides a striking example of performance and technology combining to move beyond singular, determined figures and creating transformation through continual movement. From this point there is a clear trajectory to more recent dancefilm examples. Fuller's emphasis on the performing body as force, motion, and spectacle as opposed to its traditional role as mimetic vehicle or metaphor has become a consistent characteristic of the way in which the moving body operates within dancefilm.

Dudley Murphy's 1929 film, *Black and Tan*, features the music of Duke Ellington's orchestra and a frame story about a band leader (Ellington playing himself) and his dancer girlfriend Fredi Washington (playing herself). The film includes dancing figures that are introduced in support of the storyline; however, through their filmic treatment the dancers ultimately exceed their narrative function to become abstracted moving images, spilling beyond individualized figures and containable diegetic functions.

Ellington's girlfriend has a heart condition but is forced to perform in order to secure a job for Ellington's band. At the club, a quartet of male tap dancers perform in a row in front of the band with their images reflected on a mirrored floor between them and the audience. In the second part of their routine, they dance in unison and close together so that they form one unit, their bodies and limbs locked together by an invisible force. The doubling of bodies that the mirrored floor effects is repeated by the choreography, their mechanical form simulating a hall of mirrors. The film cuts to a whoozy Washington waiting in the wings and we see the performance again through her disoriented gaze. The first shot of the quartet, which is produced through a combination of choreography and the mirrored floor, is now complicated further by a kaleidoscopic in-camera effect, the dancing quartet repeated multiple times with each repeated image itself rotating. The repetition of the entire performance requires an overlap in the temporal progression of the film and only makes sense as an attempt to maximize the impact of this visual "trick." Furthermore, the length of this sequence exceeds its function as a subjective point-of-view shot establishing Washington's poor condition, so that in this scene, the spectacle of motion—a kind of mechanistic, disembodied and abstracted motion—becomes the primary interest. The desperation of the characters' situation, struggling in a callous urban milieu, the pace of life, and the demands on the body all culminate in this rhythmic, fragmented, and intensely motile dancing image. The image expands beyond its function to suggest other meanings and broader themes.

Later in the apartment where the story began, a crowd of mourners surround Washington's deathbed, singing along to Ellington's piano. The composition of this set-up consists of Ellington in the lower right corner and the bed and mourners in the centre with the mourners' dark shadows looming large and black over the scene, covering the top left-hand quarter of the screen. The individual figures are obscure in the middle-ground but as a shadow form a clearly defined, dark, and shifting shape that moves rhythmically to the gospel-style music.[71] This disembodied, moving figure made up of a collective signifies grief, but it also fascinates as a dancerly form created through shadow play and the choreography of moving bodies. Somatic expression in this film is re-ordered, abstracted, and expanded both through choreographic direction and film techniques.

Turning to more recent examples, in Jodi Kaplan's short dancefilm, *Immersion* (1998), moving bodies, water, and fabric combine to loosen corporeal parameters and create spatial and temporal disorientation. Through superimposition, the reflection of light and the flowing quality produced underwater, fabric and bodies become indiscernible. The quality of motion comes to the fore—suspended, decelerated, evenly modulated—with random forms billowing into undefined spaces. Bodies diving into the water create a stunning change in rhythm, the center of corporeal force smothered by bubbles of air that mark its trajectory. Many contemporary dancefilms have used water, moving bodies, and fabric to achieve a visible expansion of the choreographed figure into the surrounding space-time—other notable sequences occurring in *Waterproof* (1986, d. Jean-Louis Le Tacon), based on a stage work by Daniel Larrieu, and *Blush* (2005, d. Wim Vandekeybus). *Undercurrent* (2000, d. Catherine Greenhalgh), choreographed by Rosemary Butcher, adds to such poetics an obscuring of the body through attention to the effects of air on water, the bubbles creating another layer of action with its own patterns and pace, confusing the perception of a large body moving weightlessly underwater. In this final example, the dialogue between performance and cinematic registration creates a visual poetic that realises the disappearance of the moving body into the film. In the following discussion of the operations of the close-up in dancefilm I describe how this particular shot can also release the image from the referent; how proximity can obscure the geography of the body and cause its qualities to spread out into the surrounding film space.

What Fuller achieved in performance, her realization of a moving image, would have come closer to Bergson's "duration that flows" than the "primitive" cinema, bypassing as it did clunky editing, varying film speeds, and hysterical acting styles. In pursuing this line, I am arguing for a repositioning of Fuller to a more central position within the historical and technological matrix that produced the cinematic apparatus, a position that has obvious ramifications for the history of dance, film, and dancefilm.

---

[71] The significance of jazz aesthetics and rhythms regarding *Black and Tan* is beyond the scope of my project here; however, it is important to note that my account of the cultural ascendance of continuity of movement has been limited to European and American contexts and omits the Afrocentric aesthetic that is, in fact, characterized by continual motion. This cultural influence would be felt in this same milieu in earnest shortly after Fuller's rise to fame. On the influence of jazz aesthetics on the choreographic cinema of Dudley Murphy see James Donald, "Jazz Modernism and Film Art: Dudley Murphy and *Ballet mécanique*," MODERNISM/Modernity 16, 1 (2009): 25–49.

2

The Close-up

Micro-choreographies

Dance writers have frequently acknowledged the revolution that the close-up has enacted upon the profilmic in dancefilm and video, offering new perspectives on the dancing body. In 1988, Sarah Rubidge wrote:

> Although [cameraman Tony] Keene does make use of [the close-up], he also physically moves in on the dancers.... [B]y doing so he is able to focus on particular body parts and on tiny details of movement, the touch of a hand on a leg, the gentle pressure of a foot on flesh.[1]

The proximity to the performing body that transformed the dramatic language of early cinema quite literally "witnessed" a similar transformation of the dancing body; a more intimate movement vocabulary found its medium and shifted from subtext in a live performance to text in a particular type of dancefilm. This type of screen performance thereby also created a new type of film bearing little relation to action-based dancefilms such as musicals and ballet recordings, which tend to document virtuosic feats in long-shot. The close-up in dancefilm has thus instituted new cine-choreographic terrain. Instead of Jimmy Cagney running up a wall and over into a back flip in *Yankee Doodle Dandy* (1942, d. Hal B. Wallis & William Cagney), we have a film like *Hands* (1995, d. Adam Roberts), where Jonathan Burrows's hands dance on his lap only for the camera[2] (see fig. 2.1, video 2.1 ⑤). A closed fist beats his thigh, an open palm lies still, thumb and forefinger pull out as if sewing a stitch, a finger draws along the thigh. This is followed by more obscure gestures performed in rapid sequence—hands flipping, fingers twisting, one hand becomes limp in the other's grasp. The movements of these hands fill up the frame with their dynamic choreography, tracing out its space.

As a type of cinematic shot, the close-up has traditionally had a strong connection with narrative storytelling and the construction of the star personae. More specifically, it is the *facial* close-up that has been with us since the earliest years of cinema and is most commonly cited in all manner of film discourse including critical

---

[1] See Sherril Dodds: "Through close range filming, facial expressions and subtle gestures can become a part of the dance, and so the dancing body shifts from being a general body to one that is detailed and specific" ("Televisualised," *Dance Theatre Journal* 13, 4 [1997]: 45). Sarah Rubidge, "Dancelines 2," *Dance Theatre Journal* 6, 1 (1988): 8–9.

[2] Ann Cooper Albright describes a dance that Loïe Fuller performed in 1914 that prefigures this film, *La Dans des mains*, which was "performed in total darkness, with only her hands illuminated...[and] indicated her future directions in cinema" by playing with light, shadow, and close-up framing. (*Traces of Light: Absence and Presence in the Work of Loïe Fuller* [Middletown, Connecticut: Wesleyan University Press, 2007], 176–77.)

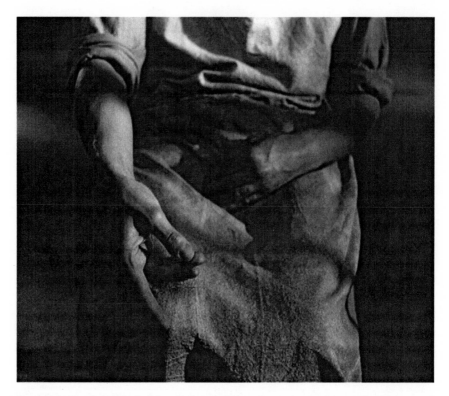

Figure 2.1 *Hands* (1995, d. Adam Roberts). Film still courtesy and copyright Adam Roberts.

theories of the cinematic image.[3] Mary Ann Doane goes so far as to suggest that the first appearance of the close-up on screen "seems to mark the moment of the very emergence of film as a discourse, as an art."[4] Doane also charts the history of theories of the cinematic close-up that go beyond narrative and star commodification, ascribing an autonomy to this particular image, an alternative function that is drawn out in this chapter. *Monoloog van Fumiyo Ikeda op het einde van Ottone, Ottone* (1989, d. Anne Teresa De Keersmaeker and Walter Verdin) exemplifies this alternative function of the close-up as it is found in dancefilm. *Monoloog* does this, ironically, by

[3] Regarding theories of the cinematic close-up I will be drawing on the writings of Béla Balázs and Gilles Deleuze but see also: Jean Epstein, "Magnification and Other Writings," trans. Stuart Liebman, *October*, 3 (Spring, 1977): 9–25; Jacques Aumont, *Du visage au cinema* (Paris: Éditions de l'Etoile/*Cahiers du cinema*, 1992); Gertrud Koch, "Face and Mass: Towards an Aesthetic of the Cross-Cut in Film," *New German Critique*, 95 (Spring/Summer 2005): 139–48; Roland Barthes, "The Face of Garbo," in *Mythologies*, ed. and trans. Annette Lavers (London: Granada, 1973), 565–67; Walter Benjamin, "The Work of Art in the Age of Mechanical Reproduction," in *Illuminations*, ed. Hannah Arendt, trans. Harry Zohn (Suffolk: Fontana/Collins, 1982), 211–44; relevant chapters in Siegfried Kracauer, *Theory of Film: The Redemption of Physical Reality* (Princeton, New Jersey: Princeton University Press, 1997); and Sergei Eisenstein, *Film Form: Essays in Film Theory*, ed. and trans. Jay Leyda (San Diego: Harcourt, 1949). For an excellent overview of the close-up in film theory see Mary Ann Doane, "The Close-Up: Scale and Detail in the Cinema," *Differences: A Journal of Feminist Cultural Studies* 14, 3 (2003): 89–97.
[4] Doane (2003), 91.

beginning with a facial close-up on Fumiyo Ikeda delivering a spoken monologue and then slowly transforming the function of the shot through carefully choreographed manipulations as the film progresses (see fig. 2.2, video 2.2⊙). The six minutes of the film consist entirely of dancer Ikeda shot in extreme close-up, speaking directly to the camera. It is a verbal tirade and as time passes Ikeda gets more irate, her face transforming under the effort to spit the words out, the movements of her features transgressing the merely expressive and becoming a kind of extreme facial gymnastics. Attention is drawn even closer to the actions of the face through a transition to slow motion and the replacement of spoken word with a music score. Now we are looking at a choreography of hypermobile facial features set to music. As her features contort, Ikeda's black bobbed hair swings around her face, framing the violent muscular activity and emphasizing and extending the physical force she exerts.

In *Monoloog* there is a transition from a focus on the communicative and expressive functions of a face in direct address to the camera, to a study in corporeal micromovements—a shift from a more traditional use of the close-up to a type of cine-choreography. Ikeda's face begins as a talking head; her facial expressions add meaning to her words in the same way that the shot has functioned in narrative cinema from silent film to the present. The ensuing transformation of the filmic performance on various levels (visual, aural, dramatic) shifts our attention from

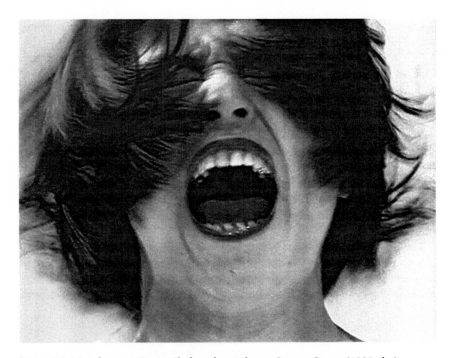

Figure 2.2 *Monoloog van Fumiyo Ikeda op het einde van Ottone, Ottone* (1989, d. Anne Teresa De Keersmaeker and Walter Verdin). Film still courtesy and copyright Walter Verdin 1989.

understanding her words to a fascination with the work of so many small muscles across the surface of the face, the various moving parts that work in combination, the physical transformation of the mouth as it opens and gapes and the eyes as they tighten and close. As the filmic treatment shifts to slow motion the attention to the physiognomic activity intensifies, loosening the bond between the diegesis and the image; the face is no longer simply part of the communication of her spoken dialogue but becomes an autonomous, fascinating, decentralized field of muscular action. At some point in the film the mise en scène takes off, becoming a cine-choreography specific to the close-up in dancefilm—a dancing field of micro-movements.

Writing in the 1920s, Hungarian film theorist Béla Balázs provides a seminal critical framework for considering the central role played by the close-up in the revolution of the dramatic representation of persons and things that the new filmic form brought about at the turn of the century.[5] The close-up drastically altered the scale of things in a process of magnification that impacted on screen performance and the manifestation of filmic space and time. Balázs's writings on silent film and the close-up are particularly valuable here because of his attention to the performing body, and they provide the conceptual foundations for this analysis of the close-up in dancefilm. The points of contact between the demands of silent cinema on filmic language and the demands of dancefilm on the same are clear and will be drawn out further in the following chapter in relation to corporeal performance in dancefilm beyond the close-up. Both silent film and dancefilm, when dealing with human subjects, depend upon modes of filmic performance that subvert the primacy of the spoken word, seeking alternative ways of drawing meaning out of the performer's body. The close-up is significant in granting *access* to these bodies.

Balázs argues that the silent era developed and perfected a cinematic language based on the close-up. He writes:

> In the first years of the movies the emphasis was mainly on movement....With the subsequent development of the silent film the place of dialogue was taken by a detailed expressive play of features and gestures, shown in close-up.[6]

Balázs emphasizes the role of the close-up in distinguishing a secondary phase from the earliest cinema, where body language was one of "exaggerated grotesque gestures," toward an intimate "gesturology."[7] He argues that, toward the end of the silent era, a close-up could provide "an entire scene," so that ultimately, "more space and time in the film was taken up by the inner drama...almost exclusively by close-ups of faces."[8]

The close-up's contribution to new film language in early cinema was not only in relation to the camera's treatment of the actor/performer and the subsequent production of dramatic meaning; it also transformed the nature of the actor's performance and, in so doing, the types of films that were being made. Attention to the performing

[5] Béla Balázs, *Theory of the Film: Character and Growth of a New Art*, trans. Edith Bone (New York: Arno Press, 1972).

[6] Ibid, 25–26.

[7] Ibid, 26.

[8] Ibid, 65, 73 and 74.

body inevitably led to new subject matter that extended beyond the central text or plot, a type of physiological subtext that began to overwhelm the films and monopolize screen time.[9] In such films, the performing body and the filmic treatment work together to produce a new type of cinema with specific characteristics of performance, dramatic language, and subject matter. Such a shift in filmic performance has an equivalent in the history of dancefilm. In *Hands*, the static camera and the other details of the shot are all drawn together in their attention to the articulations of the hands, a dance reconceived from a stage work and performed for the screen. In this example, the nature and definition of dance performance has been revolutionized. But unlike Balázs's close-up, a central and ordering dramatic arc is absent and the physiological (sub)text is front and center.

Dust (1998, d. Anthony Atanasio) is another example where the close-up creates new spaces and sites for dance. The short film begins with a close-up of sand particles blowing across surfaces, creating patterns as they dance and scatter, then hard sand cracks and a hand emerges. This begins a series of close-ups of performer Miriam King's body: her back, fingers crawling across the sand, her eyes covered by goggles. King's body emerges through fragments until we see it as a whole, attempting to swim across the sand dunes. The first full close-up of King's face is followed by a close-up of a ticking watch, then various odd angles render her face strange and unfamiliar. The second half of the film features King's body parts submerged in black water and shot in close-up, the solid form of the figure dissolving in the dark liquid and play of light (see fig. 2.3). This sequence recalls Amy Greenfield's body struggling in thick black mud in *Element* (1973), emerging and disappearing in a study almost entirely shot in close-up (see video 2.4ⓞ). Greenfield's pioneering work in the 1970s combined close-ups of the moving body with intensely motile and loose camera work that "ungrounded" the figure to a radical degree.[10] In both films, the drama is spread across various surfaces, substances, and the body of the performer equally, with detailed movements of fingers, limbs, and back muscles filling out their intensely visual tales. In such dancefilm examples, the performing body and the close-up have combined to create a new mode of filmic performance. This is often the terrain of the solo performer—a virtuoso of subtlety and detail, of mini-choreographies at the body's periphery.

This chapter examines how the close-up in dancefilm creates a specific cine-choreographic order by extending and redefining the parameters and nature of screen performance and thereby extending the parameters of dance. This is achieved through an attention to the performing body and its micro-movements—the smaller detailed movements of the body and its parts. This can often produce a

---

[9] Balázs uses the example of "the Maid's examination" scene in Carl Theodor Dreyer's *Jeanne d'Arc* (1928) (Ibid, 74). Other films/directors referred to by Balázs in his discussion of the operations of the close-up in silent film are D. W. Griffith (particularly regarding the performances of Lillian Gish), Sergei Eisenstein, Vsevolod Pudovkin, Mikhail Romm, and Alexander Dovzhenko.

[10] For more on Greenfield see Robert Haller, "Amy Greenfield: Film, Dynamic Movement, and Transformation," in *Women's Experimental Cinema: Critical Frameworks*, ed. Robin Blaetz (Duke University Press: Durham, 2007), 152–66. Haller writes: "Greenfield consistently works to place us, the spectators, inside her protagonists by bringing us close to them...[and] directs attention to no single part of the body" (154–55).

Figure 2.3 *Dust* (1998, d. Anthony Atanasio). Photo: Alan Fairbairn. Courtesy of Miriam King.

deterritorialization of the body so that any part of the corporeal whole can operate as a site for dance and, thus, meaning production and expression. Through these strategies, dancefilm institutes a bodily, dancerly model of the close-up that can operate even when the subject is not a moving body. What I am describing is a particular mode of dancefilm that can be found across the form's history, which I call *decentralized micro-choreographies*.

An engagement with theories of the cinematic close-up is essential to this end. As already mentioned, the face has a special function in most of the key readings of this particular shot. Balázs's privileging of the facial close-up can be traced to 1923 where he heralds the new technology of the silent cinema as the means to overcome the dominance of the written word: "a new machine...to turn the attention of men back to a visual culture and give them new faces."[11] He describes how the body's potential for expression and communication had deteriorated due to the printed word, with dire results:

> The emotions of men are always greater than can be expressed by gesture within the miserably narrow limits of their bodily being....Our "natural" expressive movements are always rudimentary and incomplete, because our boundless emotions are hemmed in by our bodily limitations.[12]

[11] Balázs (1972), 40.
[12] Ibid, 105.

There is a comparative thought on the body's loss of expressive capabilities and the rise of the significance of the face in the film theory of Gilles Deleuze, also in relation to the close-up during the silent and early sound period in film: "The moving body has lost its movement of extension, and movement has become movement of expression.... The face is this [intensive series]...which gathers or expresses in a free way all kinds of tiny local movements which the rest of the body usually keeps hidden."[13]

In light of the decreased capacity for expression that characterizes the body in the early twentieth century for these writers, Balázs and Deleuze develop their own theories of the close-up that posit *the face* as the ideal vehicle for "expressing" in this type of shot. While Deleuze cites Balázs's discussion of the close-up and builds on the Hungarian's ideas, it is important not to elide the huge differences between the distinct approaches taken by the two theorists to the subject. Balázs's "physiognomic" cinema is based around a particular and occurrent image within his theory of film. Deleuze's "faciality" is a much more obtuse theoretical concept within his "taxonomy" of the cinematic image; he states, "it is both a type of image and a component of all images."[14]

If, as Balázs and Deleuze put forward, there has been a suppression of the expressive potential of the body and/or its surface, either during the historical period dominated by the close-up or in our culture in general (which seems to be implicit in both writings), one of the projects of dance in the twentieth century has been to reactivate or investigate exactly this function of the body: the body as receptive surface and responsive organ that can articulate, through the most subtle micromovements, the registration of flows of energy, sensory activity, and exterior stimuli that occur through and upon the body. When applied to dancefilm, this calls for a reworking of the dominant theories of the cinematic close-up.

Conversely, a close reading of the film theories of Balázs and Deleuze reveals resonances with dancefilm beyond both writers' privileging of the face in relation to the close-up. In Balázs's model of the close-up, an expressivity independent of language is grounded in the action of the cinema upon the filmed subject, just as it is in dancefilm. Balázs also describes the transformative power of the shot—its ability to "take us out of space," distancing the image from the diegesis. Deleuze adds the process of *deterritorialization* to this attention to filmic performance—a process that liberates shots of the body in close-up from specific corporeal sites, which is also found in dancefilm. Both writers describe the micro-movements that the close-up reveals and that activate the shot's capacity for expression and autonomy.

Dance as a practice involves decentralized, antihierarchical models of the moving body and Deleuze's ideas regarding the operations of the filmic close-up are useful in unravelling how this characteristic of dance produces a novel type of close-up in dancefilm. Dance involves a bodily expressivity that attributes to the body what is

---

[13] Gilles Deleuze, *Cinema 1: The Movement-Image*, trans. Hugh Tomlinson and Barbara Habberjam (Minneapolis: University of Minnesota Press, 1986), 87–88. An exception to this theorizing of the body, face, and cinematic expression is the writings of Lev Kuleshov who, as Mikhail Yampolsky notes, "sees a far more effective means of expression in the arms and legs that in the face" ("Mask Face and Machine Face," *The Drama Review* 38, 3 [1994]: 61).

[14] Ibid, 87.

usually given to the face: expression, intensity, feeling. Deleuze's model of "faciality" is used to develop a theory of micro-choreographies in dancefilm, which, in turn, elaborates on an understanding of faciality and the close-up. Through discussions of contemporary shorts such as *Hands, Dust, Nine Cauldrons* (1997, d. Paul Hampton & Trevor Patrick), and *The Moebius Strip* (2002, d. Vincent Pluss), I will propose a theoretical reinvestment in the expressive potential of the body in close-up informed by dance theory and the writing of Jodi Brooks on the operations of the close-up in dancefilm. Characteristics specific to the close-up in dancefilm include the de-hierarchization of the performing body, an obscuring and destabilization of the corporeal geography, and the dance-like quality of the micro-movements that create a *micro-choreography*.

At the end of the chapter, I return to the writing of Balázs on the close-up and his model of a filmic expressivity grounded in the machinations of the cinema upon the filmed subject. Taking Man Ray's *Emak Bakia* (1927) as my example, Balázs's idea of "the poetry of things" is used to discuss an abstract field of motion, or *micro-choreography*, which is based on a dancerly, corporeal model but is abstracted from any recognizable human body. Other examples include Eugène Deslaw's *La Marche des Machines* (1928) and the music video clips for *All Is Full of Love* (1999, d. Chris Cunningham) and *Betty Ford* (2002, d. Oliver Husain, Michel Klöfkorn, & Anna Berger).

This chapter also establishes certain continuities or major themes across this book, beginning in Chapter 1: the release of the moving image from its referent; the marginalization of the function of language and a resistance to narrativization; and a dissolving of the boundaries between the dancing body and the dancing film image. The close-up as micro-choreography also contributes to the idea of the dancefilm form as an alternative cinematic mode, introducing cinematic forms of bodily expressivity that demand a redefining of filmic performance.

2.1 Theories of the Close-Up

> The expressive surface of our body was thus reduced to the face . . . the little surface of the face. . . .
>
> Béla Balázs[15]

Béla Balázs's consideration of the "physiognomic" function of the close-up, and the consequent "dramatic life the close-up gives to things" in *Theory of the Film*, not only suggests an approach for considering how the cinematic close-up operates in general, but is also particularly suggestive for the analysis of dancefilm.[16] According to Balázs, the close-up loosens the image from its function within the diegesis, drawing attention to the expressive activity of details within the image itself—the uncontained physiological subtext that Balázs saw leaking out beyond any diegetic function. This

---

[15] Balázs (1972), 41.
[16] Ibid, 57.

is significant for a discussion of the close-up in dancefilm as the denotative material associated with film narrative is often absent in dancefilm and the ordering function of such material is replaced by an investment in radical movement orders of and for themselves. Balázs thus provides the starting point for considering theories of the cinematic close-up and the effect a dancerly subject has on those same readings.

Balázs notes how the close-up shot discovered "the hidden life of little things"— the "cell-life" of things—and thus revealed a deeper perspective on "our vision of life."[17] He pinpoints the anthropomorphization that this entails, describing how the close-up "shows the speechless face and fate of the dumb objects that live with you in your room and whose fate is bound up with your own," finally referring to this effect as the "physiognomy" of things.[18] So this physiognomic transformation is a kind of contagion emanating from the protagonist ("objects surrounding a charming, smiling girl can all be smiling and graceful"[19]), attesting to a strong connection to the dramatic subject that Balázs insists on—what Gertrud Koch refers to as his "narrationally inscribed" effects.[20] In the next chapter, "The Face of Man," Balázs is even more specific:

> When the film close-up strips the veil of our imperceptiveness and insensitivity from the hidden little things and shows us the face of objects, it still shows us man, for what makes objects expressive are the human expressions projected on to them. The objects only reflect our own selves. . . . The close-ups of the film are the creative instruments of this mighty visual anthropomorphism.[21]

For Balázs, the face is the ideal of the close-up and physiognomic effects are the means of attaining anthropomorphic transformations that grant every *thing* an equal potential to express—that is, show us "the face of objects."

Balázs struggles with his distinction between the power of the face and that of other body parts. He writes at one point that, "the close-up can show us a quality in a gesture of the hand we never noticed before . . . a quality which is often more expressive than any play of the features."[22] But later, Balázs takes that same hand gesture and places it in opposition to the close-up of the face, which "takes us out of space, our consciousness of space is cut out and we find ourselves in another dimension: that of physiognomy." With the close-up of the hand, however, we do not for an instant forget that it "belongs to some human being"—its condition as part of a whole.[23] So there is a distinction here for Balázs between the capacity for body parts and objects to be a site for expression (*the physiognomy of the thing*) and their potential to operate as spatio-temporally independent of the imagined whole (*the physiognomic dimension*). Despite taking us "out of space," this "physiognomic"

---

[17] Ibid, 54–55, 57.
[18] Ibid, 55–57. In Gertrud Koch's article, "Béla Balázs: The Physiognomy of Things," (*New German Critique*, 40 [Winter 1987]: 167–78), she describes Balázs's theory as an "anthropomorphic poetics" or "anthropomorphic aesthetics of expression" suggesting an "animistic cosmos" within films. Koch also points to his open and flexible reading of films and the "latent progressive tendency" in his writing that leads to an emphasis on the form's visual nature.
[19] Balázs (1972), 59.
[20] Koch (1987), 169.
[21] Balázs (1972), 60.
[22] Ibid, 55.
[23] Ibid, 61.

model of the close-up cannot overcome its dividual condition due to the face's association with a hierarchical understanding of the human body where it claims supremacy. Therefore, Balázs struggles with the idea of an autonomous, nonfragmentary close-up image and this is taken up and resolved by Deleuze in *Cinema 1: The Movement-Image* in relation to the deterritorialization of the image in his "affect-image."[24]

Deleuze takes his cue from Balázs who, as we have seen, finds the facial close-up at the heart of a particular early cinematic practice. Deleuze maintains and extends the special role of the human face in relation to the close-up by making "faceicity" the basis for the affect-image—a type of movement-image that has exceptional qualities including the ability to become "pure expression" ("pure Quality") and to enable a "qualitative leap" ("pure Power") in the cinematic image.[25] This extension of the power of the face requires a huge conceptual shift.[26] As clarified in *A Thousand Plateaus*, faciality is no longer an anthropomorphic activity (as it is for Balázs), but a process of transformation enabled by the "abstract machine of faciality," which can then be applied to enable the transformation of any-thing.[27] It is this model of faciality and the related concept of *deterritorialization* that will become most useful in considering the corporeally based model of the close-up exemplified in certain dancefilms.

Deleuze's "affect-image" is the cinematic image that exists between the perception-image and the action-image in his order of movement-images. He equates this in-between or "interval" to Bergson's "living-images or matters" that have a "receptive or sensorial" facet. The living-image thus becomes a center for processing—"centres of indetermination" or "brain images":

> Affection is what occupies the interval.... It surges in the centre of indetermination, that is to say in the subject, between a perception which is troubling in certain respects and a hesitant action... the way in which the subject perceives itself, or rather experiences itself or feels itself "from the inside."[28]

We can see the relation to the human subject here and it is at this point that Deleuze introduces the face, in opposition to the body, as *the* part of "the image that we are," which can perform the "movements of expression" necessary; "*the affection-image is the close-up, and the close-up is the face.*" He writes:

> It is not surprising that, in the image that we are, it is the face, with its relative immobility and its receptive organs, which brings to light these movements of expression while they remain most frequently buried in the rest of the body.[29]

---

[24] Deleuze (1986), chap. 4, "The Movement-Image and Its Three Varieties" (56–70), and chap. 6, "The Affection-Image, Face and the Close-Up" (87–101).

[25] Ibid, 90.

[26] Deleuze's considerable shift in his ideas about film and faceicity, which take him well beyond the theories of Balázs, can be read in relation to Emmanuel Levinas's unique promotion of the face within his philosophical writings—particularly in *Totality and Infinity: An Essay on Exteriority*, trans. Alphonso Lingis (Netherlands: Kluwer Academic Publishers, 1991), which falls chronologically between the two film theorists. A similarity in concepts and terminology suggests some unattributed influence by Levinas on Deleuze's writing.

[27] Gilles Deleuze and Félix Guattari, *A Thousand Plateaus: Capitalism and Schizophrenia*, trans. Brian Massumi (London: The Athlone Press, 1988), 168. Deleuze and Guattari are explicit here: "It is not at all a question of taking a part of the body and making it *resemble* a face....No anthropomorphism here" (170).

[28] Deleuze (1986), 65.

[29] Ibid, 66.

Deleuze's affection-image, which "surges in the centre of indetermination, that is to say in the subject," being the way the subject, "experiences itself or feels itself 'from the inside'," is realized through "micro-movements," "impulsions," and "intensive series."[30] It is the *micro-movements* that enable the transformative powers of the faceified close-up to do their work, a power Balázs also attributes to the microphysiognomy that the close-up reveals. Micro-choreographies consist of *tendencies* toward movement that never actualize as a crossing from position A to position B, but constitute an expressive force as acentered resonations. What dancefilms like *Hands, Monoloog, Dust,* and *Element* discover are the micro-movements on the surface of—as well as the flows of energy through—the body in close-up, whether dealing with the face or corporeal locations other than the traditional sites for expression.

We can trace Deleuze's arrival at the face as the model for the close-up back to its *physical manifestation*: first, as the part of the body coinciding with the physical attributes of Bergson's affect; and second, as the site containing our "receptive organs"— that is, the senses. But there is another receptive organ—the skin—which covers the entire body and is also prone to experiences and feelings. Close-ups of the surface of the body in dancefilm become the site for micro-movements and impulsions that rebel against any sense of outline, being both on, under, and across the skin, spreading into undetermined locations within the corporeality.

This tendency toward deterritorialization is another characteristic of Deleuze's faciality that is relevant to the operations of the close-up in dancefilm. In *Cinema 1*, Deleuze points to Balázs's idea that the close-up "*abstracts [the object] from all spatio-temporal co-ordinates.*" This, for Deleuze, is an accurate description of how the close-up can *deterritorialize* the cinematic image in a way that "raises it to the state of Entity" and allows it to "express" rather than "translate."[31] However, Deleuze critiques Balázs's isolation of the face as the only close-up with this capacity:

> A feature of faceicity [*visagéité*] is no less a complete close-up than a whole face.... And why would a part of the body, chin, stomach or chest be more partial, more spatio-temporal and less expressive than an intensive feature of faceicity or a reflexive whole face?.... And why is expression not available to things?[32]

Deleuze departs from Balázs in insisting upon the potential for all faceified images—of faces, body parts, and things—to gain spatio-temporal independence.[33] The functions of the face—"individuating," "socialising," and "communicating"—are all dissolved as the face, or faceified object, becomes "qualities or powers considered for themselves," "that which it is as it is for itself and in itself."[34] So Deleuze arrives at a film image liberated from its referent, space, and time, free to operate as a discrete entity beyond objectification and into the realm of pure quality as an affective force.

---

[30] Ibid, 65.

[31] Ibid, 95–96: "If it is true that the cinematic image is always deterritorialised, there is therefore a very special deterritorialisation which is specific to the affection-image."

[32] Ibid, 97.

[33] It must be noted that, for Deleuze, not all affection-images attain this condition although they all have the *potential* "to tear the image away from spatio-temporal co-ordinates in order to call forth the pure affect as the expressed" (Ibid, 96).

[34] Ibid, 97–99.

In Balázs's and Deleuze's work, the face remains a touchstone regarding the potential for the close-up to bring about cinematic transformations that complicate the function of the shot within the diegesis, thereby enabling the realization of a truly cinematic, expressive force. I would argue that cinematic deterritorialization and the power to express "for itself and in itself" as an affective force is equally important for the close-up in dancefilm that takes the body or its parts as its subject. An investment in the central position of the face within the hierarchy of the body seems to be implicit to the logic of Balázs's and Deleuze's work on the close-up. There is, I believe, an assumption regarding the self-evidence of the originary status of the face regarding such things as expression, affectivity, and intensity underlying the complex of ideas built up by both theorists around the cinematic operations of the close-up. It is interesting that, theoretically, Deleuze must take the surface of the face "off" the body to complete Balázs's move toward a spatially and temporally independent, faceified close-up image.[35] Perhaps it is only in this dramatic move toward his "abstract machine of faciality" that Deleuze can distance the face from its traditional functions of communication and expression.

Deleuze's move to deterritorialize the close-up through the operations of "the abstract machine of faciality" coincides with a dancerly model of the body that is innately de-hierarchized. In contemporary dance, the face is not central and the body is not divided or hierarchized so that certain choreographic practices coincide with the operations of the close-up in film. Expression, feeling, intensity, and affect are not qualities that the face (as image) has an a priori claim over; these qualities are shared by the dancing body and its parts. The attention in Balázs and Deleuze to a subject shot in close-up that complicates the dramatic logic of the cinema—creating an opening, intensification, or transformation and deserting its signification to become movements of pure expression—could also be met by dancing bodies. A democratic, corporeal, dance-like decentralization of the focus of the close-up could look for expression in the elbow or the space behind an ear. The close-up is now a field of motion that is a decentralized micro-choreography, moving across and beneath surfaces, spreading out endlessly into the undetermined spaces of a body that can articulate even at its extremities, its periphery. In such a case, the face is returned to the body of which it is *a part*, to become one expressive possibility amongst an unlimited number in this new model of the close-up. By breaking down any centralizing tendencies in the treatment of the body, the close-up in dancefilm restores the body's expressive capabilities.

2.2 The Close-Up in Dancefilm

> *The new theme which the new means of expression of film art revealed was not a hurricane at sea or the eruption of a volcano: it was perhaps a solitary tear slowly welling up in the corner of a human eye.*
>
> Béla Balázs[36]

---

[35] See, for example: "we find ourselves before an intensive face each time that the traits break free from the outline, begin to work on their own account, and form an autonomous series which tends toward a limit or crosses a threshold" (Ibid, 89).

[36] Balázs (1972), 31.

In dancefilm, it is an understanding of the expressive capacity of the moving body engendered by a heritage of radical exploration throughout twentieth-century theater dance that reveals, discovers, and draws attention to "all kinds of tiny local movements" all over the body through the close-up.[37] Lesley Stern argues that if, as Corrine Cantrill suggests, there has been an overemphasis on the face in Western culture and a subordination of the body as a site for the production of meaning and characterization, this compulsion has been strongest in cinema, less strong in still photography, and lesser still in theater.[38] I would add that this compulsion is almost absent in most contemporary dance. Choreographic strategies generally work to develop corporeal modes of articulation or expression that involve any and every part of the body and challenge the vertical ordering resulting from the effects of gravity. When such strategies inform dancefilm aesthetics, they call for a rethinking of the operations of the close-up beyond those offered by film theory.

One model of such performance is the postmodern, non-hierarchical dancing body described by French dance theorist Laurence Louppe in relation to the work of American choreographer Trisha Brown:

> ...equalising the distribution of her body weight in lying down...relates to Brown's refusal of any expressivity dependent upon a hierarchy of body parts and their forces. It prefigures Brown's miraculous "abandon"—an abandon which has led Hubert Godard to describe Brown as "disarmed to the point of disappearance...."[39]

Kinesiologist and movement researcher Hubert Godard explains Brown's reworking of the body's relation to gravity. He describes a "plastic corporeal memory" in humans that is the "modelling of the tissues that generate the tensional organisation of our bodies."[40] This process involves the "tonic muscles which specialise in gravitational responses" and that contain our bodies' "most ancient memory":

> The essential task of the tonic muscles is to inhibit falling....In order to make a movement these muscles have to release. And it's in this release that the poetic quality of the movement is generated....Why are we moved when someone dances, when they put so much at stake in terms of their stability...? Because these activities refer to the history that is wholly inscribed in our bodies, in the very muscles that hold us upright.[41]

Brown's choreography displays a mastery over the activities of the tonic muscles, manipulating their habitual operations and everyday functions to produce dancing

---

[37] Deleuze (1986), 87–88.

[38] Lesley Stern, "As Long As This Life Lasts," *Photofile* (Winter 1987): 15–19.

[39] Laurence Louppe, "Corporeal Sources: A Journey through the Work of Trisha Brown," *Writings on Dance: The French Issue*, 15 (Winter 1996a): 8. I return to Louppe and Godard's writing on Brown in chapter five where I take up the question of the "disappearing body" in dancefilm.

[40] Laurence Louppe, "Singular, Moving Geographies: An Interview with Hubert Godard," *Writings on Dance: The French Issue*, 15 (Winter 1996b): 16.

[41] Ibid, 18. Elsewhere, Godard states that, "any gesture is literally born from the gravitational function" (Daniel Dobbels and Claude Rabant, "The Missing Gesture: An Interview with Hubert Godard," *Writings on Dance: The French Issue*, 15 [Winter 1996]: 42).

that moves us by enacting a kind of risk regarding our own tonic stability. She creates a highly skilled and poetically charged performance resulting from a de-hierarchization of the body.[42] Another of Greenfield's films from the 1970s, *Transport* (1971), recreates the performance and experience of this tonic instability *manually* (see video 2.5ⓓ). In the spirit of the choreographic experimentation occurring in the United States at the time, Greenfield creates a mise en scène crowded with bodies lifting and moving other bodies in a work-like mode, shot in close-up and mid-shot by Sandy D'Annunzio. An intensely motile camera is used again, moving under and around the performers and mimicking the experience of the one being awkwardly transported. They, like us, are cut loose from gravity yet immersed in an experience of physical effort.

That dancing involves a manipulation of our foundational, tonic stability has significance regarding filming the body in motion. If dance can challenge the centering habits of our corporeal existence, the dancing body as a type of screen performance must suggest new models for expressive film images that take as their focus any number of bodily sites in close-up. What we find in this multiplicity of bodily sites are tiny muscle movements that constitute their own micro-dance—not expressing emotions or psychological shifts, but pure movement relating only to the body and its "hidden little lives." Abstracted from the rest of the body and magnified, we find a "cell-life" jumping with micro-activity and dance-like motion: a field of shifting and moving parts or "bodies" relating to each other in a composition of movements, either random or rhythmic. Such images can provide an alternative model of the close-up where any part of a whole can be privileged with expressive potential, which is not bound to empirical systems surrounding the face, but the body, heterogeneity, and movement for movement's sake. Following Brooks's reworking of Balázs's theories of the close-up in relation to dancefilm and drawing out connections with choreographic knowledges, examples from Paul Hampton and Trevor Patrick, Vincent Pluss, and Pierre Yves Clouin illustrate how the moving body shot in close-up dissolves or disappears into the image, disarmed and open to the action of the close-up upon it, entering into a dance *with* the camera that results in micro-choreographies.

Jodi Brooks's approach to dancefilm in her essay, "Rituals of the Filmic Body," applies Balázs's film theory to thinking about the way a particular type of dancefilm can "draw our attention to movements, poses, and gestures of the body as sites of meaning and/or affect."[43] She uses Balázs's notion of a physiognomic cinema to describe the particular way the body is framed in Stephen Cummins and Simon Hunt's short film *Resonance* (1991), a theorization that emphasizes the possibilities for a physiognomy of the *body*, shifting away from the privileging of the face in Balázs.

---

[42] There is an interesting comparison to be drawn here to Gilles Deleuze's description of "aberrant movement," which is set in opposition to a "normality" dominated by "centres": "centres of the revolution of movement itself...and of observation for a viewer able to recognize or perceive the moving body, and to assign movement. A movement that avoids centring, in whatever way, is as such abnormal, aberrant" (*Cinema 2: The Time-Image*, trans. Hugh Tomlinson and Robert Galeta [Minneapolis: University of Minnesota Press, 1989], 36).

[43] Jodi Brooks, "Rituals of the Filmic Body," *Writings on Dance: Dance on Screen*, 17 (Summer 1997–1998): 17.

Brooks's understanding of Balázs's approach to screen performance is evidenced in the appropriateness of Cummins's film to his particular notion of physiognomy. *Resonance* is, as Brooks points out, a "more narrative based film" whose "dominant sentiment...could be seen as belonging to the figure of the lover."[44] The film tells the story of two relationships with little use of dialogue: the first between two gay men dealing with a violent attack on one of them, the second between the aggressive perpetrator of the violence and his girlfriend. Close-ups on the naked bodies of the gay couple, particularly where their bodies make contact sexually or choreographically, have a floating sensual quality that elaborates on their love story (see fig. 2.6, video 2.6⬤). These shots contrast with a close-up on the crossed arms of the girl as her boyfriend wraps himself protectively around her.

Brooks's definition of *Resonance* as a "narrative" film suits Balázs's consistent referencing of the physiognomic image to a dramatic subject. She uses "physiognomy" to describe the way in which "gestures are offered forth for scrutiny and unravelling" and how the film reads the "attitudes and gestures" of the "central male bodies."[45] This is a reworking of Balázs's model with the body and its potential for meaning production replacing the face as the central focus. In this way, Brooks describes a restaging of the profilmic via the close-up that is particular to the dancefilm form.

Figure 2.6 *Resonance* (1991, d. Stephen Cummins and Simon Hunt). Photo: Toula Anastas. Courtesy and copyright Estate of Stephen Cummins.

---

[44] Ibid, 17–18. The choreography and performance in the duet sequences is by Chad Courtney and Mathew Bergan.

[45] Brooks (1997–1998), 17–18.

Figure 2.7 *Vivarium* (1993, d. Mahalya Middlemist). Film still courtesy and copyright Mahalya Middlemist.

In Brooks's discussion of *Vivarium* (1993, d. Mahalya Middlemist) she goes even further, leaving Balázs and physiognomy behind (see fig. 2.7, video 2.7⊙). This is due to the nature of the film that is nonnarrative and concentrates instead on the action of the film upon the moving body and the moving body upon the space of the film—their dance with each other. Brooks describes this engagement as a "struggle," this demanding filmic body "recharting" the space of the film.[46] The film consists mostly of close-ups on Sue-Ellen Kohler's moving body. The body is pale against a dark background and is lit with colored light, mostly blue, which sculpts the corporeal form in space. Shots of curled-up limbs create a confusion of body parts, and a close-up of shifting back muscles and a rolling torso highlights the mechanics of the body. The action of the close-up on the surface of the body in *Vivarium* produces a filmic body Brooks describes as "similar to a mobius strip—it is as if it has no distinguishable inside or outside, front or back."[47]

Here we have a description of the distancing of the image from what is behind it, describing a motile, cinematic expressivity via the close-up that exemplifies a bodily, dancerly model, negotiating the space between the subject and film as a dancer negotiates their partner. Instead of a determined and contained reference (the face)

[46] Ibid, 18.
[47] Ibid, 19.

that refers to something "behind the image" like an emotion or intention, we have a decentralized, mutable, "constantly changing surface," a "sensory surface" that responds and articulates through consistent motion. And the movement does not only shift across the surface of the body, but beneath, exploring the "relationship between the figure's skin and muscle," creating the "mobius strip" effect.[48] Because, in the dancefilm, the liberation of the camera's gaze means seeing more than ever before given that the subject has a capacity for articulation and expression extending equally throughout the entire body, from head to toe, from inside to outside. The nature of filmic performance in dancefilm dominated by the close-up is thus redefined.

Nine Cauldrons features a combination of close-ups and long-shots on the dancing body of Trevor Patrick dressed in a variety of outfits. There are close-ups of his feet walking slowly in high heels and male dress shoes; of his back moving beneath a suit jacket, organza, or the rippling of muscle under bare skin; of his chest shifting under a crisp white shirt or a silky blouse; of hips instigating weight changes under a lace skirt; and of his hands folding and unfolding or smoothing along the textures of his garments. The close-up shots linger over the detail of small movements that are caused by major muscular and skeletal action so that the screen becomes the site for the micro-choreography of the folds of fabric, muscle under flesh, and articulations of the hand joints. The choreography unfolds across these various corporeal sites with each carrying the same degree of expressive power.

Patrick's sharper, full-bodied movements often play with the body's center of gravity, enacting the risk to stability that distinguishes the dancing body from the everyday, utilitarian body. The exploratory nature of the physical performance in this film, its challenge to centralized, stable, and hierarchically organized on-screen bodies, is explained by Patrick in his article, "Subtle Bodies":

> ...any performance is affected by the largely invisible play of energy through the mind and body.... [H]ow can these forces move and be seen to move the body?... The desire to answer these questions for myself was fundamentally what attracted me to the use of technology in dance—to film and video.[49]

Patrick describes here a project that seeks to reveal the subject of the film—his own dance performance—the "dialogue between body and mind," which constitutes his practice. He goes on:

> The camera attempts to see that experience which is recorded in the tissues of the body, in ways which can be apprehended by an audience.... The camera contemplates the action of breath, the subtle suggestion of movement under fabric, over skin, the details of gesture, posture, and facial expression. Each of these elements offers the viewer a point of entry into the experience of the body. Detail may be seen at the level of imagining.[50]

---

[48] Idem.

[49] Trevor Patrick, "Subtle Bodies," in *MAP Movement and Performance Symposium Papers*, ed. Erin Brannigan (Canberra: Ausdance Inc., 1999), 31–32.

[50] Ibid, 34.

Patrick is describing how the close-up, in Balázs's words, reveals the "hidden little life of things," and *Nine Cauldrons* does reveal something *more* regarding the profilmic performance. But it is the expressive potential of the micro-movements in this film that impress, their ability to take on a life of their own *cut out* of the choreographic continuity. These movements of expression complicate any sense of an exterior logic, creating an opening, intensification, and transformation.

Louppe and Godard's reading of Brown's de-hierarchized corporeal performance helps unravel the deterritorialization the close-up effects in certain dancefilms—an obscuring of any means of identification or location within the corporeal geography. The term *disarm* and the notion of a disappearing body are perfect for the images produced in these films: an anthropomorphic surface that leaks meaning from every part equally, obscuring any means of identification or location within the corporeal geography. In *Nine Cauldrons*, while the dancer and corporeal location are always identifiable, this information becomes redundant as the body disappears into the details of the micro-choreography.

In *The Moebius Strip*, the camera follows the bodies of Gilles Jobin's dancers in close-up as they play out a series of tasks, providing each other with bodies on which to climb, slide over, tunnel through, crawl upon, lie on, and stretch (see fig. 2.8). Toward the beginning of the film, the dancers undress to white t-shirts and black underpants, which reveals the machinations of their bodies and renders them interchangeable. The constantly altering camera angles also complicate the position of the bodies in relation to a gravitational center. Close-ups isolate hands grabbing unidentifiable body parts, these fragments becoming tangled and confused until in one sequence—an extreme close-up on a web of bodies—the light source is obscured so that the camera only registers dark, mobile shapes. The expression of physical

Figure 2.8 *The Moebius Strip* (2002, d. Vincent Pluss). Film still courtesy and copyright Vincent Pluss.

utility is spread out across the corporeal fragments and surfaces extending the idea of deterritorialization across various bodies, so that the dancers' heads—which are seen every now and again—become a means of identification that seems defunct.

The French filmmaker Pierre Yves Clouin takes this potential of the close-up to an extreme, maximizing the tendency toward obscurity to create his intimate signature aesthetic. Clouin's films are autoportraits of his body shot in close-range and at strange angles, creating uncanny images to the sound of his physical exertions. In *Kangaroo* (1998), fingers and then a hand emerge through what looks like buttock cheeks but could be knees. In *The Little Big* (1999), a barely lit anthropomorphic shape moving slightly back and forth is discerned, again resembling buttocks, but a burst of light reveals it is a shot of his back, down his body from behind his head, his bare buttocks creating another similar shape below. In *Workman* (1998), a shot of Clouin's back and thighs with his bottom raised high in the air focuses on the action of the muscles in his back and hip, the gluteus muscle pumping in and out as his knee bends and straightens. The crease in his hip begins to look like that between forearm and upper arm or any other corporeal joint. The resulting movements have an uncanny quality that departs from corporeal specificity, expressing the materiality of the human condition humorously through unlikely and undisclosed bodily sites.

2.3 The Poetry of Things

> ...*It is not an "abstract" film nor a story-teller; its reasons for being are its inventions of light forms and movements* ...
>
> Man Ray (on *Emak Bakia*)[51]

Some dancefilms, such as *Emak Bakia*, have as their subject a dancing field of micromovements completely abstracted from a recognizable human body. Balázs's reference to a poetic of "things" can assist in thinking through the way these films still operate as cine-choreographies. Balázs describes an aberrant type of cinema resulting from an overindulgence in close-ups unrelated to the narrative drive. The *poetics of things* refers to a more abstract approach to filmmaking, which, when combined with the corporeal model of the close-up being proposed here, provides a framework for considering such dancefilms. These films may not even make direct use of the close-up, but they replicate the pure movement of micro-choreographies: the field of shifting and moving parts that have been found in films such as *Vivarium*. If we look at Balázs's description of what he saw as the extreme, later period in silent films we find something akin to this more experimental or abstract use of micro-choreographies.[52]

Returning to Balázs's discussion of the close-up at the point where Deleuze leaves him, his intensifying concentration on the close-up's revelation of a material world

---

[51] Man Ray, "Emak Bakia," in *Close Up 1927–1933: Cinema and Modernism*, eds. James Donald, Anne Friedberg, and Laura Marcus (Princeton NJ: Princeton University Press, 1999), 43.

[52] Balázs is not specific about dates here but describes the period as the "last years of the silent film" and refers to Dreyer's *Jeanne d'Arc*, which was released in 1928 (Ibid, 74).

made newly visible—and somehow transformed—is an approach to cinema that could help describe a new type of expressivity grounded in the dancing body (or equivalent) shot in close-up. Balázs's position on the close-up and expression is much more complex than Deleuze's reading allows and I believe this is because of the tension in Balázs's writing between his advocacy of a cinema of human expression and his recognition of the potential for cinema to go beyond this dramaturgically bound function and toward a realization of its own particularly cinematic possibilities. As a result, there is a two-way pull between the attention to the subject and its specific "rules," and how the cinematic activity that enables this newly enhanced attention makes its presence felt beyond its service to the subject.

When Balázs releases the face from its condition of partiality, it is only to become the pure expression of "emotions, moods, intentions and thoughts"—aspects dependent upon the diegesis of the narrative film.[53] His notion of expression never quite makes the leap into the independent model proposed by Deleuze. But it does suggest a filmic expressivity grounded in the machinations of the filmic image upon the filmed subject, such as the expressivity that micro-choreographies produce where the interest is in the action of the camera on the moving body. Balázs's fascination with such a cinema is held in check as he oscillates between his dramatically determined model of the close-up and the possibility of something else, warning against:

> the temptation of showing the "hidden little life" as an end in itself, divorced from human destinies; it strayed away from the dramatic plot and presented the "poetry of things" instead of human beings.[54]

Balázs's notion of "the poetry of things" offers possibilities for dancefilms that feature a field of micro-movements where "human destinies" and a "dramatic plot" are often absent. For example, in Man Ray's *Emak Bakia* (subtitled "Cinepoem") we have a "hidden little life" of and for itself: The details of objects and things are rendered by the action of the camera on its subject, revealing an intense play of micro-movements that create choreographies for the screen.

In her introduction to Siegfried Kracauer's *Theory of Film: The Redemption of Physical Reality*, Miriam Hansen places "physiognomic approaches in 1920s film theory" (which would include the work of Balázs) alongside Deleuze's cinema books within a lineage of "theorists of the nonnarrative aspects of cinema," and rightly so.[55] The deeper Balázs gets into the details of the visual life revealed by the close-up, the more he moves away from the demands of the narrative drive. His theoretical commitment to the face and anthropomorphism may curb his departure into what he refers to as "the poetics of cinema," but this emphasis in his writing should be considered in relation to his conviction that the cinema's main function is to reignite

[53] Ibid, 61.
[54] Ibid, 59.
[55] Miriam Bratu Hansen, "Introduction," in Kracauer (1997), xxxii. Koch's recent article on the face in close-up, which draws on ideas from Balázs and Kracauer, continues this tradition reading the use of the shot in Weimer Cinema cut together with images of the "mass" as evidence of "the *a priori* self-reflexivity of film," its central role in the historical crisis of the image, and early cinema's avant-garde status (Koch [2005], 142).

humanity's expressive potential.[56] Seen in this context, the powers Balázs gives the close-up as an integrated, nonpartial image provide a way out of the closure of narrative diegesis and must be recognized as a radical shift.

Balázs traces the development of the close-up to the final years of the silent era where he notes an intensification of the aspects he has already outlined; the face isolated on the screen reveals to us the hidden life of things, "the world of microphysiognomy."[57] It is here, beyond his merely physiognomic cinema that the amount of screen time given to the close-up is at its highest, the movements are at their most subtle, and the degree of abstraction is at its most extreme. He describes an "intensity" in the filmic image in opposition to "a piling of event on event," and this "microdramatics" goes beyond the demands of the story, spreading out moments "in the ritardando of detail [sic] close-ups, showing that crucial moment in instantaneous sections of time when everything still hangs in the balance."[58] Balázs is describing intensified micro-movements that mark a departure from the demands of the narrative and have an affinity with the abstract micro-choreographies of motion studies such as *Emak Bakia*.

In *Emak Bakia*, objects that *could* be a glass prism, the shimmering fabric of a woman's dress, reflections on black glass, and out-of-focus reflected lights, are fragmented and distorted, becoming unspecified "dancing" images made up of a multiplicity of smaller moving parts (see fig. 2.9). One image that resembles bacteria under a microscope is revealed to be a field of daisies. These effects are achieved through a close-up on spinning objects or their reflections. The spinning creates repetitions and patterns that are definitely dance-like, and the dispersion of focus produced by the variety of moving parts is drawn into sharp contrast by Man Ray's inclusion of facial close-ups. These relatively still subjects centralize our gaze as, on all three occasions, eyes slowly open to pull our focus even further, taking the centralizing power of the face as image to an extreme. This "cinepoem" shows us "the poetry of things," not just revealing the "hidden little lives" of static objects that reflect the surrounding drama, but making them dance seemingly just for themselves, bringing them to life by giving them a type of motion that transforms them. This is how far the close-up can take the image in dancefilm, beyond the narrative and the profilmic performance, creating independent, animated microchoreographies.

Rather than confirming the dimensions and physical nature of the subject, micromovements make any type of stability in the image—of shape, nature, or identity—contentious. This recalls Trisha Brown's abandon and disarmament produced through overriding any hierarchical tendencies in the moving "body." Brown's fluid,

---

[56] In the first few pages of *Theory of Film*, Balázs describes the relationship between the cinema and the public as collaborative, with the public having a very direct role in its creative development. In arguing for a commitment to cinema studies he writes, "what is at stake is not merely the proper valuation of the film, but the fate of the film itself, for this depends on our appreciation, and we are responsible for it." He says that the exchange between art and the public "is a hundred times more so" in the case of film than any other art form, as the considerable economics involved depend upon audience "appreciation" (Balázs [1972], 19). Cinema, for Balázs, should ultimately serve the expressive demands of humanity.

[57] Ibid, 65.

[58] Ibid, 84–87. Deleuze's concept of the affection-image has much in common with Balázs's physiognomic image, including "ritardando," which also recalls Deleuze's affection-image as "interval."

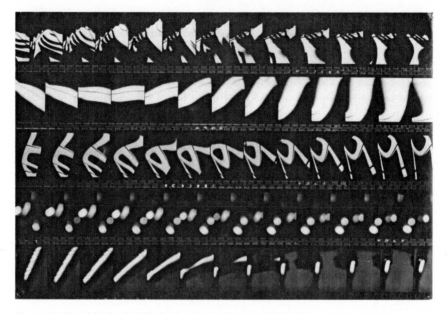

Figure 2.9 *Emak Bakia* (1927, d. Man Ray). Courtesy BFI Stills.

mutable, and intensely motile dancing body is the perfect reference point for these dancing images that create an entirely cinematic dance form—independent of, yet deeply affiliated with, the human body. What is of primary significance in cases such as *Emak Bakia* is the quality of the movement of the image, how it transforms the inanimate and creates meaning through "dance."

Another film that creates a micro-choreography for the screen through the close-up and abstraction of moving objects is Eugène Deslaw's *La Marche des Machines*. In this film, working machinery is shot in close-up so that the place of the part within the whole and its function is obscured. The camera transforms the movements of the pumping metal machinery revealing its human quality, such as the grasping action of two hooks facing each other and moving together in a smooth arc, perfectly in unison and clawing at the air. The micro-choreography of the moving machine parts is arranged through camera work and editing. A close-up on water jets creates a very different quality of movement, more akin to Man Ray's smooth and rhythmic spinning images, an organic swirl of liquid forms.

Chris Cunningham's music video for Björk's *All is Full of Love* takes Deslaw's theme even further—the camera lovingly laboring over the shiny, pumping machinery that is constructing a robotic clone of the pop star. This activity is overseen by a first robotic clone who caresses and kisses her new mate when complete. The close-up of liquid sprayed onto, and dripping off, the machine parts in this context has a particularly sexual subtext. This is reiterated by the detailed shots of the pumping actions and the rhythm of the camera and edit, which is less objective and work-like than Deslaw's, moving at a slow and seductive pace. The micro-choreography of the machinery is also shot in low-light and often in silhouette, creating a romantic and slightly noir mood further complicating any human/robot/machine categorization.

A final contemporary example is *Betty Ford*. This German music video features a variety of athletes and dancers (rowers, gymnasts, breakdancers, flamenco dancers) in white, often shot in close-up or mid-shot, fragmenting their bodies and actions. These images are then multiplied across split-screens that divide and divide until the simultaneous and varying micro-movements across the screen resemble the multiple, moving parts of the close-up in dancefilm.

The micro-movements that the use of the close-up enables in such films can be connected to the micro-movements described by Balázs and Deleuze in relation to the close-up in general. These micro-choreographies are not limited to human content, or even to the close-up shot as traditionally understood. Micro-choreographies describe a cine-choreographic order characterized by micro-movements or small impulsions, dancerly motility across and through a variety of surfaces, movement consisting of related parts that form a choreographic whole across equal and indeterminate sites. Throughout this book, micro-choreographies will return in other types of dancefilm as an important operation within the broader field of work.

3

Gesture-Dance

There appears to be a third realm between the speaker's gestures and the decorative expressive movements of the dancer, and this realm has its own form of interiority. The gestural language *of film is as far removed from the* linguistic gestures *of theatre as it is from dance.*

Béla Balázs[1]

boy (1995, d. Peter Anderson and Rosemary Lee) opens with a face appearing through grass at the top of a sand dune. The young boy, dressed in a khaki jumpsuit and lying on his stomach, peers intensely out to sea from a beach. He sees a Boy (the same performer) running along the water's edge. They gesture to each other. He moves quickly with work-like actions, grabbing in toward himself then throwing his arms out. He bends over and circles his elbows, as if running. The Boy on the beach answers with a jump to the sky, then a rotating leg kick and spin. This action is then retrograded, further complicating the message he is sending back. The boy hits the sand and looks up, the Boy appearing in the distance out of the beach haze, running with aeroplane arms. The boy works quickly with the sand, busy fingers and hands flicking and patting. Intermittently he looks up, his hands framing a view of the Boy moving through the landscape (see fig. 3.1, video 3.1 ⏺). The boy jumps off dunes and slides down in a slow, covert manner. He creeps along a ridge, arms moving awkwardly, high behind him like the wings of a bird. The Boy runs along the beach on all fours like a dog, stopping and sniffing the air in close-up. Other close-ups frame rapid head turns and searching eyes, the camera watching the surveyor. An empty jumpsuit floats in the water, a final dive off the dune, and the film ends.

boy features a solo performance by Tom Evans and focuses attention on his gestural performance, which gives the impression of responding to invisible stimuli. The gestures in *boy* conjure imaginary colleagues, tasks, responsibilities, secret signals—this is serious play with cinematic resonances. The thriller, the spy film, the war movie are all evoked, toppling from the mind of the young protagonist who is oblivious, lost in the communications and orientations between himself and his "playmate." The gestures performed are familiar but they slip away from easy definitions—earnest, busy, awkward, and virtuosic with the tone of work but with no clear purpose beyond play.

A certain type of dancefilm can be described as a *gestural cinema* with an internal economy dominated by corporeal gesture. In the dancefilms of Peter Anderson and

---

[1] Béla Balázs, "Visible Man, or the Culture of Film (1924)," trans. Rodney Livingstone, *Screen* 48, 1 (Spring 2007): 99.

Figure 3.1 *boy* (1995, d. Peter Anderson and Rosemary Lee). Film still courtesy and copyright Rosemary Lee and Peter Anderson.

Rosemary Lee, Pina Bausch, Wim Vandekeybus, Miranda Pennell, and others, there is a preoccupation with choreographed gestures of the body and their ability to express meaning, connect with the everyday, and evoke character and story.[2] Often the scenario is familiar cinematic territory associated with narrative fiction-film—a family gathering for a birth or death, teenagers congregating at a local haunt, an intimate domestic interior, an epic or dramatic landscape—and the gestural performance is grounded in that scenario—the physical contact between loved ones, a greeting or salute, dressing for the day. But those gestures are inevitably treated to a whole new process that shifts us away from the familiar and results in a cine-choreographic mode that I will refer to as a *gesture-dance*.

The "third realm" of gesture in Béla Balázs's quote above, "the gestural language of cinema," provides a starting point for examining where the history of cinematic performance and gesture-based choreographic practices come into direct contact with each other in dancefilm. I follow Balázs in distinguishing the gestural language of cinema from an understanding of gesture as a companion to speech (both everyday and dramatic), defining it as a *medial* modality that emerged in the early years of narrative film from a confluence of performance and cinematic technologies. I then trace how this gestural modality has informed choreographic research in the twentieth century and vice versa. So while Balázs places dance in opposition to the gestural language of cinema, I will describe a particular strand of choreographic practice,

[2] Other dance filmmakers analyzed elsewhere in this book who are distinguished for the use of gesture in their films are Pascal Magnin, Clara van Gool, and David Hinton.

running from Ruth St. Denis through to Pina Bausch, that has been in dialogue with corporeal cinematic performance.

For many dance makers, gesture is everything dance is not: functional, task-based, object-oriented. Isadora Duncan articulates a tradition of hostility toward this field of human action in modern dance when she refers to "gestures" in describing the movements of pantomime and how they "stand in" for language.[3] Martha Graham links the term to communication as does Merce Cunningham, who refers to gestures as "referential movement" related to speech.[4] Gesture is not only practical and functional, but it is a term collocated with signification and communication. For other choreographers, often associated with dance theater, gestures are the raw material for dance and are treated to processes of translation or transformation utilizing a variety of techniques (exhaustion, exaggeration, juxtaposition, intensification, adaptation) to produce original movement. This gestural choreographic process produces a very different type of dancefilm to those practices associated with more formalist movement research. In dealing with recognizable, familiar movements of the body and a corporeal attitude more connected to the everyday, these films often work from the assumption that the body is inherently *expressive* and foreground the corporeal production of meaning in a way that is unique within dancefilm practice. Where micro-choreographies, for instance, tend toward producing an abstract, poetic mode of dancefilm, the gesture-dance can be suggestive of themes such as loneliness or frustration utilizing character and motivation. This, in turn, suggests narrative, the literary model that has dominated the development of cinematic language since it first appeared in silent cinema. The way in which these dancefilms "stage" choreographed gestural performance in relation to character, scenario, and theme mimics aspects of classic narrative feature filmmaking. In this way the gesture-dance can evoke memories of *other* gestures in *other* films; the historical background of gestural performance in cinema weighs in as an influence on our spectatorial experience.

Belgian choreographer and filmmaker Wim Vandekeybus depends upon corporeal expression in his films, bringing some elements of narrative filmmaking and dramatic acting into play with his choreographic skills. But at the heart of this interdisciplinary process is his use of corporeal gesture. In *Inasmuch* (2000), birth and death scenes comprise familiar cinematic terrain, but there is no dialogue, actions diverge from expectations, and emotional journeys are rerouted. A woman is in the throes of childbirth and her husband, children, and a mid-wife are at hand. Anxious glances and sweaty brows are all in order, but when the newborn boy is taken out to the waiting family in the arms of his father, the family have gone. The baby then quickly morphs through the male family members, from toddler to old man, with varying reactions from the father struggling under their weight. Later, the old man lies dying and, once more, family members gather around. Gestures of grief and concern give way to amazement as the old man stands up and attempts to dress before abruptly passing away. The gestures of melodrama are subverted in this film through the use of

[3] Isadora Duncan, *My Life* (London: Victor Gollanz, 1928), 41.
[4] Martha Graham, *Blood Memory* (London: Macmillan, 1991), 7; and Merce Cunningham, *Changes: Notes on Choreography*, ed. Frances Starr (New York: Something Else Press, 1969), 157.

fantastic plots and unstable performer/role connections, a technique Vandekeybus exploits in other films such as *Elba and Frederico* (1993) and *Blush* (2005).

To get to the heart of the resonance between the gesture-dance in dancefilm and the history of gestural performance in cinema, I return to the origins of the narrative tendency in film. This occurs during the first decades of the silent era and, as we have already seen, silent cinema and dancefilm have much in common; they share a suppression of spoken word, which brings into focus the corporeal articulations of performers, which then impacts on the filmic treatment. Between 1905 and 1920, the directors and actors of the silent cinema were developing new gestural practices that were specific to the film form. The seminal writings of Balázs again provide a historical and critical framework, this time for considering the shift in screen performance from reflecting a *body in crisis*, to realizing a *gestural revolution*. Dating back to 1924, Balázs's writings on film not only elucidate the significance of the close-up regarding the development of filmic performance as seen in the previous chapter, but they also constitute a foundational body of literature on gestural cinema. Erica Carter writes that Balázs's film theory draws a focus on "shifts in actorly performance engendered by the new interrelation of camera and the gestural body" since the silent era.[5] For Balázs, the dominance of the close-up in silent film followed a period of "exaggerated grotesque gestures," a period exemplified by the Pathé Frères films of French stage productions shot in long shot and made in conjunction with the Société des Auteurs Dramatiques. Balázs explains that during this period the actors' attempts to compensate for both the silence of the new film form and the absence of detailed facial expressions due to camera distance resulted in a performance style "customized" for the screen. But this new form was not quite liberated from the stage and was most appropriate to a "dramaturgy of strictly pantomimic comic situations."[6]

The era Balázs describes has traditionally followed the "primitive" years (1893–1904), covering the period 1905 to 1916 when the narrative imperative was emergent but not yet dominant and screen technology was developing at a rapid rate. I will refer to this as the *transitional period* in early silent cinema, a period characterized by a *gestural mediality* that draws attention to the performing body. During this time new techniques and technologies result in a cinema where the performing body and cinematic mise en scène combine in a choreographic staging that exceeds narrative imperatives and is fascinated with the unassimilable, expressive potential of the moving body. Early film stars like Lillian Gish provide fertile territory for analyzing gestural performance typical of this transitional period where actors and directors combined existing performance methodologies such as François Delsarte's system of expression with new corporeal performance modes such as modern dance, psychological realism, and an experimentation with observation and improvization. The resulting filmic performances challenge the reduction of the body to a definable totality and allow for gestural activity beyond the demands of any ruling, prescriptive order, evoking Jean-François Lyotard's *Acinema*. This gestural mediality resonates with the gesture-dance in contemporary dancefilm, which is the product of a

[5] Erica Carter, "Introduction to Balazs," *Screen* 48, 1 (Spring 2007): 91.
[6] Béla Balázs, *Theory of the Film: Character and Growth of a New Art*, trans. Edith Bone (New York: Arno Press, 1972), 26–27.

comparative confluence of everyday gestures, acting techniques, and somatic-based forms of expression.

Delsarte, mentioned in Chapter 1 in relation to Genevieve Stebbins's seminal theater dance practice, is a key figure in discovering a historical exchange between the gestural spheres of cinema and dance. Delsarte's theories regarding a correspondence between our internal life and our gestural habits provided the foundations for training in both acting and dance from the mid-nineteenth to the early twentieth century. Delsarte, a French singer and actor who developed an original training system for voice and gesture applicable to singing, oratory, and acting (referred to as a *system of expression*), opened his school in Paris in 1839. The word *Delsarte* has come to stand for two things over the last 160 years: (a) a scientific approach to uncovering the *correspondences* between physical movement and our interior life, and (b) *histrionic* theatricality in performance. The latter has unfortunately distorted the revolutionary contributions he made to the former. Delsarte believed in a natural correspondence between mind and body and had faith in corporeal knowledge and the expressive potential of the body beyond the spoken word. For Delsarte, the body is always producing some kind of meaning.

At the same time, dance was developing new modes of corporeal expression and the work of Ruth St. Denis, whose Denishawn School provided training in Delsartean methods and would contribute to the training of silent film stars, represents a specifically gestural form of dance that shared many qualities with the new film form. St. Denis's creation of historic or exotic characters, her use of dramatic scenarios, mimetic gestures, and poses within a choreographed whole, and her commitment to corporeal expression corresponded with the aesthetics of nascent narrative cinema. This also made her the natural choice to collaborate with D. W. Griffiths in creating the Babylonian ballets for *Intolerance* (1916).

The *gestural revolution* that took place in the spheres of early theater dance and silent cinema can be seen as a recuperative process in the broader historical context of the fin de siècle *crisis of the body* touched on previously. According to theorists such as Balázs, the expressive capacity of the body deteriorated between 1850 and 1900. The physical arts floundered with the proliferation of the printed word, the populist dilution of the Romantic period in ballet, the rise of the melodramatic spectacle with its emphasis on pantomime, and a dominance of burlesque dance on the popular stage. A *gestural crisis* occurred and its symptoms were manifested in physical maladies such as neurasthenia and hysteria. According to Giorgio Agamben, this would register in the first films made between 1893 and 1904 that perhaps signal a turning point when cinema, like a distorted mirror, showed the world what its gestures had been reduced to.[7] In this particular story of the body in crisis, Delsarte's ideas return as part of a body culture industry that contributed to the gestural revolution, impacting upon almost every strata of society.

Delsarte's research into gestural performance not only provides key concepts for my analysis of gesture-dance but also constitutes a pioneering, rigorous approach to

---

[7] Giorgio Agamben, "Notes on Gesture," in *Means without End: Notes on Politics*, trans. Vincenzo Binetti and Cesare Casarino, (Minneapolis: University of Minnesota Press, 2000), 53.

corporeal performance and gestural processes that resonates with the contemporary ideas of Hubert Godard. Godard works across the fields of dance studies, movement analysis or kinesiology, rehabilitation, and biomechanics. In highlighting this connection, the early period of gestural experimentation and research is reflected in the most recent and progressive choreographic and analytical work engaging with gesture. I return to a key concept of Godard's, the *pre-movement zone*, later in this book, but his ideas about the role of gesture in current choreographic practice provide a framework for considering the work of contemporary dancefilm makers. Godard writes:

> The body mythologies circulating in a social group write themselves in the postural system and reciprocally, the corporeal attitude of individuals makes itself the medium of this mythology. A certain representation of the body which appears today on all film and television screens participates in the constitution of this mythology.[8]

Godard's writings on gesture develop links between the everyday operations of corporeal gesture, their manifestation in performance, and the cultural mythologies that underwrite this exchange.

We can compare his sentiments with Balázs's understanding of the interface between gesture and culture at the beginning of the twentieth century:

> Culture does not just refer to the beautiful poses of statues in art galleries, but to the gait and the everyday gestures of people in the street or at work. Culture means the penetration of the ordinary material of life by the human spirit, and a visual culture would have to find new and different forms [of expression].... The art of dance cannot do this; it is a task that will be accomplished by film.[9]

Contradicting Balázs, Godard describes an exchange between professional (dance and theater), amateur (therapeutic body practices), and quotidian gestural processes, and it is this complex network of gestural production that is exemplified in current cine-choreographic examples of gesture-dance. We could then say that dancefilm meets Balázs's call for a gestural cinema combining aesthetics with an "everyday" humanity. These dancefilms are also unique within the broader field of practice in recuperating dance from its strong association with formal abstraction in the twentieth century, returning to *expression* and *intentionality* while prodding at the cinematic conventions relating to the same.

The films of Miranda Pennell beautifully combine the everyday gestures and postures of the body with local social movement practices and her choreographic sense of movement and composition. *Magnetic North* (2003) is a portrait of teenagers in a small Finnish town consisting of short scenes where girls skate in repetitive patterns to the Doors's "Wild Child," boys play electric guitars in their bedrooms, and teenagers pose for the camera, their gaze locked to ours and their posture speaking

---

[8] Hubert Godard, "Gesture and Its Perception," trans. Sally Gardner, *Writings on Dance* 22 (Summer 2003–2004): 59.

[9] Balázs (2007), 97.

for itself. The performances of the young skaters and guitarists in their cultural environment is staged in a tender and poetic film that juxtaposes their gestures with images of their apartment blocks, frozen lakes, and power cables. The patterns of corporeal behavior in this world are broken when Pennell has a gang of young girls bark like dogs at the camera, or she choreographs a spiralling string of skaters.[10] (video 3.2▶)

For Agamben, cinema is the homeland of gesture. For the rendering of human gesture, nothing beats cinema for its ability to provide focus, access, revision, quotation, manipulation, framing, and exploration. Yet, surprisingly little analytical work has been done on gesture in cinema, let alone the exceptional gestures of silent cinema.[11] Already in this book I have suggested new analytical frameworks for considering corporeal screen performance in the absence of spoken words. Throughout this chapter I focus on the gestural process, the gesture in process, drawing on Agamben's definition of the gesture as a "means without end," inevitably describing corporeal actions that subvert the economy of production where actions work toward a predetermined end.

3.1 The Body in Crisis and Gestural Mediality

> By the end of the nineteenth century, the Western bourgeoisie had definitely lost its gestures.
>
> Giorgio Agamben[12]

As outlined in the previous chapter, the film theory of Béla Balázs and Gilles Deleuze suggested that the close-up as a film image dominated during the silent era due to a decreased capacity for corporeal expression. Across critical writing on early twentieth-century modernity, one can find numerous accounts of, what was fundamentally and for our purposes *productively*, a crisis of the body. It was this crisis of the corporeal sphere and its gestures that opened up possibilities for the moving body beyond coded or prescribed action and created, in screen performance, a transitional period of gestural mediality. And it is in gestures characterized by this medial condition that we find the influence of choreographic and somatic knowledges, both historically and currently.

---

[10] Other films of Pennell's that are based on culturally specific gestural spheres are *You Made Me Love You* (2005), *Fisticuffs* (2004), *Human Radio* (2002), and *Tattoo* (2001).

[11] A preoccupation with the performing body in the work of early film theorists, such as James Naremore, Roberta Pearson, Jennifer Bean, Rebecca Swender, and the recent work of Jonathan Auerbach, provides critical discourse around screen acting and actor training. Lesley Stern's work on gesture in cinema has also provided an important reference point, especially: "Putting on a Show, or the Ghostliness of Gesture," *Senses of Cinema*, [Online] 21 (July–August 2002), available at: http://www.sensesofcinema.com/contents/02/21/sd_stern.html [October 1, 2005]; "Paths That Wind through the Thicket of Things," *Critical Inquiry* 28, 1 (2001): 317–54; and "Acting Out of Character: *The King of Comedy* As Histrionic Text," in *Falling for You: Essays on Cinema and Performance*, ed. Stern and George Kouvaros (Sydney: Power Institute, 1995), 277–305. Also influential has been Jodi Brooks, "Crisis and the Everyday: Some Thoughts on Gesture and Crisis in Cassavetes and Benjamin," in Stern and Kouvaros (1999), 73–104. For an overview of writings on gesture more broadly see Carrie Noland's introductory essay in *Migrations of Gesture*, ed. Carrie Noland and Sally Ann Ness (Minneapolis: University of Minnesota Press, 2008), ix–xvii.

[12] Agamben (2000), 49.

Leo Charney and Vanessa R. Shwartz define *modernity* as "an expression of change in so-called subjective experience" brought on by "talismanic innovations: the telegraph and telephone, railroad and automobile, photograph and cinema."[13] The setting is the late nineteenth-century metropolis, and the conditions for the individual subject are characterized by ephemerality, fragmentation, displacement, speed, danger, and rapid transformation. The earlier writings of Georg Simmel, Siegfried Kracauer, and Walter Benjamin (among others) provide the basis for a large body of social, aesthetic, and cultural theory produced in the 1980s and 1990s on this subject.[14] Benjamin Singer writes that these particular early theorists of modernity:

> ...focused on what might be called a *neurological* conception of modernity...a fundamentally different register of subjective experience, characterized by the physical and perceptual shocks of the modern urban environment.[15]

Throughout the writings on this period, the body figures prominently as a traumatized site, struggling to negotiate new manifestations of space, time, and matter. Charles Baudelaire provides a particularly poetic image of modern man "hurrying across the boulevarde":

> ...amidst this moving chaos in which death comes galloping at you from all sides at once I must have made an awkward movement, for the halo slipped off my head and fell onto the muddy asphalt pavement.[16]

This image of the lyric poet with a slippery halo, his coordination hampered by the bustle of the urban street, provides a vivid image of the challenges that the city presented to everyday existence. What emerged from these conditions was a "fugitive physicality," to use Tom Gunning's term, whose materiality was ungrounded by the sensual and perceptual bombardments of the city.[17] This process was intensified by the rapid shift for a large percentage of the population from rural to urban environments, as well as the emerging technologies of reproduction with their phantom moving figures.

Anson Rabinbach surveys particular health problems resulting from this assault on the human body, charting the emergence of "fatigue" as a major concern in the 1870s, and its culmination in a new condition termed "neurasthenia" by New York

---

[13] Leo Charney and Vanessa R. Schwartz, "Introduction," in *Cinema and the Invention of Modern Life*, ed. Leo Charney and Vanessa R. Shwartz (Berkeley: University of California Press, 1995), 1.

[14] Other theorists of modernity would be Max Weber, Emile Durkheim, Georg Lukács, Theodor Adorno, and Max Horkheimer. For writings drawing on these earlier theorists see: Charney and Shwartz (1995); Stephen Kern, *The Culture of Time and Space, 1880–1918* (Massachusetts: Harvard University Press, 1983); Anson Rabinbach, *The Human Motor: Energy, Fatigue, and the Origins of Modernity* (Berkeley: University of California Press, 1990); Miriam Hansen, "Benjamin, Cinema and Experience: 'The Blue Flower in the Land of Technology,'" *New German Critique*, 40 (Winter 1987): 179–224; David Frisby, *Fragments of Modernity: Theories of Modernity in the Work of Simmel, Kracauer and Benjamin* (Cambridge: MIT Press, 1986); Eugene Lunn, *Marxism and Modernism: An Historical Study of Lukács, Brecht, Benjamin and Adorno* (Berkeley: University of California Press, 1982); and Marshall Berman, *All That is Solid Melts Into Air: The Experience of Modernity* (New York: Viking Penguin, 1988).

[15] Benjamin Singer, "Modernity, Hyperstimulus, and the Rise of Pop Sensationalism," in Charney and Shwartz (1995), 72.

[16] Charles Baudelaire quoted in Walter Benjamin, "On Some Motifs in Baudelaire," in *Illuminations*, ed. Hannah Arendt, trans. Harry Zohn (London: Fontana Press, 1992), 189.

[17] Tom Gunning, "Tracing the Individual Body: Photography, Detectives and Early Cinema," in Charney and Shwartz (1995), 19.

physician George Miller Beard.[18] This condition manifested as various symptoms including weakness in the limbs, bad digestion, depression, sensitivity to cold, and a pallid complexion, but the outstanding issue was the patient's difficulty in articulating their symptoms and the physician's subsequent role as sounding-board and advisor. Beard, along with Dr. Achille-Adrien Proust, believed neurasthenia directly resulted from the conditions of modernity.[19] Rabinbach writes:

> The identification of neurasthenia with modernity was also reflected in the symptomology of the illness itself.... The growth rate of fatigue and nervous disorders seemed to be directly proportional to the intensity of energy necessary to contend with modern society.[20]

Others, such as Jean-Martin Charcot's student, Charles Féré, believed the condition to be hereditary. Charcot diagnosed one quarter of his patients as neurasthenics, distinguishing this condition from travel-related disorders and "more extreme hysteria."[21]

Whether it was the new shocks and disorientations of everyday perception, the debilitating effects of neurasthenia, or the drastic and disabling impact of hysteria, the fin de siècle body was feeling the impact of, and dealing symptomatically with, the sensual and perceptual challenges of modern urban life. As Jodi Brooks summarizes, "Modernity is marked by a crisis of experience and an experience of crisis".[22] And it was in the clinics, the arts—particularly the physical art of dance—in popular entertainment and on the cinematographic screen that the crisis of human experience and its impact on the human body would be negotiated, explored, and played out.

Giorgio Agamben describes how the late nineteenth-century gestural crisis was captured in very early cinema and addressed in the "recuperative" work of contemporaneous dancers, writers, and poets. Agamben thus sets the scene for a gestural revolution involving body cultures, new dance forms, and actor training and performance techniques. Like Deleuze, Agamben makes a connection between early modern dance and the emergence of cinema, but significantly for my project here, he brings film and physical movement into relationship via the notion of gesture.[23]

According to Agamben, sequential photographic movement studies of the late nineteenth century document the shift from the pose, featured in photography and painting, to the gestures and movements that film records. Static images predating the cinema can now be seen as contingent, lacking the motility offered by this technological revolution, so that "cinema leads images back into the homeland of gesture":

---

[18] Rabinbach (1990), 146–78.

[19] Neurasthenia's most comprehensive textbook, *Hygiène du neurasthénique* (Paris: Masson et Cie., 1879) was co-written by Beard and Marcel Proust's father, Dr. Achille-Adrien Proust. Rabinbach comments that Marcel, who spent up to six and a half days a week in bed writing, could have been his father's primary subject (Ibid, 156–57).

[20] Ibid, 154–55.

[21] Ibid, 154.

[22] Brooks (1999), 80.

[23] In his article, "Gestural Cinema?: Giorgio Agamben on Film," Benjamin Noys provides a rare commentary on this much cited essay. He describes Agamben's "new theory of gestural cinema" as an alternative to Deleuze's approach, as it argues "that cinema belongs, essentially, to the realm of ethics and politics, and not aesthetics." [Online] Rev. 7/05/2004. Available at: http://www.film-philosophy.com/vol8-2004/n22noys. [December 20, 2008].

And that is so because a certain kind of *litigatio*, a paralyzing power whose spell we need to break, is continuously at work in every image; it is as if a silent invocation calling for the liberation of the image into gesture arose from the entire history of art.[24]

Agamben thus presents another version of the transformation described in Chapter 1 from ancient to modern movement at the beginning of the twentieth century, noting a general shift from *image* to *gesture*.[25] The new technology of the cinema, which would dissolve the postures and poses of portraiture back into the actions from which they were drawn, had a special significance in relation to dance. For what art form suffers more through the isolation of one image from the continuity to which that image belongs?

Cinema would become the natural home for gestural expression. But, given the crisis of the body outlined above, what condition were those gestures in? Agamben characterizes gestures at the turn of the century as being under the influence of a "polar tension"—between their "obliteration" and their transformation into "destiny":

> …And when the age realised this, it then began (but it was too late!) the precipitous attempt to recover the lost gestures in extremis. The dance of Isadora Duncan and Sergei Diaghilev, the novel of Proust, the great *Jugendstil* poetry from Pascoli to Rilke, and, finally and most exemplarily, the silent movie trace the magic circle in which humanity tried for the last time to evoke what was slipping through its fingers forever.[26]

In the work of these artists, along with the new medium of film, Agamben finds efforts to reclaim and utilize, often "in extremis," the gestural articulations of the body that were at the time, as Felicia McCarren also points out, becoming strongly associated with hysteria.[27]

Agamben hypothesises that since the "generalized catastrophe of the sphere of gestures" around the turn of the twentieth century as evidenced by Gilles de la Tourette's walking studies and encyclopaedia of "an amazing proliferation of tics, spasmodic jerks, and mannerisms," there was a loss of gestural control in the twentieth century on a grand scale.[28] Physical behaviors were depicted on the

---

[24] Agamben (2000), 56.

[25] Hillel Schwartz wrote convincingly in 1992 of the shift from pose to gesture during this period, the role played by emerging theater dance and cinematic performance modes, and connections with the ideas of Delsarte and associated body practices ("Torque: The New Kinaesthetic of the Twentieth Century," in *Incorporations*, eds. Jonathan Crary and Sanford Kwinter [New York: Zone, 1992], 71–127). His discussion of a "new kinaesthetic" also resonates with the ideas of Deleuze and Bergson regarding "modern movement".

[26] Agamben (2000), 53–54. The polarity Agamben appears to be setting up is the obliteration of gestures through loss of "naturalness" and gestural control/clarity leading to reification into a frozen image (i.e., "destiny") versus the transfiguration of the gesture by returning it to the dynamic continuity to which it belongs. He compares the latter to Eadweard Muybridge's consecutive images and Aby Warburg's ambitious and unfinished *Mnemosyne Atlas*, which he describes as a "virtual movement of Western humanity's gestures from classical Greece to Fascism," like a flick book of stills describing the attempted redemption of gesture through art (55–56).

[27] Felicia McCarren, "The 'Symptomatic' Act Circa 1900: Hysteria, Hypnosis, Electricity and Dance," *Critical Inquiry*, 21 (Summer 1995a): 748–74. For more on the relation between dance, hysteria, and the unconscious, see this article and McCarren's book, *Dance Pathologies: Performance, Poetics, Medicine* (California: Stanford University Press, 1998), where she draws out the relationship between Fuller's dancing, electricity, and the "theater" of Jean-Martin Charcot. McCarren's clinching evidence is the origin of Fuller's dance as a representation of hypnosis in a medical parody called *Quack MD*, along with Fuller's own revelation of her familiarity with the clinical use of electricity in her account of an electric shock treatment she underwent in Sweden (McCarren 1995a, 762).

[28] Agamben 2000, 51.

contemporary silent screen that seem to have imported the corporeal anomalies charted in the clinics, accounting for their disappearance from medical records after the birth of cinema:

> One of the hypotheses that could be put forth in order to explain this disappearance is that in the meantime ataxia, tics, and dystonia had become the norm and that at some point everybody had lost control of their gestures and was walking and gesticulating frantically. This is the impression, at any rate, that one has when watching the films that Marey and Lumière began to shoot exactly in those years.[29]

Agamben thus suggests that cinema has somehow acted as a sensitive plate, recording and refiguring the gestures of the body throughout crisis, liberation, and loss.

In his book on the rhetoric of human form in very early cinema, Jonathan Auerbach echoes Agamben's impression of performance in these films. He distinguishes human action from other moving bodies that appear on screen via their agency, volition, or motivation, and it is the link between mind and body that he finds defamiliarized in early film:

> …figures in these early films often seem possessed, at the mercy of mysterious powerful forces, unseen but felt, beyond personal control; they are seized by fits of near hysteria…or insanity…or governed by gravity…or nervous electrical impulses…suggesting how neither filmmakers nor viewers nor bodies on-screen quite knew what to make of or do with themselves.[30]

In the group of ten films programmed at the first commercial screening at Salon Indien du Grand Café in 1895, amongst the "home movies" of the Lumière family and people at work and play, are three films containing some directed performances and the structure of a gag: L' Arroseur arrosé, La Voltige, and Saut à la couverture. In these films, the actors perform physical tricks that are choreographed, but retain a sense of improvisation and proximity between virtuosity and failure. The punishment of the naughty boy who stops the gardener's water supply in L' Arroseur arrosé is swift and awkward—chasing, ear pulling, and smacking abruptly played out in a self-conscious interaction between the two players. The policeman who cannot successfully mount his horse in La Voltige reappears in a similar scenario in Saut à la couverture where he is attempting to throw himself into a blanket held by four colleagues. His repeated attempts to master the physical tasks at hand are reduced to unconvincing blunders; he lands flat like a plank on the horse and slides off, swings one leg over only to have it come right round and he is off again, or he somersaults on to the blanket to be bounced out and onto the ground. Running quickly between attempts and throwing himself in again and again, he does appear to have lost control of an apparently agile body and be at the mercy of an oddly powerful force of gravity.

In a slightly later film, Edwin S. Porter's The Whole Dam Family and the Dam Dog (1905), a picture frame presents a variety of characters in direct address to the "camera"

---

[29] Ibid, 52–53.
[30] Jonathan Auerbach, Body Shots: Early Cinema's Incarnations (Berkeley: University of California Press, 2007), 11.

but, rather than still poses, each family member is moving about in unaccountable ways. Mr. I. B. Dam sneezes uncontrollably and Mrs. Hellen Dam is nagging so violently she loses her words as well as her breath. Jimmy Dam smiles, blows off large amounts of smoke, and wipes his face in manic succession. Miss U. B. Dam fusses quickly with her hair and pins on a hat while smiling, laughing, and chatting nervously. Miss I. P. Dam swings violently from side to side in a dance, also frantically donning a hat, and even Baby Dam, The Dam Cook, and The Dam Dog busy themselves with grimaces and rapid actions, the dog actually having to get up and leave frame. Each character seems driven by some outside and unnatural force, moving with such detail and speed that they *could* be stimulated by "nervous electrical impulses."

Beyond Agamben's fantastic vision of a general population suffering from Tourette's Syndrome, one could conclude that the cinema absorbed, and provided a safe place for the enactment of, excessive bodily expression outside the clinic. It is in the visual recording and demonstration of this historical moment where body technologies are "out of step" with visual technologies that we find evidence of a gestural crisis. As Auerbach states, the moving image "made people acutely aware of their bodies," and it could be that this visual evidence then played a *therapeutic* role in the following gestural revolution involving professionals, amateurs, and innocent bystanders alike.[31] Hillel Shwartz writes:

> ... motion pictures as theatre were literally instrumental in reeducating old and young alike in posture, gesture, and gracious or efficacious movement.[32]

This revolution would not be played out in cinema alone, but in combination with an influential body culture industry and the new theater and dance forms that emerged from this milieu. These three phenomena of early twentieth-century modernity would effectively counter the gestural crisis and provide the conditions for a transitional phase of gestural mediality, a mediality that persists in gestural dancefilm.[33]

Agamben's definition of gesture as *medial* is central to thinking through the type of corporeal performance I am dealing with in the silent films and contemporary dancefilms analyzed in this chapter. Agamben distinguishes between (a) an action as a means to an end, or a medial action in respect to an end, and (b) an end in itself, or finality without means. He proposes a third category of action, which is *gesture*: an action as an "event" or as "pure mediality."[34] He writes that dance as aesthetics would correspond to category (b), but that:

> If dance is gesture, it is so, rather, because it is nothing more than the endurance and the exhibition of the media character of corporal movements. *The gesture is the exhibition of a mediality: it is the process of making a means visible as such.*[35]

---

[31] Ibid, 7.

[32] Schwartz (1992), 101.

[33] Carrie Asman describes a new interest in gesture during the first decades of the twentieth century, beginning with Walter Benjamin's writings on Bertolt Brecht and Franz Kafka, but observing the trend in other fields beyond epic theater and drama including philosophy, film, sociology, and enthnography. While this supports the idea of a "gestural revolution," Asman makes no reference to the role of body cultures or dance (Carrie Asman, "Return of the Sign to the Body: Benjamin and Gesture in the Age of Retheatricalization," *Discourse* 16, 3 [1993]: 46–64).

[34] Agamben (2000), 56–59. His references for these definitions of gesture are Aristotle and Marcus Terentius Varro (116 BC–27 BC).

[35] Ibid, 58.

Across the films under discussion here, the corporeal activity has an irreducible quality, whether in the absence of, or *despite*, narrative imperatives; there is less emphasis on an *end* to be arrived at or expressed. To return to the Pennell and Vandekeybus examples, in *Magnetic North* narrative is replaced with an observational mode that expresses the world of the Finnish teenagers through their corporeal activities and the dramatic, snow-bound environment. Electricity, music, and speed on the ice combine to describe the personal expression and release that these young people exploit, but the film is by no means reducible to this reading. While in *Inasmuch*, the narrative itself has the radical qualities of magical realism, and the actions of the performers, whether pretending to fly only to crash into a wall, or secretly slipping lollies into the mouths of those under duress, is unpredictable and open to a variety of readings.

What distinguishes these dancefilms from others is that they perfectly fit Agamben's description of gesture as a *means without end*. They investigate the gestural capacities of the body and its ability to express through an inclusive interrogation of exploratory, cliché, and quotable gestures. If "the gesture is essentially always a gesture of not being able to figure something out in language," then the interrogation of somatic knowledge initiated by figures such as François Delsarte, and continuing in the research of artists such as Pennell, Vandekeybus, and Bausch, produces *gesturality* on screen.[36]

3.2 François Delsarte and the Gestural Revolution

> *I saw the lack of musical rhythm to be the result of a general "a-rhythm," whose cure appeared to depend on a special training designed to regulate nervous reactions and effect a co-ordination of muscles and nerves; in short, to harmonise mind and body.*
>
> Émile Jaques-Dalcroze[37]

Agamben has identified both cinema and dance as places that were addressing the gestural crisis and indulging in the transitional, medial condition of the body and its gestures at the beginning of the twentieth century. What kinds of research and practices were supporting this period of experimentation? And what can those body technologies offer us in thinking through the most recent dancefilms exploring gesture and the moving image? In the opening quote, Émile Jaques-Dalcroze articulates the role that physical cultures would play in the recuperation of the health and expressivity of the body in the first decades of the twentieth century. As composer and Professor of Harmony at the Conservatoire in Geneva in 1892, Jaques-Dalcroze's radical ideas led to his dismissal and the establishment of his own successful school in Hellerau, Germany in 1910. Here, he set about developing a new training system for his music students to compensate for the lack of harmony he found in the

---

[36] Ibid, 59.
[37] Emile Jaques-Dalcroze, *Rhythm, Music and Education*, trans. Harold F. Rubenstein (London: The Dalcroze Society, 1973), viii.

connection of body and mind ("a-rhythm"), "to liberate their particular rhythms of individual life from every trammelling influence."[38] While not central to my discussion of gesture and performance, Jaques-Dalcroze's Eurythmics is one example (and a particularly significant one for dance) amongst the diverse body systems that emerged in the early twentieth century.[39] But some of the foundational and most influential ideas in the field, particularly in America, were those developed by François Delsarte.

Previously, we saw how American Delsartism dovetailed with Henri Bergson's theories of movement and the emergence of modern dance and cinema. Looking more closely at the role of movement and gesture in the Delsarte system we find that his most innovative ideas take us through silent cinema and contemporary dance forms to a gestural mode of dancefilm. Those ideas include recognition of a correspondence between mind and body, the development of methodologies to regain control over this relation, unswerving faith in corporeal knowledge, and his passionate promotion of gesture over spoken word in relation to *expression*.

Manifesting in teachings at Denishawn and informing performance techniques across the board, the intense corporeal research undertaken by Delsarte and others would encourage an exchange between performance disciplines, resulting in a gestural revolution on stage and screen.

In the draft Delsarte made for his unpublished book, he recounts an early episode with a drama teacher where he is failing to perform as required and declares, "I don't know how to go to work to imitate you; I don't seize the details of your gesture." He bores tutors and fellow students with his persistent working over of a single line and accompanying gesture until an "unstudied attitude which I had assumed under the action of a genuine emotion" at the sight of his cousin approaching satisfies him, producing a "harmonious and natural" gesture.[40] Delsarte thus describes a shift from dramatic training via mimetic reproduction of stock gestures and postures, "the working of a rule without a reason," to a "natural," "genuine" response.[41] This anecdote gives a sense of Delsarte's radical efforts to produce a correspondence between an emotional truth and physical articulation.

Delsarte's system of expression was based on a return to everyday gestures, researched through observation to establish "basic principles underlying what was specific and individual."[42] This project was carried out in the period prior to the

---

[38] Ibid, x. Nina Lara Rosenblatt and Michael Cowan draw a direct line from neurasthenia to the physical regime of Eurythmics. See Nina Lara Rosenblatt, "Photogenic Neurasthenia: On Mass and Medium in the 1920s," *October* 86 (1998): 47–62; and Michael Cowan, "The Heart Machine: 'Rhythm' and Body in Weimer Film and Fritz Lang's *Metropolis*," *Modernism/Modernity* 14, 2 (2007): 225–48.

[39] Other systems contemporary with Jaques-Dalcroze and the Delsartean influence include American physician Dudley Sargent's fitness regimes, Hellerau student Rudolf Bode's expressive gymnastics, Rudolf Steiner's Eurythmy, Frederick Matthias Alexander's technique, and Bess Mensendieck's system. Important precedents were the German gymnastics system instigated by Friedrich Ludwig Jahn (1778–1852) and the Swedish Ling System developed by Per Henrik Ling (1776–1839).

[40] François Delsarte, "The Literary Remains of François Delsarte," trans. Abby L. Alger, in *Delsarte System of Oratory* (New York: Edgar S. Werner, 1893), 385–89. Delsarte did not document his theories so accounts of his work come primarily from a draft manuscript for a book that is mostly anecdotal, and from the writings of his students and disciples. I will refer to Nancy Lee Chalfa Ruyter's comprehensive research as well as primary material translated in Delsarte 1893.

[41] Delsarte (1893), 397.

[42] Nancy Lee Chalfa Ruyter, *The Cultivation of Mind and Body in Nineteenth Century American Delsartism* (Connecticut: Greenwood Press, 1999), 76.

gestural crisis when it was possible to invest in the idea of a universal rationale for human movement, and it marks the beginning of the modern period of research into performance. Delsarte's process included visiting morgues, observing the dying, studying the depiction of human form and action in art, and observing people in the streets, especially children and their caretakers (the aristocrats promenading the Tuileries were useless beings "false from head to foot"). From specific examples he developed "laws" relating to the minutiae of human gesture including the position of the thumb as a "thermometer of life" and how the shoulder effects the "expression of the passions."[43] His research resulted in a detailed training system for voice, gesture, and speech based on such universal laws, but their application was dependent upon a natural match between "sentiment" and "form." As Delsarte states, "nothing is more deplorable than a gesture without a motive."[44] It was his balance between the specific and universal, between art and technique, that would be lost in the Chinese whispers that replaced a comprehensive thesis from the master himself. The proliferation of incomplete and secondary literature reduced his methodologies to a documented system, but it was also this very reduction that ensured the dissemination, application, and popularity of Delsartism.[45]

Central to Delsarte's ideas is the Law of Correspondence, which promoted a direct relationship between the physical and non-physical, the body and the mind, between "movement and meaning." This idea had popular currency in the mid- to late-nineteenth century and, as Nancy Lee Chalfa Ruyter points out, would be an essential component of later acting methodologies developed by Constantin Stanislavsky, Jerzy Grotowski, and Eugenio Barba.[46] But specific to Delsarte is the comprehensive taxonomy that he developed and the underlying, pre-Freudian understanding of "the self to be more or less transparent."[47] An account of a demonstration during Delsarte's lecture presentation in Paris gives a sense of his comprehensive approach to gestural training and a hint of the artist behind the system:

> He depicted the various passions and emotions of the human soul, by means of expression and gesture only, without uttering a single syllable; moving the spectators to tears, exciting them to enthusiasm, or thrilling them with terror at his will; in a word completely magnetising them. Not a discord in his diatonic scale. You were forced to admit that every gesture, every movement of a facial muscle, had a true purpose, a raison d'être.[48]

It is tempting to imagine a whirlwind of exaggerated gestures and grimaces, but Delsarte taught restraint: "... true artists never let their gestures reveal more than a

[43] Delsarte (1893), 401–11.
[44] Ibid, 524.
[45] See an interview and transcript of a lecture given by Delsarte's daughter, Mme. Marie Delsarte-Géraldy, while in America in 1892 regarding how far the system had diverged from her father's original intentions (Delsarte 1893, 533–42).
[46] Ruyter (1999), 76–77. The other significant principle of Delsarte's system was the Law of Trinity, which structured his taxonomy; however, it has less direct relevance to this discussion of his understanding of gestural performance.
[47] Julia A. Walker, "'In the Grip of an Obsession': Delsarte and the Quest for Self-Possession in *The Cabinet of Dr. Caligari*," *Theatre Journal* 58 (2006): 619. The ideas of Sigmund Freud (1856–1939) gained currency in America after he lectured there in 1909.
[48] Francis A. Durivage, "Delsarte," in Delsarte (1893), 577.

tenth part of the secret emotion that they apparently feel and would hide from the audience to spare their sensibility."[49] This sentiment would be repeated by the "new school" of acting in the late nineteenth century, "correcting" the transgressions that were attributed to the Delsarte method.

The "sovereign," "superior," "infallible," "divine reason" that Delsarte defers to in the schoolyard episode cited above is actually the truth of the body—an instinctual physical response to the emotions aroused by the sight of his cousin approaching him. In this anecdote he reveals his trust in the intelligence, knowledge, and authority of the body and its gestures in relation to authentic expression. Here is his definition of gesture first published in English in 1882, a description that must have resonated with potential actors of the silent screen:

> Gesture corresponds to the soul, to the heart; language to the life, to the thought, to the mind. The life and the mind being subordinate to the heart, to the soul, gesture is the chief organic agent.... It prepares the way, in fact, for language and thought; it goes before them and foretells their coming; it accentuates them. By its silent eloquence it predisposes, it guides the listener. It makes him a witness to the secret labor performed by the immanences which are about to burst forth.... Gesture is the direct agent of the heart. It is the fit manifestation of feeling. It is the revealer of thought and the commentator upon speech.... [I]t is the spirit of which speech is merely the letter. Gesture is parallel to the impression received; it is, therefore, always anterior to speech, which is but a reflected and subordinate expression.[50]

In this passage Delsarte describes: (a) a direct and emphatic link from gesture to our interior lives; (b) how gesture preempts or provides the context for speech and thought, revealing the moments prior to speech where the body is already heavy with meaning; (c) how it "fleshes out" speech for the listener but is also "anterior," providing commentary that goes beyond the limitations of spoken word; and (d) gesture is "parallel" or equal to "the impression received," an impression experienced in the body of the spectator and providing evidence of a *gestural exchange*.[51] These ideas are echoed in the writings of early film theorists such as Balázs, supporting the notion that Delsarte's work resonates in the gestural language of the silent screen:

> In [silent] film... the play of facial expressions is not an optional extra, and this distinction means not only that gestures in film are more explicit and detailed, but that they operate on an entirely different plane.... A speaker's gestures have the same emotional content as his words.... It is merely that they refer to words as yet unborn.[52]

The important role of gesture in the communication of ideas and emotions in silent cinema, and its capacity to exceed language in this regard is clear in the performances of Lillian Gish. In *Broken Blossoms* (1919, d. D. W. Griffith), Gish/Lucy Burrows embodies fear in scenes with her physically abusive father. She expresses a range from timidity to blind terror, saying much more with her body than the minimal intertitles. When her father accuses her of returning home late she turns

[49] Delsarte (1893), 526.
[50] Ibid, 465–67.
[51] The idea of *gestural exchange* will be taken up in chapter seven, where the body of the spectator is introduced to my discussion of dancefilm.
[52] Balázs (2007), 98.

her shoulders away from him, nodding nervously and speaking to him over her shoulder, gesturing toward the food she has bought. When she locks herself in a cupboard in fear of her life, she claws at the wall opposite the door as her father takes to it with an axe, slouches against it in defeat, shakes her head from side to side with glazed eyes, and turns around and around in futile panic. In the latter example she seems beyond thought, and the variety and detail in her gestures go well beyond the limitations of language. Early cinema was the perfect stage for the "silent eloquences" of gesture, expressing the "secret labor" that preempts and exceeds the spoken word.

The direct influence of Delsarte's ideas upon American acting and theatrical dance would be via American Delsartism, the product of theater actor, producer, and director Steele Mackaye. Mackaye studied and worked with Delsarte from 1869 to 1870 and brought the system to America in 1871, the year in which Delsarte died. Mackaye's promotion of the system in America, and his training courses instituted in New York in 1875, have been credited with establishing formal actor training in that country.[53] James Naremore writes that Mackaye's version of a Delsartean training system was "the principle method of formal instruction for American actors between 1870 and 1895," with its effects lasting well beyond these years.[54] Naremore describes Delsarte as representative of a "prescriptive, formulaic" gestural style of performance predating the revolution of Stanislavsky:

> The entire tradition of Delsartean and expressionist theatre…has something of this feeling—a slowing down and drawing out of the actor's movements, a reduction of the performance to a series of *gests*, or moments when the body pauses in a slightly exaggerated posture so that the audience can contemplate the figure.[55]

As I have shown, this is a simplification of Delsarte's original ideas based on secondary sources and, while Naremore cites Delsartism as representing a codified gestural language, he does not ultimately place his methods in opposition to Stanislavsky's. He also refers to the co-existence of Delsarte's influence with "psychological realism" throughout the silent era, and he links Delsarte's system of expression to training techniques for the avant-garde including those developed by Antonin Artaud and Jerzy Grotowski—and modern dance.[56] These contradictory comments by Naremore signal the uneasy position Delsarte has held within performance theory.

The reach of Delsartism in America quickly spread from the male-dominated professional context exemplified by Mackaye to become part of the body culture industry that was addressing the gestural crisis and was associated with the women's reform movement. Mackaye's student Genevieve Stebbins's work and teachings involved a rigorous and well-researched adaptation of Delsarte's ideas that was

---

[53] Ruyter (1999), 17–21. Mackaye set up the New York School of Expression in 1877 and founded the Lyceum Theatre School with Franklin Sargent in 1884. That school would become the American Academy of Dramatic Arts. For more on this period in American theater see: Benjamin McCarthur, *Actors and American Culture, 1880–1920* (Philadelphia: Temple University Press, 1984); and Julie A. Walker, *Expressionism and Modernism in American Theatre: Bodies, Voices, Words* (New York: Cambridge University Press, 2005).

[54] James Naremore, *Acting in the Cinema* (Berkeley: University of California Press, 1988), 53.

[55] Ibid, 52 and 140. Here he refers to Dietrich in *Morocco* (d. Josef von Sternberg, 1930).

[56] Ibid 1988, 52–65.

widely disseminated through her publications and the teachers she produced at her New York School of Expression, established in 1893.[57] Stebbins's development of performative practices and artistic principles founded in Delsartism, along with her significance regarding the shift from pose to flow outlined elsewhere, would open the way for Duncan and St. Denis.

Mackaye's Delsartism had an even more direct influence on the development of American modern dance through the work of Ted Shawn, who was Ruth St. Denis's partner in life and work. He employed Henrietta Hovey at Denishawn, who studied with Delsarte's son Gustave in Paris and whose lectures Shawn snuck into.[58] Delsarte's overall categories of movement were oppositional, parallel and successional, with nine aspects—altitude, force, motion (magnitude), sequence, direction, form, velocity, reaction, and extension.[59] These all related to the production of meaning and, while information on Mackaye's system of expression is sparse, it is known that he added "harmonic gymnastics" to Delsarte's program extending the system beyond expressive gesture and toward the choreographic. One innovative concept of Mackaye's was "ease," "relaxation," or "decomposition," which, in balance with "tension," would become fundamental to the generation of movement in modern dance and the key to its dynamics.[60] Shawn demonstrates how these principles can be applied to dance in his book, *Every Little Movement*, and his compositional techniques gained longevity through the work of his famous students: Martha Graham, Doris Humphries, and Charles Weidman.

Dance critic and biographer Walter Terry states, "A case may be made that America's modern dance is rooted in Delsarte principles and that Ted Shawn, who became the world's foremost dance authority on Delsarte, nurtured those roots."[61] So through Mackaye we can see the link between Delsartean principles for acting and, via his students Stebbins and Hovey, the development of body cultures that would lay the groundwork for theater dance to develop in America. And, through Hovey's student Shawn, we can connect Delsarte directly to the early development of modern dance.[62] Delsarte's rigorous approach to corporeal performance and belief in somatic

[57] Stebbins studied with Mackaye from 1876 to 1878 as well as Delsarte pupil and author Abbé Delaumosne, and she had access to some of Delsarte's unpublished manuscripts. She published five books on her Delsartean practice between 1885 and 1913, with her foundational text, *The Delsarte System of Expression*, having six editions over this period (Nancy Lee Chalfa Ruyter, *Reformers and Visionaries* [New York: Dance Horizons, 1979], 134–37). For more on the links between American Delsartism, the women's reform movement, and early modern dance see: Elizabeth Kendall, *Where She Danced* (New York: Alfred A. Knopf, 1979); Ruyter (1999) and (1979); Helen Thomas, *Dance Modernity and Culture* (London and New York: Routledge, 1995); Deborah Jowitt, *Time and the Dancing Image* (Berkeley and Los Angeles: University of California Press, 1988); and Sally Banes *Dancing Women: Female Bodies on Stage* (London: Routledge, 1998).

[58] Hovey is also known as Henrietta Crane and Henrietta Russell and, having studied with Delsarte's son Gustave in Paris and Mackaye in America, is another subject of Ruyter's research into American Delsartism. Ruyter concludes that "the woman herself and what she imparted are elusive" (Ruyter 1999, 43).

[59] Ibid, 79–80.

[60] Ibid, 84–85.

[61] Walter Terry, *Miss Ruth: The 'More Living Life' of Ruth St. Denis* (New York: Dodd, Mead & Co., 1969), 69. In support of this, Olga Maynard's important book, *American Modern Dance: The Pioneers* (Boston, Toronto: Little, Brown and Company, 1965), contains sections on both Delsarte and Dalcroze and a "genealogy" indicating their profound legacies in relation to American dance (178). It is important to note that the repeated connection of Delsarte and Jacques-Dalcroze to an American canon of twentieth-century theater dance promotes a geneology that omits the influence of Afrocentric aesthetics and relegates artists not directly linked to the Denishawn-Graham-Cunningham-Judson Church lineage to the margins.

[62] Ironically, as Ruyter notes, Delsarte had no professional interest in dance, nor did his contemporary mid-nineteenth-century dance community show any interest in his ideas (Ruyter 1999, 8–9).

knowledge, along with his ideas about a correspondence between our internal life and authentic gesture and the expressive potential of gesture beyond spoken word, constitute a strong current of ideas running across gestural performance in both dance and film in the early twentieth century. The Delsartean system is one element in a complex of body technologies and methods that constituted an experimental milieu for gestural development in the performing arts during this time, and this experimentation continues in the gesture-dance of contemporary dancefilm.

3.3 Modern Dance—Silent Drama

> *Every little movement has a meaning all its own.*
>
> Otto Harbach[63]

This quote is from the lyrics to "Every Little Movement" by Otto Harbach, the hit song of a 1910 musical that provides the title for Shawn's book on Delsarte, *Every Little Movement*. Shawn suggests that the popularity of this song in the first decade of the twentieth century was due to "the epoch-making new chapter which had been opened in the world of the dance."[64] From tango teas to the salons of the best families in New York, America was dancing and the hub of new performance practices—Hollywood—was caught up in the general cultural hysteria surrounding dance halls, folk dance, Isadora Duncan, Irene and Vernon Castle, Anna Pavlova and Mikhail Mordkin, the Ballets Russes, and Ruth St. Denis.

In the previous section, the recovery from the gestural crisis and the ensuing gestural revolution that would manifest on the silent screen and in early modern dance training and performance in America in the 1910s and 1920s was traced to popular body cultures such as American Delsartism and Eurhythmics, along with the new technology of the cinema. This revolution would revive Delsarte's original project: recognising the expressive potential of the body and bringing the mind-body relation back into dialogue. The resulting new form of gestural cinema staged the moving body choreographically and resonated with a new gestural style of theater dance that followed cinema's shift from the order of the pose to gesture as continuity of motion. The following considers the cinematic in the choreography of Ruth St. Denis and the choreographic in silent cinema.

In 1906, St. Denis would conjure a new dance form that, like Genevieve Stebbins's performances, constitutes a transition from the codified gestures and poses of Delsarte's followers to the continuity of movement that Fuller performed like a premonition in the late nineteenth, and into the twenty-first, century. St. Denis's mute, gestural dance performed in exotic costumes and staged in dramatic mise en scène occupied a performance scenario matched in the emerging narrative form of cinema. Her physical language would resonate with the demands of the silent screen as noted

---

[63] Quoted in Ted Shawn, *Every Little Movement: A Book About François Delsarte* (New York: Dance Horizons, 1963), 10.
[64] Ibid, 10.

by Balázs, who cites her art to corroborate his belief that cinema was part of a general and widespread recuperation of the physiognomic and gestural life of man.[65]

Two practical matters relating to the proximity of early cinema and the emerging theater dance practice would also play a part in the gestural revolution. First, there was the presentation of film screenings and dance performances side-by-side in the same venues—the vaudeville houses of America.[66] And second, the geographic proximity of the film studios in Los Angeles to the first American school devoted to the new art form of theater dance, Denishawn. The significant role that dance played in actor training from the very earliest years of cinema in America is an undeveloped field of critical inquiry. The details of this history can go some way toward explaining the affinity between the modern dance charter and silent film acting regarding the central role of expression, an increase in physical range, gestural transformation, and a new relationship between performance and the everyday. And it will be these same aspects of dancefilm that will define the cine-choreographic mode of gesture-dance in contemporary examples.

Modern theater dance and silent cinema share the same nonnarrative, variety hall origins and professional reference points (circus, slapstick, spectacle, acrobatics, melodrama, social dance). Gunning describes how vaudeville, melodrama, and pantomime were closer to early film culture than the "legitimate theater" and offered more cinematically compatible theatrical contexts lacking in "unity of space and point of view" and time, and with a strong emphasis on spectacular visual effects.[67] This theatrical world was also a point of departure for Ruth St. Denis who, like D. W. Griffith, would ultimately combine the influence of the legitimate theater with these populist elements to create an entirely new creative practice.[68] The resulting dance and screen genres would reach unprecedented audiences and fall completely into step with contemporary popular culture. For both forms this involved developing a mute, physical language that was distinguishable from vaudeville and classicism and in line with a new realism in popular stage melodrama and physical training regimes.

Peter Wollen and Vicky Allen point out that many of the early modern dance artists appeared at one time or another on the vaudeville and music hall stage.[69]

---

[65] Balázs cited in Miriam Hansen, *Babel and Babylon: Spectatorship in American Silent Film* (Cambridge: Harvard University Press, 1991), 342. Hansen makes, what she herself describes as, the "crucial" connection between Balázs's theory that cinema could resolve the Tower of Babel resulting from diverse national languages, and St. Denis's choreography of the Babylonian dance scenes in *Intolerance*.

[66] A list of nickelodeons written by New York's police commissioner in 1908 includes ninety-three vaudeville theaters that featured film in their programs (Benjamin Singer, "Manhattan Nickelodeons: New Data on Audiences and Exhibitors," in *The Silent Cinema Reader*, ed. Lee Grieveson and Peter Krämer [London: Routledge, 2004], 120). Koritz describes Maude Allen's big break in London in 1907 in a mixed programme including film screenings: "Alfred Butt, manager of a major music hall, the Palace Theatre, arranged for her appearance as a turn in a programme of typical acts: jugglers, trained animals, comedians, and 'The Bioscope'" (Amy Koritz, *Gendering Bodies/Performing Art: Dance and Literature in Early Twentieth Century British Culture* [Ann Arbor: The University of Michigan Press, 1995], 34).

[67] Tom Gunning, *D. W. Griffith and the Origins of American Narrative Cinema: The Early Years at Biograph* (Urbana: University of Illinois Press, 1991), 36.

[68] Other things St. Denis and Griffith share are themes and aesthetic references: the redemption motif, which went some way toward their effective cross-over from popular to mainstream/high art; and Orientalism, a connection made by Miriam Hansen (Hansen [1991], 237–38 and 353). For a discussion of the impact of Orientalist concert dance on silent cinema aesthetics see: Gaylan Studlar "Valentino, 'Optic Intoxication,' and Dance Madness," in *Screening the Male: Exploring Masculinities in Hollywood Cinema*, eds. Steven Cohan and Ina Rae Hark (London: Routledge, 1993), 23–45; and "Out Salomeing Salome: Dance, the New Woman, and Fan Magazine Orientalism," in *Visions of the East*, eds. Matthew Berstein and Gaylan Studlar (New Brunswick, New Jersey: Rutgers University Press, 1997), 99–129.

[69] Peter Wollen and Vicky Allen, "A-Z of Cinema: D-Dance," *Sight and Sound*, 6, 9 (1996): 30.

Isadora Duncan, Loïe Fuller, and St. Denis all had some experience performing dance as "light entertainment." In her autobiography, Duncan describes being asked to add "some pep" to her dancing by a certain manager and, in desperation, added frills to her costume, "pepper" to her steps, and performed to "popular" music.[70] Fuller's "skirt dance" gained its first major success at the Folies Bergère in Paris and went on to raise the artistic reputation of that venue.

Of the modern dance pioneers, St. Denis was the most consistent in her associations with vaudeville. Terry identifies the first stage of her career as being the years 1894 to 1904 which she spent in Manhattan and describes her specialization in "leg work, in the kicks, splits, and the skirt manipulations popular in vaudeville."[71] In the 1906 season when she relaunched herself, St. Denis's *Radha* was performed twice a day "on a variety bill that included Nena Blake and her Bronco Beauties, and Kosta, 'The Man with the Revolving Head.'"[72] And at the height of their fame, the Denishawn company toured the vaudeville circuit where "those who spent hard earned quarters to see a seal twirl a trumpet were not always receptive to the dances."[73] Denishawn managed to strike a happy balance between artistic innovation and popular culture kudos, an approach that became increasingly unfashionable within theater dance circles and was not repeated until Katherine Dunham's popular programs in the 1940s. As St. Denis's brother would put it, "[Ruth] was interested in many things, but show business first."[74] The primary influence that inspired St. Denis's reinvention and debut as a radical new style of solo dancer on variety stages, such as the New York Theatre and Grand Theatre, was the fashion for all things Oriental in the first decades of the twentieth century.

Particularly influential was the melodramatic theater of David Belsaco with whom she once toured, popular entertainments featured at New York's Coney Island, and graphic design featured in the increasingly ubiquitous advertising industry.[75]

At Denishawn, a school set up in 1915 with Ted Shawn, her dance partner and husband of one-year, the Dalcroze and Delsartean training systems were combined with ballet classes, "free movement," and "oriental dance" as taught by St. Denis.[76] The latter classes were made up of movement exercises derived from her famous "Oriental" routines; as Terry explains, "most of her academic approach reversed the customary method of employing a technique in preparation for a dance."[77] In footage shot at Denishawn in 1915, St. Denis leads the students who copy her sequence of gestures: walking rhythmically with a basket held on her head, scooping the basket forward and up, waving in an odd salutation, and quicker, smaller

---

[70] Duncan (1928), 34–35.

[71] Terry (1969), 10. Thomas Edison made a film of her during this period, *Ruth Dennis, Skirt Dancer* (1894, Edison Co.).

[72] Jowitt (1988), 133.

[73] Ted Shawn, *One Thousand and One Night Stands*, with Gray Poole (New York: Da Capo Press, 1979), 61.

[74] Terry (1969), 58.

[75] It is worth noting that Steele Mackaye's stage melodramas, which immediately predate Belasco's, have been described as prefiguring D. W. Griffith's silent epics (Naremore [1988], 53).

[76] St. Denis had her own links to Delsarte. She saw Stebbins in a "pure dance expression" in 1892 at Madison Square Theater and her mother passed on some dubious Delsarte training; she recalls "being told that my emotions were in the middle of me, and that my physical impulses were from the hips down…and that from the shoulders up, *all* was spiritual" (Terry [1969], 3, 15, and 192).

[77] Walter Terry, *Ted Shawn: Father of American Dance* (New York: The Dial Press, 1976), 69.

hand actions as if passing objects to a crowd. Pedagogy was a priority for Shawn, who did the lion's share of teaching and choreographing for students, and this aspect of Denishawn activities cemented the duo's place in the American modern dance canon.[78] As with Delsarte, the development and training in new, more comprehensive physical techniques at Denishawn was never an end in itself, but always to serve *expression*, "for the sole purpose of conveying deeper, wider, more cogent meanings than it had been possible to express through the techniques and vocabulary of 19th Century ballet."[79] Defining new relationships between movement and meaning would become a preoccupation of American modern dance, from the mute dramas of St. Denis to the epic distancing of Graham and random connections in Cunningham. But at Denishawn the right or "authentic" gesture would be preceded by "the thought, emotion, purpose, intent"; there would be an explicit and direct correspondence between gesture and meaning[80] (see fig. 3.2).

St. Denis's performances were steeped in theatricality, often being "scenes" from some distant exotic place. The use of characterization, along with a framing narrative of enlightenment, brings her dancing much closer to the theatrical traditions that fed into the emerging narrative cinematic language of the silent screen than, say, the abstract moving image of Fuller or the personal and theatrically sparse approach of Duncan. Compared with Fuller and Duncan, there was also a much stronger use of gesture (she was sometimes described as a gestural dancer) and a minimum of virtuosic, choreographed phrases of steps. For example, *Incense*, one of three dances making up her first public program as a solo dancer at the Hudson Theatre in New York in 1906, consists mainly of walking and arm gestures.[81] The costume is an Indian sari and there are two incense stands downstage. It begins with slow walks forward carrying a tray of incense, which is moved around in small circles and raised above the head with slight backbends. Deliberate walks toward the incense stands are followed by a pinch of incense being thrown into the flames and undulating hand gestures mimicking the rising smoke. The tray is placed on the ground and simple wave-like arm movements are performed. Other dances were performed by St. Denis and recorded in the late 1940s and 1950s and, due to her more advanced years, may be deceptively pared back. But the profusion of photographs of St. Denis in static poses, far outnumbering those of her midmovement, suggest that her earliest dances such as *The Incense*, *Radha*, and *The Cobra* were based on recognizable and choreographically formulated gestures and poses[82] (see figs. 3.3 and 3.4).

---

[78] Shawn (1979), 62–63 and 69. He also developed film ideas in his early years in Los Angeles, writing and starring in a film for Thomas Edison in 1912, *Dance of the Ages*, with Norma Gould as his dancing partner.

[79] Shawn (1963), 62.

[80] Ibid, 69. "Certainly every dancer should study pantomimic movement—that is to say, how to convey realistically emotions, dramatic episodes, human situations, and activities, without the use of words" (71). Shawn is most likely referring to the Delsartean taxonomy of gesture, which, as I have discussed, is not equivalent to pantomime.

[81] This analysis of *Incense* is based on a film by Phillip Baribault of St. Denis performing the dance, shot in 1953 when St. Denis was 74, and a reconstruction performed by Deborah Zall in *Denishawn: The Birth of Modern Dance* (1988, New Jersey Center Dance Collective).

[82] By 1913 she had begun choreographing more abstract, lyrical, and choreographically complex dances that did not reference the Orient, beginning with *The Scherzo Waltz*. But it is her Oriental, gestural dances that she is remembered for.

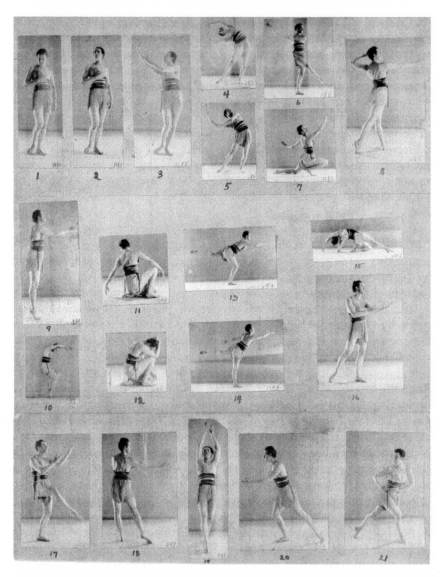

Figure 3.2 Ted Shawn in poses from a class dance called Sculpture Plastique, created by him in 1916. These pictures accompanied the notes and music of the dance which the pupils bought. Denishawn Collection. Jerome Robbins Dance Division, New York Public Library for the Performing Arts, Astor, Lenox and Tilden Foundations.

Given her slight exposure to Delsarte methods but her lack of any other formal training, what were the choreographic processes she utilised in generating her movement material? In interviews with Terry, she describes the sourcing of poses and gestures for the composition of her dances which she would combine using simple transitions such as stylised walks or changes in level, signalling her 'transitional'

Figure 3.3 Otto Sarony. Ruth St. Denis in *Radha*, 1908. Denishawn Collection. Jerome Robbins Dance Division, New York Public Library for the Performing Arts, Astor, Lenox and Tilden Foundations.

Figure 3.4 Ruth St. Denis in *The Incense*, 1916. Denishawn Collection. Jerome Robbins Dance Division, New York Public Library for the Performing Arts, Astor, Lenox and Tilden Foundations.

status between the ancient and modern movement described by Bergson. She also describes "translating" gestures of communication into other "languages": for example, creating a movement to express *no* inspired by Egyptian bas-reliefs and paintings. She states:

> ... if I cannot speak it correctly, in the movement sense, I will spend six weeks hunting up a particular gesture until I'm justified in using that gesture, justified in that it is authentic and can be properly included in my total plan of expression.[83]

It is beyond the scope of this chapter to discuss St. Denis's appropriation, insensitive or otherwise, of foreign cultural expression. The fact is, St. Denis did appropriate the corporeal languages of Eastern cultures, which she would eventually visit, and, in imagining what those lost and existing languages might be, she created something that was authentic to her own creative research and expressive purposes.[84] As demonstrated through my descriptions, representational gestures were treated to a process that removed them from the directly mimetic and interfered with their corporeal production through manipulation of tempo, tension, balance, and compositional context.

The important point here is that the nascent dance practices at the Denishawn School in Los Angeles drew from the same training sources, body cultures, and popular theater references as the performance modalities of the silent screen, and the expressive qualities of the body, face, and hands were a preoccupation for both performance genres. In fact, the school was advertised in *Photoplay* and many silent film stars trained there in order "to acquire new mimetic skills so essential to the silent screen," as Terry says.[85] Film theorists such as Jerome Delamater and Wollen have commented on the important role that dance played in performance training for the silent screen. And Naremore writes:

> In the nineteenth century, actors were taught balance and movement by dancing masters, so that a good deal of silent film behaviour—with its air of grace and refinement, its flexibility and sentimental lyricism—seems vaguely related to classical ballet; thus [Lillian] Gish has an erect posture and a quality of delicacy mixed with strength that might have been learnt in a dancing class, and Chaplin is the most balletic of actors.[86]

Audiences of Hollywood films during this period were watching actors with varying degrees of dance training and expertise.

Many other early screen actors underwent dance training, some at Denishawn. Once set up in Los Angeles, Griffith often sent his stars to study there, as was the

---

[83] Terry (1969), 82–83.

[84] For more on this see Jane Desmond, "Dancing out the Difference: Cultural Imperialism and Ruth St. Denis's 'Radha' of 1906," *signs*, 17, 1 (1991): 28–49; Banes (1998), 80–93; and Ramsay Burt, *Alien Bodies: Representations of Modernity, 'Race' and Nation in Early Modern Dance* (London: Routledge, 1998), 164–65.

[85] Terry (1976), 67.

[86] Naremore (1988), 50. (Chaplin is obviously a special case regarding corporeal expression, choreography, and film but a discussion of physical comedy is beyond the scope of my project here.) Jerome Delamater states that, "many stars of the silent era either came from dance backgrounds or studied dance to improve their ability to move with grace and ease" (Jerome Delamater's *Dance in the Hollywood Musical* [Michigan: Ann Arbor, 1981], 13). And Peter Wollen summarizes the relationship between Griffith and Denishawn in a succinct paragraph in *Singing in the Rain*, (London: BFI, 1992) commenting that, "in the early silent period, there was an explicit affinity between pantomime acting and dance, which was not only demonstrated in spectacular dance sequences, but also inflected a whole style of acting" (61).

case with Lillian and Dorothy Gish, Blanche Sweet, Mabel Normand, and Mae Marsh. Others like Carol Dempster he lured from the studio to the screen.[87] As Lillian Gish recalls:

> I also joined the Denishawn Dancing School, studying with Ruth St. Denis and Ted Shawn.... Their large living room had been converted into a studio with mirrors and practice bars, and later...Mother rented it so that we could practice early in the morning and late at night. Within a few years my body was to show the effects of all this discipline; it was as trained and responsive as that of a dancer or an athlete.[88]

Griffith's encouragement for his actresses to attend Denishawn classes is an example of the experimentation that the transitional phase allowed—a chance for reflection on the operations of corporeal performance at the same time that filmmakers were reflecting on the parameters of filmic performance more generally. Griffith understood the special significance of corporeal performance in silent film. When the theatrically experienced Gish sisters presented themselves at the Biograph studios in New York, Griffith said, "we don't deal in words here," and after a traumatic audition process involving the discharge of firearms he revealed his satisfaction with the comment, "you have expressive bodies."[89]

Roberta Pearson has written about the significant change in performance style in Griffith's Biograph films between 1908 and 1913, stating that this slate of films provides the key to "the emergence of a performance style that came to dominate the classical Hollywood cinema, and, by extension, world cinema."[90] Just as the term *Delsartean* has come to blanket a diverse range of performance examples, Pearson's identification of an acting style representative of cinema per se is fraught. But the idea that Griffith's innovations formed the basis of a performance mode specific to cinema is useful. It suggests that there exists a repository of corporeal behavior that is identifiably "cinematic'"—a *gesturology of cinema*—behavior that was born of a confluence of performance styles and modes and was deeply *medial* in nature. As we have seen, this gestural profile appears to owe much to the somatic cultural forms so influential at the beginning of the twentieth century, constituting a historical precedent for the cinema-dance exchange in contemporary examples of *gestural dancefilm*.

Pearson refers to the style of acting from which Griffith departed as the *histrionic code* and the new style developed during Griffith's time at Biograph as the *verisimilar code*. The former she connects to the most prominent style of theater concurrent with Griffith—melodrama—where the emphasis was on a display of virtuosic and

---

[87] For more on dancers in early cinema see Delamater (1981); Garafola (1998); Studlar (1993); Jowitt (1988); Shawn (1979); Maynard (1965); Wollen and Allen (1996); Jane Pritchard, "Movement on the Silent Screen," *Dance Theatre Journal*, 12, 3 (1996): 26–30; and Arthur Todd, "From Chaplin to Kelly: The Dance on Film," *Theatre Arts*, XXXV, 8 (1951): 50. Non-Griffith actresses who attended classes at Denishawn include Myrna Loy, Colleen Moore, Margaret Loomis, Lenore Ulric, Ina Claire, Carmel Myers, Claire Niles, Florence Vidor, Barbara and Joan Bennett, and Ruth Chatterton. Modern dance training for actors continued beyond the silent era. Martha Graham taught "movement" to many actors; Bette Davis, Gregory Peck, Liza Minnelli, Joanne Woodward, Tony Randall, and Woody Allen (Graham 1991, 120).

[88] Lillian Gish and Ann Pinchot, *The Movies, Mr Griffith, and Me* (New Jersey: Prentice-Hall, 1969), 100.

[89] Ibid, 36–37.

[90] Roberta E. Pearson, *Eloquent Gestures: The Transformation of Performance Style in the Griffith Biograph Films* (Berkeley: University of California Press, 1992), 5.

coded acting skills with little concern for illusions of reality.[91] This leads Pearson to Delsarte. Rather than sustaining the chronological separation of "histrionic" or melodramatic acting and "verisimilar" or natural acting established in key texts such as Pearson's, I would like to return to Delsarte's ideas on *correspondence* and *universal or codified gestures* and add to this Agamben's body in crisis to account for the medial quality of gestural performance during this era of transition and experimentation.

These historic influences produce three different gestural modes that are evidenced in the performances of Lillian Gish: (a) excessive and exaggerated gestures that can be seen as a hangover from the gestural crisis and associated lack of physical control (exemplified in Jean Epstein's description of Gish)[92]; (b) the histrionic gestures of the pantomime tradition that had simplified Delsarte's research; and (c) the new psychological realism emerging on the European dramatic stage that can be seen as a revision of Delsarte's ideas on correspondence. The variety of body practices in use during this time are evidence of an intense focus on, and interest in, the moving body and its ability to express. What these techniques collectively produce is also more than mere variety of register. In foregrounding technique per se, these performances reveal *the process of making a means visible as such.*

Armed with a better understanding of the parameters of human locomotion gleaned from the new body culture industry, in combination with dance training and gestural experimentation, we begin to see a resolution of the crisis of the body associated with very early cinema in the staging of corporeal performance on screen in the second decade of the twentieth century. The silent screen provided a new stage for the gestural articulations of the performing body and demanded a new approach that adapted to the special conditions of film. The transitional period placed the actor in a radical proximity to everyday scenarios and the contingencies of everyday life, as Jennifer M. Bean argues.[93] Not only was the action moved to less controlled environments than the proscenium stage, whether the early chaos of the film studio or the great outdoors, but lack of scripts during film production placed an emphasis on improvisation, and single-takes left little room for error, capturing edgy and sharp performances. Directors like Griffith would stage the cinematic gesture *as, and in, process*, registering the shift from an oscillation between anarchy/hysteria and codification to a new mediation between these two poles of corporeal expressivity. This developmental period of screen performance is marked by the mediality that Agamben ascribes to the term *gesture*: "*The gesture is the exhibition of a mediality: it is the process of making a means visible as such.*"[94]

Gish's performance as Henrietta Girard in *Orphans of the Storm* (1921, d. D. W. Griffith) exemplifies a virtuosic use of gesture that draws from a number of performance registers, illustrating Naremore's description of Gish's graceful,

---

[91] Ibid, 21–23. See Naremore (1988), 52–67 and Gunning (1991), 227–28 on the coexistence of both codes in actors like Mary Pickford.

[92] "…the little, short, rapid, spare, one might say involuntary, gestures of Lillian Gish who runs like the hand of a chronometer!" (Jean Epstein, "Magnification and Other Writings," trans. Stuart Liebman, *October*, 3 [Spring, 1977]: 1).

[93] Jennifer M. Bean, "Technologies of Early Stardom and the Extraordinary Body," *Camera Obscura* 48, 16, 3 (2001): 8–57. Bean describes how proximity to real life on set impacted on the corporeal performance, as "the terms of the *realness* structured in ostensible opposition to the anachronistic, secure, and comfortable gestures of the stage" (29–30).

[94] Agamben (2000), 58.

refined, flexible, and lyrical corporeal style. Telling her sister, Louise/Dorothy Gish that she is blind, Henrietta/Lillian delicately touches her own fingers to her eyes, sparking Louise/Dorothy's hysterical response. (She performs many more complex gestures in communicating with her blind sister that are, of course, redundant within the logic of the fictional world.) Her frantic gesturing to the aristocrats who could save her from the lecherous Le Fleur consists mainly of a begging gesture, hands forward of her body and facing each other. When refusing her love interest Chevalier de Vaudrey because of her commitment to her lost, blind sister, she clenches her first to her mouth and turns her back to the camera, her face hardly visible under a large hat. When the truth is revealed, their heads are close together in intimacy and they cover each other in small gentle kisses. And on being told that her sister is dead, she mauls her sister's shawl and, in close-up, her eyes roll back in her head.

In adapting narrative drama for the screen, Griffith helped define a theatrical idea of cinematic language that would come to dominate the film industry, eclipsing other alternatives represented elsewhere in this book such as movement studies and experimental film. The dancefilms under discussion here are aligned with this turn to drama in film—character, storytelling, the everyday—and in contrast to the more strictly choreographic examples such as the films of Babette Mangolte and Maya Deren. The transitional gestural performances of Griffith's actors provide a model of gestural mediality that resonates with gestural performance in contemporary dance-film. Here we find bodies heavy with narrative potential and connected to an expressive charge, whether through connection to the everyday, the use of codified gestures, through a direct link to an intention or emotion, or an unconscious impetus beyond corporeal control.

3.4 Staging Gesture-Dance in Dancefilm

If Pearson is right, if Griffith's "eloquent gestures" set a precedent in screen performance that would come to dominate world cinema, then we should be able to trace the influence of Gish's corporeal performance through to the gestural cine-choreographies of the present. But even if Pearson is only half-right, the gestural performances resulting from the dance/film exchange that occurred in the first two decades of the twentieth century will have some resonances with contemporary dancefilm through *gestural circulation*. As Lesley Stern states:

> The interesting thing about the gestural as it manifests cinematically is its propensity for migration. Gestures migrate from one movie to another, from the movies into social milieux and vice versa, they resonate, disappear and reappear—differently, and the differences pertain to cultural and historical context as well as to media and genre.[95]

My understanding of a *circuit of gestural exchange* in relation to dancefilm will be developed more fully in my final chapter, but what is pertinent here is *the transformation of*

---

[95] Stern (2002).

gestures as they cross cultural, historical, technological, generic, and disciplinary boundaries in the production of the cine-choreographic order of *gesture-dance*. As stated elsewhere, choreography in the twentieth century has involved a pursuit of *original movement*. For the dance artists under discussion here that quest has involved bringing techniques of movement invention to the *translation* and *transformation* of all kinds of gestures. When St. Denis was seeking a corporeal expression for *no* in her "Egyptian" dance, she was researching and developing a unique corporeal language. If Delsartean methodologies and screen acting aesthetics informed the gestural choreography of St. Denis, what contemporary body technologies produce the *gesture-dance* of Vandekeybus and Bausch?

The mind-body research undertaken by Delsarte, the context of physical health and therapy in which his ideas flourished, and connections with emerging dance practices have a contemporary counterpart in Hubert Godard's work on gesture. Godard provides a methodological bridge from Delsarte to an understanding of gestural operations in contemporary dance and dancefilm. His current and more physiologically (rather than spiritually) grounded approach to the connections between corporeal movement and expression brings Delsarte's Law of Correspondence up to date.[96] Godard also describes the status of gesture as inherently contingent and details the complex matrix of influences both localized *in* as well as *surrounding* the body that render gesture as medial. His insight into gestural production, and the specific work of contemporary dance in interfering with the processes involved in that production, provides analytical tools for describing the exceptional quality of gestural performance in contemporary dancefilm.

Godard's essay, "Gesture and Its Perception," focuses on how we experience gesture as it occurs in life, performance, and dance. He describes how gestures are produced by *forces* that create, regulate, and censor "mythologies of the body in motion"—individual, social, cultural, historical, environmental—and these same *forces* produce "frames of perception" through which we encounter gesture. Godard's description of *gestural production* emphasizes complexity—the infinite number of variables, invisible forces, and the degree of unconscious physiological work that is involved. This complexity correlates with Agamben's definition of *gesture* as "*an exhibition of a mediality: it is the process of making a means visible as such.*"[97] According to Godard, gesture is always contingent and can be open to many readings, which may be part of the appeal for artists such as Bausch, whose work is rigorously open-ended. Godard suggests that these conditions of gestural production and reception may be the reason that classification has become the task, and this is corroborated by the enduring and controversial influence of Delsarte's taxonomy.[98]

For Godard there is only one certainty in relation to gesture: that it is inseparable from an "expressive charge." Godard states:

---

[96] Resonances with Delsarte's therapeutic connections can be found in the special relationship between contemporary dance and healing in the late twentieth and early twenty-first centuries, a relationship that Godard has contributed to in his work with the National Cancer Institute in Milan, among other things. For one perspective on this contemporary link see Emily Wilcox, "Dance as L'intervention: Health and Aesthetics of Experience in French Contemporary Dance," *Body & Society*, 11, 4 (2005): 109–39.

[97] Agamben (2000), 58.

[98] Godard (2003–2004), 57–59.

The relationship to one's weight, that is to gravity, already contains a temperament or intention towards the world.[99]

This is not dissimilar to Auerbach's claim that all "human action is motivated," and both point to the processes between mind and body that were so central to Delsarte's project.[100] Godard's connection of our corporeal habits, both conscious and unconscious, to an *intentionality* is supported by the example of our ability to recognize a footfall on a staircase. Even beyond vision, gestural traces constitute unique phenomena attached to us all as unique and inherently expressive beings.

The significance of this link between gesture and *expression*, first established in the discussion of Delsarte's work and so important to the choreographic work of Bausch (whose lineage shares links with German Expressionism), relates to the role of gestural performance as an alternative to dialogue in both silent film and dancefilm. If human movement is inherently expressive, then gesture-dance as a cinechoreographic order can provide an alternative to literary-based, narrative film form while bringing the genre of dancefilm closest to the terrain occupied by the same. In *The Lament of the Empress* (1989, d. Pina Bausch), a male character in drag walks around a dance studio, his hand sliding along the ballet bars that line the walls. He walks slowly and evenly and is mumbling. This simple action located in this particular setting, along with his dancers' gait and introspective posture, suggest various scenarios: a performer preparing to go on stage, an injured dancer mourning a lost career. The expressive charge of this corporeal activity projects a character and story suitable for cinematic development, but Bausch's episodic film structure leaves this moment isolated and ambiguous. While character, mood, intention, and motivation may all be present, the medial nature of gesture is highlighted in gesture-dance examples such as *The Lament of the Empress* through an absence of any linear "order of production," so that expression is liberated and allowed to meander along the more dispersive trajectories of somatic knowledge. As Bausch expert Norbert Servos writes, recalling Agamben's gestural mediality, in her work "the body is no longer a means to an end, it is now the subject."[101]

Godard describes how/where the expressive charge of a gesture happens:

> The perception of a gesture functions by a global apprehension and only with difficulty allows us to distinguish the elements and stages which ground, for the actor as much as the observer, the expressive charge of that gesture.[102]

Godard is fairly obtuse here, but a few ideas can be drawn from this assertion. Expression is grounded in the various stages of gestural performance, from initial impulse to its completion, but also in what he refers to as a "global apprehension" that encompasses both actor and observer and takes in all of the variable forces described above that are involved in the gestural process. For Godard, the static standing position already contains this *expressive charge*; the tonic or gravitational

[99] Ibid, 58.
[100] Auerbach (2007), 11. Even Yvonne Rainer, whose choreographic project of the 1960s and 1970s went so far in challenging the role of expression in dance, writes: "...the body speaks no matter how you suppress it" (quoted in Thryza Nichols Goodeve, "Rainer Talking Pictures," *Art in America* July [1997]: 58).
[101] Norbert Servos, *Pina Bausch Dance Theatre* (Munich: K.Keiser, 2008), 25.
[102] Godard (2003–2004), 57.

muscles that work to maintain our equilibrium "are also those that register changes in our affective and emotional state":

> The internal resistances to disequilibrium, which are organised by the system of gravitational muscles, will induce the quality and affective charge of the gesture. The psychic apparatus expresses itself through this gravitational system. It is through its investment that it charges movement with meaning, modulates and colours it with desire, inhibition and emotion.... and this happens unknown to the subject, being upstream of her/his conscious awareness.[103]

It seems, if we follow Godard, that Delsarte was right in determining a direct correspondence between an emotional truth and physical articulation, and the methodology of assuming a posture to conjure a mood. And with the inclusion of the gestural recipient or spectator in Godard's account of gestural production, we have an inkling of the depths to which gestural circulation and exchange will run.

What Godard *can* elaborate on are the conditions for gestural production in the body, "the richly meaningful internal dynamics of gesture," and the variables involved at this stage that produce "the quality, the specific colour of each gesture": mood, physique, the initiating body part, "the flows of intensity organizing it," how the movement is visualized, the play around the center of gravity and the degree of tension.[104] Godard then describes the ways in which choreographers interfere with the processes of gesture:

> Dance is the pre-eminent site for making visible the disturbances where these forces of cultural evolution meet and conflict.[105]

The example given by Godard is a moment in Bausch's live work where her performers deliver a text "while developing movement that bears a signifying charge opposed to what is being said."[106] In *Kontakthof* (1978), a character recalls her early dancing days and the cruelty of her teacher, violently brushing another women's hair and then thrusting her face into a bucket of water yelling, "Smile... why don't you smile?" The disjunction between "signifying charge" and signifier can also be mute in Bausch's live work; in *Nelken* (1982), the domestic action of peeling potatoes is transformed into an act of seduction as a woman attracts the attention of a menacing group of men who literally, and repetitively, throw themselves at her across a table.

This disjunction is possible due to the dancers' ability to manipulate the conditions for gestural production through corporeal research and training. And this is the real appeal that Delsarte's ideas held for dance—a system that offered tools for adapting human motion to new expressive demands. How can we produce gestures that reveal something new about modern life? How can we get outside the forces that shape current "mythologies of the body in motion" and codependent corporeal "frames of perception"? How can we find new gestures to express new "intentions towards the world"? These are questions that Delsarte tackled, early cinema was

---

[103] Ibid, 59.
[104] Ibid, 57–59.
[105] Ibid, 57.
[106] Ibid, 59.

confronted with, and dance pioneers like Ruth St. Denis explored. They are also questions that certain forms of contemporary dance and dancefilm make central to aesthetic projects grounded in somatic expression.

In the work of Pina Bausch we can see how cultural, technological, and aesthetic influences play a role in an exemplary process of gestural transformation. The *technological* in this instance refers to methodologies and knowledges of the body (*technologies of the body*) *as well as* experimentation with the mechanical aspects of cinematic production that have impacted on many levels of Bausch's work (*technologies of cinema*). Throughout her career, Bausch utilized filmic devices such as montage, cross-fades, and fade-outs to structure her stage productions, as touched on briefly in my Introduction. It is important to acknowledge that her choreographic language is also steeped in the *gesturology of cinema*. Her performers generally assume the attitude and poise of glamorous, urbane socialites and are often clothed in evening wear. They throw back champagne and laugh in an exaggerated manner, strut in heels across the stage with murderous intent, request papers from people in an overtly officious manner, and run forward—reaching out—as if into the arms of a loved one. These overblown gestures evoke cinematic moments but always depart from our expectations: the champagne is gargled and spat, the woman in heels cannot quite keep her balance, the request for papers recurs again and again throughout the performance with no consequences, and the lovers that the performers run to are us, the audience beyond the footlights.

Bausch has interrogated the sphere of human gesture and created her own style of dance theater, or tanzteater.[107] Her work is an interrogation of performance per se and the performance of gesture specifically, and her central theme is human relations:

> I have only seen human relations or I have tried to see them and talk about them. That's what I'm interested in. I don't know anything more important.[108]

With some use of spoken word or vocal utterance but with an emphasis on physicalization, her work is, inevitably, based on the gestures of social relationships.[109] As human interaction is a significant ingredient of drama, these gestures are always heavy with the potential for narrative. As Jochen Schmidt puts it, "Bausch pieces are narrative. They tell things, but they don't tell stories."[110] Bausch's dance theater employs limited continuity regarding character. The distance between character and performer is collapsed as individuals completely transform between scenes or have continuity across a whole series of works. Together with designer Rolf Borzik she creates an ambiguous or abstract mise en scène: Her stage sets resemble art installa-

---

[107] Bausch began choreographing in 1968 and was the director of Tanztheater Wuppertal Pina Bausch from 1973 until the time of her death in 2009. Studying with Kurt Joos who had trained with Rudolf von Laban, Bausch's points of reference include Laban's redrawing of the kinetic parameters of the body, the German Expressionist tradition, and the American modern ballet and dance that she encountered during her studies at the Juilliard School of Music in New York and dancing for Antony Tudor between 1959 and 1962.

[108] Raimund Hoghe, "The Theatre of Pina Bausch," trans. Stephen Tree, *The Drama Review: TDR* 24, 1 (1980): 65.

[109] Hoghe on Bausch's use of spoken word: "Words that keep one from getting lost, sentences one can cling to—Pina Bausch's work denies such safety anchors... words are something slight, fragmentary, and blurred" (Hoghe [1980], 69).

[110] Jochen Schmidt quoted in Ann Daly, "Tanztheater: The Thrill of the Lynch Mob or the Rage of a Woman?" *Critical Gestures: Writings on Dance and Culture* (Middletown, Connecticut: Wesleyan University Press, 2002), 12.

tions rather than the sparse open spaces of most contemporary dance of the 1980s and 1990s. And there is no conclusiveness, judgement, or commentary; just showing.

There is no "moral" in the Griffith sense and not even an anticlimax. Bausch says:

> Somehow I am always a kind of "counsel for the defense".... Somehow at these points, where one ordinarily says, "This is uncomfortable" or "This isn't right," or whatever— there I try to understand somehow why it is as it is.... [To give answers] would be conceited.... I'm just as lost as all the others.... You can see it like this or like that. It just depends on the way you watch.[111]

This open-ended approach would confuse and infuriate her audiences in the early years. In a public forum on Bausch's work in New York in 1985, dance critic Joan Acocella states:

> It's not repetition that bothers me. It's repetition without development, variation, exploration. Development is something that we in America associate with intelligence.[112]

Bausch's subversion of the order of production that Acocella is referring to exemplifies the way that gesture-dance operates in cinema: as an interrogation of the means of expression in this "homeland of gesture." The moral ambiguity of Bausch's work is written in her choreographed gestures, which exemplify mediality in dance-film: Objects are moved, ground is covered, emotions are expressed, but the corporeal condition is weighed down with "a dream vision of what remains of movies after their stories have gone," to borrow an evocative phrase from Geoffrey O'Brien.[113] The gestures are presented with no dramatic context to hang on. As her one-time dramaturg Raimund Hoghe puts it, corporeal performance in her work depicts "visible reactions to invisible situations.... They themselves constitute the story."[114]

The Lament of the Empress returns the montage structures Bausch developed for the stage to the screen. As Ana Sanchez-Colberg writes:

> If, in previous theatrical work, it was critically acknowledged that Bausch incorporated filmic devices to create her stage pieces, in *Die Klage Der Kaiserin* Bausch has inverted the process.[115]

The opening scenes of women under various states of physical duress in a lush European landscape are edited together as isolated incidents, linked by score, location, mood, and a certain attitude to performance. One woman pushes a leaf blower

[111] Hoghe (1980), 72.
[112] Joan Acocella quoted in Daly (2002), 15. Acocella's comments are supported by Daly herself who, in her editorial commentary, criticizes Bausch for not providing commentary on the violence against women that she depicts (18).
[113] Geoffrey O'Brien, quoted in Auerbach (2007), 2.
[114] Hoghe (1980), 65.
[115] Ana Sanchez-Colberg, "Reflections on Meaning and Making, in Pina Bausch's *The Lament of the Empress*," in *Parallel Lines*, ed. Stephanie Jordan and Dave Allen (London: John Libbey and Co., 1993), 219. This follows Claudia Rosiny's observation: "...the choreographer transfers her production method to another medium. The montage principle of her pieces in the eighties is continued in the succession and repetition of images" ("Film Review: The Lament of the Empress," *Ballett International*, 6–7 [1990]: 74).

around a forest in autumn, pointing a pistol at the leaves that dance around her. The machine is heavy and she is alternatively pushing and pulling, dressed in a tiny party frock on a very cold day. Another woman wears a burlesque costume—fishnet tights, a corseted, strapless leotard, and a black mask that shoots up into the air like bunny ears (fig. 3.5). She is staggering around in circles on rocky terrain with a helicopter hovering out of sight, bent over and exhausted but compelled to go on, pulling her top up over her breasts. Another woman in a glamorous blue swimsuit wanders in a dark part of the forest calling out for her "mama" and turns up later beside the road with a friend, both trying to shelter from the rain and the cold with a bundle of clothes held over their heads. Two women in coats with dark, bobbed hair walk with purpose amongst the trees led by enormous dogs on leashes.

Still more women appear in this prolonged sequence of cuts between intensely dramatic and profoundly dark situations. The consistently mobile camera follows a girl in a dolly shot as she walks quickly down a path, wearing a jacket, underpants, and high heels and smoking a cigarette. Another woman in heels, a bathing suit, and a head scarf hauls sheep and goats around. The music is a slow lament played by a brass band. The performances in this opening section of the film exemplify Hoghe's description of actions that are responding to situations unknown or invisible to the spectator, and this *cutting out* of dramatic intention brings notions of performance itself to the fore. The girl in the bunny ears is looking for something and she cannot leave it alone, as if her life depends on it. Her outfit suggests this moment as a tragic outcome of a prior engagement—they gesture to another time and place that has led her to this.

Figure 3.5 *The Lament of the Empress* (1989, d. Pina Bausch). Film still courtesy La Cinémathèque de la Danse, Paris. Rights Reserved.

Walking, as *the* basic human gesture, recurs across the film. And this connection back to our most simple movement exemplifies Bausch's relationship to dance, which is not, for her, the starting point, but somewhere to finish:

> ...what I consider beautiful and important there, I do not want to touch for the time being—because I think it is so important. You have to learn something different first...then perhaps you can dance again.[116]

Hoghe adds: "An inviting gesture, a gentle turn of the head, a glance, a walk towards each other and a touch—everyday motions or already a dance?"[117] It is as if Bausch must find the choreographic in the familiar before she can move fully into what we recognize as contemporary dance. Such dance sequences are rare in this film (as is the case with Vandekeybus and Pennell's work as well) and are often relegated to a black box space with the ambience and lighting effects of a "legitimate" performance. The shift from everyday movement to dance will become a major topic in my discussion of the musical, but here it demonstrates why Bausch's work is so significant in relation to dance, gesture, and links to the gestural language of the cinema. These are bodies we feel we know—their gestures are lifted from stories, games, and films and somehow made uncanny. And in their capacity to express they exceed the limitations of language, recalling Delsarte's words: how gesture is "a witness to the secret labor performed by the immanences which are about to burst forth....Gesture is the direct agent of the heart. It is the fit manifestation of feeling."[118]

So how does Bausch *transform* gestures in creating gesture-dance on film? How does she get beyond dominant body mythologies to physically express something new about the world? In some instances there is an intensification or exaggeration comparable to the dramatic scenarios that frame the gestures of silent cinema. Desire, frustration, and despair dominate these performances as bodies carry out actions with no satisfying conclusions. Something drives these bodies to acts of endurance, of labor without results: stumbling over rocky terrain or waiting out in the cold. A man carries a wardrobe on his back, his legs trembling under the strain. Another woman performs a dance with her arms, balancing on an icy pathway with the wind and snow nearly knocking her over. These figures are caught out, locked in a moment that is inescapable because each time they get where they are going (lug that animal, fall with exhaustion) there is another drama to deal with, like a series of traumatic climaxes that will not end. Duration and repetition play an important role both within and across scenes as we cut back to a figure throughout the length of the film.[119]

Adaptation and juxtaposition are other techniques that transform familiar gestures and short-circuit any development of character and narrative. In *Lament of the*

---

[116] Quoted in Hoghe (1980), 64.
[117] Idem.
[118] Delsarte (1893), 466–68.
[119] Ciane Fernandes discusses Bausch's use of repetition regarding duration and transformation at length in *Pina Bausch and the Wuppertal Dance Theater: The Aesthetics of Repetition and Transformation* (New York: Peter Lang, 2005). This Bauschian compositional element features more prominently in her stage works than it does in *The Lament of the Empress*.

Empress, these processes are often tied to specific scenarios where performances sit uneasily with our expectations. Bausch has structured the film around three main locations: the forest, the interior of a studio/apartment, and a theater/performance space. The recognizable cinematic locations of nature, domestic spaces, and theatrical contexts frame specific performance registers that make contact with cinematic conventions and then depart. A woman and a man are alone in a vast domestic interior. She is agitated and flies at him in anger, they tussle physically, and then the action takes off as she climbs up his frame and stands on his shoulders. A man in drag sits at a pristine breakfast table, baring a stockinged leg, wearing sunglasses, and smoking a cigarette. Nothing happens (see fig. 3.6). And particular cinematic treatments also resonate gesturally only to take off in other directions. The close-up on a meticulously made-up face in a diva-like pose, lying back and looking up to the camera, is deconstructed as a hand comes into frame and tweaks her nose, or fingers walk over her face. Other close-ups on various crying faces sit alone, unconnected to character or action. Legs are framed to carry out a drama: pairs tango together, bright red stilettos strut across a stage. And performers in various stages of undress render particular scenes uncomfortable. Breasts slip out of dresses as bodies succumb to fatigue, distress, duress. A woman sits bare-breasted at a meal, her Egyptian headdress empowering her in her storytelling: a monologue involving a demonstration of the sphinx position.

Belgian choreographer Wim Vandekeybus's short films also bring the processes of dance composition to the rendering of gesture. Actions, gestures, and postures speak louder than words, which may also be present but are always multilingual and intensely poetic. In *Elba and Frederico*, the crossover time in the morning between a

Figure 3.6 *The Lament of the Empress* (1989, d. Pina Bausch). Film still courtesy La Cinémathèque de la Danse, Paris. Rights Reserved.

night-worker and his day-working partner is multiplied through montage, the characters repeating actions—brushing teeth, dressing, making coffee, getting out the door—with slight variation. The sleeping/waking moments have the same intentionality as the inane physical games that they invent to relieve the boredom—flicking cigarette filters with rubber bands and blowing tissues into the air while changing clothes. We thus become familiar with these bodies and these gestures and, with the addition of a very close and mobile camera, they accumulate to express the claustrophobic and repressive cycle of their daily routine. What is wrung out of these gestures beyond the thin plotline is the unassimilable, and the final rape scene releases this excess into violence.

In *Blush*, an engagement party is full of tension, bravado, teasing, games, and alcohol; people undress and dance on the table; the bride and groom tussle verbally. But actions occur that take these bodies beyond the excesses of celebration: Revellers collectively bite the table and try to lift it off the ground, a frog is mixed in a blender and drunk on a dare, and a toast—the gesture of celebration and joy—is shattered as the bride and groom squeeze their glasses until the bride's explodes, shot in crystal clear slow-motion. *Blush* takes us from joyful ritual to the dark side of mythology. The bride throws herself from a cliff top and her presence at the wedding as a ghost registers in the final group pose for the camera, where she is missing from the wedding party who are dressed in black. These "scenes" are interspersed with choreographic sequences that shift the action from the everyday to the underworld and back again. But the gestures of celebration and grief gone wrong, such as the insulting, seductive manoeuvres by the women around the groom at the wake, demonstrate where gestural transformation can take cinema in this type of dancefilm.

In this film, along with my other examples, it is a cine-choreographic approach to gesture that creates a new type of screen performance. The dancerly attention to physical articulation and the cinematic staging of the body reveals what the body knows and can express in scenarios that would usually depend on spoken word. The irreducible nature of this corporeal activity takes us where language cannot, revelling in the mediality that links this particular cine-choreographic mode with other types of dance, film, and dancefilm.

4

Maya Deren

Strategies for Dancefilm

INTERVIEWER: *Was there anything like* Choreography for the Camera *before Deren?*
SNYDER: *No. Well, I take that back, because we don't really know. There was another woman named Loïe Fuller, fifty years before Maya, who in her later years was doing experimental films in Europe.*[1]

The quote above, taken from a 1977 interview with friend of Maya Deren and dance scholar Allegra Fuller Snyder, locates the films of Deren within a specific genealogy: the history of film utilizing choreographic content and form. Deren is the second of three twentieth-century artists, all women, whose work provides a historical framework for this book. Loïe Fuller was a fin de siècle artist whose work can be read as embodying the conditions of movement, performance, and technology that led to the emergence of dancefilm. Creating work half a century later, Deren was the filmmaker who reintroduced dance into the film avant-garde at the height of the modern dance movement. Later in the century, choreographer and filmmaker Yvonne Rainer would develop theories and practices that are taken up in the following chapter to provide some initial terms for considering the most radical and recent screen dance practices.[2]

Fuller is the logical precursor of Deren in relation to the history of dancefilm for several reasons. Most significantly, Deren, like Fuller, embraced contemporary technologies and made them part of the aesthetic fabric of her work. Deren utilized the full technological range of her medium in exploring what she saw as its distinguishing elements, realizing its condition as a "time-space art."[3] Multiple exposures, jump cuts, slow-motion, negative film sequences, superimposition, matches-on-action, freeze-frame, and acute camera angles are just a few of the cinematic techniques and effects she employed. Second, Fuller and Deren pioneered radical aesthetic roles for the human body in motion, placing it at the center of their aesthetic and technological explorations. This combination of technological innovation and a privileging of the moving body leads to the third point of comparison: Fuller was the first artist, male or female, to claim credit as both director and choreographer for her films.[4]

---

[1] Allegra Fuller Snyder, "Interview with Allegra Fuller Snyder," in *The Legend of Maya Deren: A Documentary Biography and Collected Works. Volume 1 Part Two: Chambers (1942–47)*, ed. VèVè A. Clark, Millicent Hodson and Catrina Neiman (New York: Anthology Film Archives, 1988), 288.
[2] Connections between Deren and Rainer are made in two essays in Bill Nichols anthology, *Maya Deren and the American Avant-Garde*, ed. Bill Nichols (Berkeley: University of California Press, 2001); Renata Jackson's "The Modernist Poetics of Maya Deren" (47–76) and Maureen Turim's "The Ethics of Form: Structure and Gender in Maya Deren's Challenge to the Cinema" (77–102).
[3] Clark et al. (1988), 460.
[4] For details of Fuller's film productions see Chapter 1.

While Deren never credits herself as "choreographer," she shares a general credit with Talley Beatty for *A Study in Choreography for Camera* (1945), and a "choreographic collaboration" credit is given to Frank Westbrook for *Ritual in Transfigured Time* (1945–56).[5] Deren certainly compared her filmmaking process to that of a choreographer by stating, for example, that *A Study in Choreography for Camera* is a "duet" between dancer and filmmaker and *Ritual in Transfigured Time* is a "dance film" because all the various movements within the film are combined "according to a choreographic concept."[6]

What is also of note regarding Snyder's quote is the role of the two artists within their milieu, Fuller's fame emerging out of fin de siècle Paris and the innovations of modernity, with Deren at the beginning of a new, mid-century era of avant-garde filmmaking and working within the bohemian artistic and political culture of New York's Greenwich Village. Both artists were at the vanguard of their fields and influenced other artists: Deren's work and model of independent cinematic practice directly impacted on a generation of American filmmakers including Charles Atlas, Shirley Clarke, Yvonne Rainer, Amy Greenfield, Norman McLaren, and Hilary Harris. Both women pushed the boundaries of their form, making these artists fundamental to the historical connection between dancefilm and the avant-garde described throughout this book.[7]

Deren's writing plays an important role in any understanding of her film practice including the key cinematic strategies discussed in this chapter: *verticality, depersonalization,* and *stylization of gesture. Vertical film form* is a concept developed by Deren to account for the different film structure in non-narrative films—what she calls "poetic film." Rather than progressing "horizontally" with the logic of the narrative, vertical films or sequences explore the quality of moments, images, ideas, and movements outside of such imperatives. *Depersonalization* refers to a type of screen performance that subsumes the individual into the choreography of the film as a whole. Actors become figures across whom movement transfers as an "event." The manipulation of gestural action through *stylization* occurs through individual performances as well as cinematic effects—the two levels of filmic performance combining to create screen choreographies. These three concepts are bound to Deren's utilization of dance as a performative mode and illustrate her significance regarding the development of dancefilm.

Considering Deren's work in light of her connections with, and interest in, dance focuses attention on questions of corporeal performance in her films. Beginning with Deren's own films, I will explore the privileged role given to the

---

[5] When asked about the choreographic content of *A Study in Choreography for the Camera*, Hella Hammid who was camera-operator, said, "Maya thought it out and [Talley Beatty] executed it perfectly" (Clark et al [1988], 280). And in an article Deren wrote for *Dance* magazine she describes her choreographic collaboration with Frank Westbrook during the making of *Ritual in Transfigured Time*: "In the actual dance passage, Frank Westbrook collaborated with me in the effort to design dance movements which would not be suddenly new, but which, in their stylization, would seem but the climactic extension of the ordinary, casual movements of the party scene" (458).

[6] Ibid, 458.

[7] Their shared connections to literary Symbolism shed some light on their experimental practices. Deren's MA thesis was titled "The Influence of the French Symbolist School on Anglo-American Poetry." Like the Symbolists, both artists resist narrativization in their work, aiming at a transcendental aesthetic by turning their attention to the concrete terms of their medium.

moving body in films like *Meshes of the Afternoon* (1943), *A Study in Choreography for Camera*, *Ritual in Transfigured Time*, and *Meditation on Violence* (1948). Deren's characteristic film strategies outlined above consolidate tendencies found in earlier avant-garde dancefilms, such as Jean Renoir's *Sur un air de Charleston* (1926) and Francis Picabia and René Clair's *Entr'Acte* (1924), and can be traced through to contemporary work, such as the films of UK director David Hinton in his collaborations with choreographer Lloyd Newson and his company, DV8 Physical Theatre, and dancer/choreographer Wendy Houstoun. Such connections demonstrate the significance of Deren within the history of dancefilm and point to the continuing relevance of her aesthetics and practices, which assist in mapping the broad field of dance screen.

The question of the influence of dance on Deren's radical film aesthetic has been generally avoided by film theorists, perhaps due to the challenges presented by interdisciplinary work.[8] That dance had a special significance and aesthetic function for Deren is clear. Having migrated to America from Russia with her parents at age five, Deren graduated from Smith College with an MA in literature in 1939 and, in the same year, became secretary to Katherine Dunham. Dunham was a commercially and critically successful African-American choreographer and anthropological researcher of Caribbean dance. Her fieldwork and writing on Haitian dance had a strong impact on Deren, who went on to pursue her own research in Haiti. In the documentary, *In the Mirror of Maya Deren* (2001, d. Martina Kudlácek), Dunham describes Deren "performing" at a company party dancing wildly to drumming music, and there are other references to Deren's aspirations as a dancer in accounts of her time with the Dunham company.[9] Jonas Mekas also recounts Deren dancing often in her own home at social gatherings.[10]

This history prior to her first completed film project in 1943, *Meshes of the Afternoon*, clearly informs Deren's work, not least of all in her collaborations with Dunham dancers Talley Beatty and Rita Christiani. Deren's finished films are black-and-white experimental shorts, all around fifteen minutes long, except for *A Study in Choreography for Camera*, which is shorter at two-and-a-half minutes. Working against the conventions of mainstream cinema, and rejecting documentary, abstract, and surrealist traditions, Deren developed her own aesthetic and dancefilm

---

[8] Renata Jackson's *The Modernist Aesthetics and Experimental Film Practice of Maya Deren (1917–1961)* (Lewiston, New York: The Edwin Meller Press, 2002) gives an account of some choreographic influences on Deren's work, and one particular essay in Nichols's anthology deals directly with the dance content in her films head on: Mark Franko's "Aesthetic Agencies in Flux: Talley Beatty, Maya Deren and the Modern Dance Tradition in *Study in Choreography for Camera*," in Nichols (2001), 131–49. The lack of attention to Deren's work from within dance academia is pointed to by Franko: "There has been to my knowledge that links Maya Deren to the American modern dance tradition" (Nichols [2001], 131). This observation remains true in 2010, with the exception of Ok Hee Jeong's "Reflections on Maya Deren's Forgotten Film, *The Very Eye of Night*," (*Dance Chronicle*, 32, 3 (2009): 412–441).

[9] Some Dunham dancers believed that Deren "aspired to become a dancer with the company," but was disappointed due to her apparently unsuitable physicality, her racial background (the company members were all African American at the time), and the fact that "Dunham would prevent her from joining the dance classes, reminding her that she had been hired as a secretary and not as a dancer" (Clark et al., 1984, footnote 51, 504).

[10] Mekas says, "We used to also play drums together.... Maya would put on exotic dresses and dance ... dancing for hours on end with a wildness and excitement and also a total seriousness" (Jonas Mekas, "A Few Notes on Maya Deren," in *Inverted Odysseys: Claude Cahun, Maya Deren and Cindy Sherman*, ed. Shelley Rice [Massachusetts: MIT Press, 1999], 129–30).

form. Using performers with no acting training and often casting herself as the protagonist, her films are underscored by a preoccupation with figures moving through a variety of natural and domestic locations, a distortion of time and space continuity, destabilized/fragmented subjects, mobile and ambiguous sources of agency and desire, stylized figural action, and dream-like narratives. These elements come together to create a carefully structured, "choreographed" whole, translating "the magic of thoughts and dreams to film."[11] Five of Deren's films contain explicit dance content: *A Study in Choreography for Camera, Ritual in Transfigured Time, Meditation on Violence, The Very Eye of Night* (1952–55, released 1959), and her Haitian Voudou footage shot between 1947 and 1954 (posthumously assembled by Teiji and Cherel Ito to create *Divine Horsemen* in 1977). Beyond these explicit examples, a choreographic sensibility regarding cinematic production (camera movement, framing, editing, special effects), an attention to the articulations of the performing body, and the use of movements and gestures outside the familiar are all elements that can be found across Deren's oeuvre.

Deren's interest in dance, play, and ritual as modes of physical performance would appear to be due, in part, to their resistance to language and to those models of film dominated by it. Deren was opposed to what she terms "the literary approach" to filmmaking—a process she describes as involving the employment of "'intellectual' writers" regardless of their appropriateness to the project at hand. These films are often screen adaptations of novels and plays that maintain the literary form and have a consequent impact on acting, which she describes as stylistically "cliché." Deren sees such practices as improper for film, arguing for a cinema where "the elements, whatever their original context, are related according to the special character of the instrument itself." She suggests that the art form would be better off had it pursued the silent film form, a point that underscores connections between her work and the gestural cinema described in the previous chapter.[12] Her films are marked by an absence of score and dialogue; *At Land* (1944), *A Study in Choreography for Camera*, and *Ritual in Transfigured Time* are all silent, and none of her films feature spoken word. Deren's pursuit of an alternative to language-based cinema not only led to her institution of a film practice dominated by corporeal performance, but it also called for a merging of profilmic and filmic elements into a truly cinematic form independent of all other art forms:

> In discussing the formal emergent whole of a work of art, I pointed out that the elements, or parts, lose their original individual value and assume those conferred upon them by their function in this specific whole.[13]

---

[11] Clark et al. (1988), 615.

[12] Maya Deren, "An Anagram of Ideas on Art, Form and Film," in Nichols (2001), 39, reproduced with original page numbers. French filmmaker Germaine Dulac put this argument forward in 1926 in "Aesthetics, Obstacles, Integral Cinégraphie" where she writes: "Sympathetic study of mechanical movement was scorned.... The cinema thus became an outlet for bad literature" (trans. Stuart Liebman, reproduced in *French Film Theory and Criticism Vol.1 1907–1929*, ed. Richard Abel [Princeton: Princeton University Press, 1988], 390–91). Tom Gunning sets out a lineage of what he calls "non-patriachal cinema, challenging the formats of drama and narrative with new forms of sensuous abstraction," from Fuller, through Dulac to Deren in "Light, Motion, Cinema! The Heritage of Loie Fuller and Germaine Dulac," (*Framework*, 46 1 [2005]: 125). See also Deren's acknowledgment of her debt to silent comedies (Clark et al. [1988], 287–88).

[13] Deren (2001), 40.

In the case of films dominated by the activities of moving bodies, we shall see how for Deren this produced a filmic whole characterized by the quality of its mobile elements, constituting the production of a new form—the dancefilm. Such ideas, along with Deren's repeated use of the term *dancefilm*, have directly informed my own use of the term in referring to a cinema of movement where the dance and film elements become indistinguishable.

Deren's meandering and often dream-like plot structures are further proof of her rejection of language-based models for film—in this case cause and effect linearity. Her disregard for traditional film credits, including her own role as a performer, are evidence of Deren's resistance to the hierarchical structures that still dominate mainstream film production.[14] The lack of cast and crew hierarchies, scripts, and set shot-lists in early silent cinema, along with the use of extreme close-ups, suggested another cinematic alternative to Deren.[15] The framing of fragments of the performing body in close-up, such as Chao-li Chi's skin sliding over his ribs in *Meditation on Violence*, reveal the micro-choreographies at the body's periphery, unravelling the privileging of the face and spoken word in narrative-based cinema. Such shots are sometimes enhanced by Deren's use of temporal distortions such as slow-motion, effecting a kind of motion study that also evokes early cinema practices.

4.1 Vertical Film Form

> *...she attempted to work with the moment, distending it into a structure of exquisite ambiguity, underwritten by the braver spatial strategies that came perhaps more easily to the developed kinetic sense of a dancer.*
>
> Annette Michelson[16]

In a 1953 symposium on "Poetry and the Film," Deren describes a model of cinema that reveals her insight into contemporaneous conventions of filmic structure.[17] She describes "horizontal" film structure as affiliated with drama, "one circumstance—one action—leading to another," and discusses how this develops and delineates narrative and characterization in film. "Vertical" film structure, or "poetic structure," on the other hand:

---

[14] Deren omits a performance credit for herself from the films in which she stars, *Meshes of the Afternoon*, *At Land*, *and Ritual in Transfigured Time*. She does not credit performers in general except for the dancers she collaborated with.

[15] Deren (2001), 50.

[16] Annette Michelson, "Film and Radical Aspiration," in *Film Theory and Criticism*, ed. Gerald Mast and Marshall Cohen (New York: Oxford University Press, 1979), 633.

[17] This symposium was organized by Amos Vogel for Cinema 16, an early New York film society. The other panellists were Willard Maas (filmmaker), Arthur Miller (playwright), Dylan Thomas (poet), and Parker Tyler (poet and film critic). The male panel members are dismissive of Deren's ideas, even mocking, and the symposium ends with a confrontation between Miller and Deren. Miller does not grasp Deren's cinematic concepts, turning the discussion back to poetry as an aural rather than visual element within film. The papers from the symposium were published at the time in Jonas Mekas's *Film Culture*, and republished as "Poetry and the Film: A Symposium," in *The Film Culture Reader*, ed. P. Adams Sitney (New York: Prager Publishers, 1971), 171–86. Michelson contextualizes this symposium, and specifically Deren's contributions, as a significant event in the history of film theory in her articles "Film and Radical Aspiration" (Mast and Cohen [1979], 617–35), and "Poetics and Savage Thought," (Nichols [2001], 21–45).

...probes the ramifications of the moment, and is concerned with its qualities and its depth, so that you have poetry concerned, in a sense, not with what is occurring but with *what it feels like or with what it means.*[18]

Deren refers to such cinematic moments as "retardations" that focus on the *how* rather than the *what*, drawing attention away from the narrative logic and toward the images for and of themselves: to "visible and auditory forms for something that is invisible which is the feeling, emotion, or metaphysical content of the *movement.*"[19] These filmic moments/movements may consist of a variety of images joined through montage that are "brought to a center, gathered up, and collected by the fact that they all refer to a common emotion" or idea.[20]

The *movement* of the cinematic forms or elements are pivotal to Deren's film practice and, in this respect, verticality in her work does not mean inertia, but consists of a variety of movements on various levels of the filmic performance that "fill out" a moment. This aspect of Deren's model of cinematic verticality demonstrates that, while the concept clearly pertains to avant-garde or alternative film practices, the kinetic quality of Deren's verticality points to the specifically choreographic nature of her film work. It also preempts Jean-François Lyotard's Acinema, rejecting the "order of oppression" that is associated with the horizontal thrust of narrative cinema. The Acinematic film form bleeds out vertically, allowing space for the two poles of "immobility and excessive movement" that Lyotard associates with avant-garde cinema.[21] These poles are exemplified in Deren's short films through her use of slow-motion, freeze-frame, and the extreme kineticism of her performers: figures running along a beach or into water, spinning around in a garden, performing the expansive movements of modern dance in a domestic setting, swinging a blade in close proximity to the lens. Such movements create resonances that expand the idea or meaning in both time and space, elaborating on the quality of a central theme without resorting to language. The order of verticality dominates these films and prefigures a major tendency in contemporary short dancefilms.

As Wendy Haslem has pointed out, Deren's writing has not received the attention of filmmaker-theorists such as Sergei Eisenstein and, as a result, the importance of her work in relation to the development of film theory has often been overlooked.[22] I have compared Deren's poetic film form with Lyotard's more recent Acinematic

---

[18] Sitney (1971), 173–74. My emphasis.
[19] Ibid, 174. My emphasis.
[20] Ibid, 178.
[21] Jean-François Lyotard, "Acinema," *Wide Angle*, 2, 3 (1978): 53–54.
[22] Wendy Haslam, "Maya Deren: The High Priestess of Experimental Cinema," *Senses of Cinema*, www.sensesofcinema.com/contents/directors/02/deren.html. Writing in 1988, Michael O'Pray states that, "there is no substantial critical writing on Deren in this country and her own writings, particularly the fascinating 'An Anagram of Ideas on Art, Form and Film,' have been virtually ignored" (Michael O'Pray, "Maya Deren: 9 Times a Life," *Monthly Film Bulletin*, 55, 653 [1988]: 185). Nichols's anthology filled a large gap in theoretical work on Deren at the time of its publication, which Nichols suggests may have been due to a delay in the publication of a second volume of her collected writing. The first volume, which is in two parts—*The Legend of Maya Deren: A Documentary Biography and Collected Works. Volume 1 Part One: Signatures (1917–42)*, ed. VèVè A. Clark, Millicent Hodson and Catrina Neiman (New York City: Anthology Film Archives, 1984) and Clark et al. (1988)—has provided the backbone for research on Deren since its publication. Since Nichols's anthology, Jackson's monograph has been published along with articles by Theresa L. Geller, Catherine Russell, Alison Butler, and an earlier version of this paper, "Maya Deren, Dance, and Gestural Encounters, in *Ritual Transfigured Time*," *Senses of Cinema* 22 (2002). Online: http://archive.sensesofcinema.com/contents/02/22/deren.html. Accessed 4/6/10 http://archive.sensesofcinema.com/contents/02/22/deren.html. Accessed 4/6/10.

model of film. Deren's articulation of an interruption/alternative to the narrative drive of classic fiction film, particularly her choice of terminology, also precedes and perhaps informs Gilles Deleuze's treatment of the issue in his cinema books.[23] His model of the "movement-image" describes the basis of the linear progression of an action-reaction film structure (Deren describes it as "one action leads to another action," "the logic of actions"[24]), while his "time-image," found in the revolutionary postwar fiction films of the Italian Neo-realists and the French New Wave, is characterized by "purely optical and sound situations." For Deleuze, these images fill the space where something is, for example, "too powerful, or too unjust, but sometimes also too beautiful, and which henceforth outstrips our sensory-motor capacities."[25] Deleuze calls the type of image that occurs in the interval between an action and reaction an "affection-image" and describes it as "a coincidence of subject and object, or the way in which the subject perceives itself, *or rather experiences itself or feels itself 'from the inside'*.... It relates movement to a *'quality'* as lived state."[26] His description and terminology bears some resemblance to Deren's explication of verticality as a film structure concerned with the "qualities" and "depths" of a moment, "with *what it feels like or with what it means*."[27]

Deren suggests that examples of vertical film structure occur in opening sequences of films and in dream sequences, or in completely vertical shorts such as those that she directs. In such films, she believes the intensity of prolonged verticality cannot be sustained for too long, explaining the short length of her films.[28] It is the oppositional relation that Deren sets up between narrative and verticality that is criticized by other panellists in the 1953 symposium. Arthur Miller says, "There is no separation in my mind between a horizontal story and the plumbing of its meaning in depth."[29] To this, Deren replies:

> Now I am speaking for a combination, although personally, in my films, there has not been such a combination. I'm speaking of other films and the way poetry occurs in them, either as an image—the sudden development of a poetic image, which you might have in a dream sequence of a film that was otherwise narrative in its structure.[30]

In defence of Deren's contribution to the symposium, Annette Michelson asks whether the "polarity" Deren sets up between the vertical and horizontal, disjunctiveness and linearity, is valid, answering "no" while acknowledging the idea as a

[23] Gilles Deleuze, *Cinema 1: The Movement-Image*, trans. Hugh Tomlinson and Barbara Habberjam (Minneapolis: University of Minnesota Press, 1986) and *Cinema 2: The Time-Image*, trans. Hugh Tomlinson and Robert Galeta (Minneapolis: University of Minnesota Press, 1989).

[24] Sitney (1971), 178.

[25] Deleuze (1989), 18. As Alison Butler points out, for Deleuze "the distinction between the movement-image and the time-image is not absolute" but rather they are "interpenetrating tendencies" ("'Motor-Driven Metaphysics': Movement, Time and Action in the Films of Maya Deren," *Screen*, 48, 1 [2007]: 6).

[26] Deleuze (1986), 65. My emphasis.

[27] Sitney (1971), 173–74. My emphasis. Renata Jackson also makes this connection to Deleuze's film theory (Jackson [2001], 66–67). Butler discusses Deren's film form in relation to Deleuzian film theory at length, ultimately stating that, while her overwhelming interest in film time suggests her work prefigured the postwar period that was dominated by the time-image, she actually created "a movement-image in which time was the most prominent dimension" and thus "seems to belong to a transitional phase" (Butler [2007], 23 and 5). Both Jackson and Butler also note Bergsonian language in Deren's writings on film.

[28] Ibid, 174–75.

[29] Ibid, 183.

[30] Ibid, 185.

Figure 4.1 A *Study in Choreography for Camera* (1945, d. Maya Deren). Film still courtesy Anthology Film Archives.

step toward theorizing radical formal innovation in film.[31] Deren's argument does indeed set up an exemplary model based on a binary opposition. However, her films, with their dream narratives and multiple, detailed film movements, demonstrate a much more complex interplay between a linear drive and verticality, despite her argument to the contrary, as I shall demonstrate in my discussion of examples of her work. The idea that verticality can occur in horizontal film forms will also be drawn out in the chapter on the musical, where opening sequences and fantastic dance routines demonstrate qualities outlined here—vertical qualities that actually escape the limitations of discrete "moments," informing entire, feature-length films.

A very literal application of the concept of cinematic verticality can be discussed in relation to Talley Beatty's edited leap in Deren's A *Study in Choreography for Camera*[32] (see fig. 4.1). This film follows a choreographed sequence through a variety of settings—a "horizontal" continuity of motion in time across disparate spaces. In the final leap, the inevitability of the subject's relation to the ground and the effects of gravity undergo a transformation as the figure is unbound or ungrounded through

[31] Michelson (1979), 632. Michelson discusses Deren's verticality mainly in relation to her radical strategies regarding time and space.

[32] Sitney describes how this film instituted "a completely new kind of film . . . a dance film with equal participation by both arts." He also places the film at the cusp of a shift within avant-garde film away from "abstracted narrative forms," stating that "Maya Deren introduced the possibility of isolating a single gesture as a complete form" (Sitney [1979], 24–26).

the use of overlapping edits and multiple perspectives. As Deren states, "In the film a leap is sustained for almost a half-minute, a much longer period than is humanly possible."[33] The cinematic play with the real effects of gravity captures the dancer's radical and "moving" destabilizations: the manipulation of verticality and balance that constitute dance practice. Such moments in Deren's films demonstrate a play along another axis that interrupts the drive or logic of a linear thrust, and in this, perhaps her simplest film, that logic is the temporal continuity of the choreography itself played out against spatial discontinuity. Here, play and flux around the gravitational center are combined with spatial discontinuity to create a "vertical" window inside the film onto the spectacle of motion. These sequences create a poetics of human motion that is dancerly and, like dance, operate outside function-ality and the laws of everyday movement.

Verticality does not always involve a dramatic manipulation of time, but it will always include movements that exceed the logic of the action. Another example is Deren's intense movement study, *Meditation on Violence*. Chao-li Chi performs the Chinese boxing styles Wudang Tai Chi and Shaolin Kung Fu against a white wall; the lack of depth and close camera create a volatile filmic space. The theme of violence is elaborated upon through the performer's movements, which begin with smooth and gentle circular actions and accelerate into sharp punches and strikes. At the peak of the action the setting changes to an outdoor environment, where Chao-li Chi, dressed in more formal traditional clothes, wields a sword and performs large dramatic movements including leaps that are shown in slow-motion and freeze-frame (see fig. 4.2). The movement of the camera also plays a part, circling the performer and moving in tight to meet Chao-li Chi's direct gaze and action. There are few full-length shots of the per-former, so the emphasis is not so much on the *what* (what style, what steps) as the *how* (how does it feel or mean). The film is not merely a demonstration of a physical disci-pline, but "the meditating mind turned inwards upon the idea of movement."[34] Rhythm and repetition give the movements a circular quality that assists the spiral structure of the film, which ends where it begins, with the softer opening actions against the white wall. This meditation on violence—the dynamic quality of the performance as an enactment of the theme of the film, "the self-contained *idea* of violence"—completes itself with no reference beyond body and camera.[35]

Deren's ideas regarding poetic film form also articulate an aspect of filmmaking that preceded her own work and can be linked to dancefilm. Vertical sequences can be found in the first wave of the cinematic avant-garde—for instance in Jean Renoir's *Sur un air de Charleston* and Francis Picabia and René Clair's *Entr'Acte*. In the former, Catherine Hessling performs a Charleston, which is shown in slow-motion. The film is a series of scenes between Hessling (who appears as a white "savage"), Johnny Hudgin (dressed as an African academic), and a figure in a monkey suit. There is no dramatic development—the structure of the film resembles a vaudeville variety show—but the slow-motion sequence acts as an interruption nonetheless—a prolonged, sideways shift where details of figural motion become the primary subject.

[33] Clark et al. (1988), 267.
[34] Maya Deren, "Chamber Films," *Filmwise*, 2 (1961): 38–39.
[35] Maya Deren, "Notes, Essays, Letters," *Film Culture*, 39 (1965): 18.

Figure 4.2 *Meditation on Violence* (1948, d. Maya Deren). Film still courtesy Anthology Film Archives. All Rights Reserved.

This scene constitutes another example of, in Fernand Léger's words, "the moving image as the leading character," through the use of slow-motion.[36] The dramatic change in the speed of the cinematic movement disturbs any kind of continuity, even an episodic one, drawing us into a moment that is "filled out" with excessive and detailed cinematic movements.

In *Entr'Acte* a dancer in a tutu spins on a glass floor, the camera set up underneath so that the viewer looks up her skirts (see fig. 4.3). This shot is repeatedly cut into a series of scenes (the film structure being similar to that of Renoir's film), all shot outdoors with a large cast. The film itself was made to be screened during a performance of Picabia and Erik Satie's ballet *Relâche* by Rolf De Maré's Swedish Ballet, and the dancing figure almost serves as a kind of interval within the film, linking it back to the performance. But it is also another example of a discrete moment of spectacular motion, operating independently of any other element in the film and completing itself with the punch line of a bearded face revealed above the skirts. In both this and the Renoir example, the activity of dancing is itself disjunctive, introducing an order of movement that, particularly when highlighted through repetition, duration, or altered temporality, is "out of step" with the rest of the film.

Perhaps the "what it feels like" of Deren's verticality refers here to a particularly corporeal experience—a kinaesthetic empathy on the part of the viewer with the

---

[36] Fernand Léger, quoted by Dalia Judovitz, "Dada Cinema: At the Limits of Modernity," *Art & Text*, 34 (1989): 56.

Figure 4.3 *Entr'Acte* (1924, d. Francis Picabia and René Clair). Courtesy BFI Stills.

moving body scrutinized by the camera. Attention shifts from the mechanics of the action to something more like the "quality" of the movement and its relevance to one's own physicality. The duration of the shot of Hessling performing the Charleston in *Sur un air de Charleston* creates a space for the contemplation of the physical dynamics of the dance. The action of the muscles and momentum of the limbs are vividly apparent and the extension to contemplating how such a performance would feel in one's own body is inevitable. This type of kinaesthetic empathy on the part of the spectator should also be considered in relation to Deren's films. In *Meditation on Violence*, the experience has a dual quality as the viewer takes the position of the fighting partner who Chao-li Chi looks at and directs his actions toward, as well as Chao-li Chi himself. A sense of discomfort is created due to the camera's proximity to the action and the "attack" of the performance, while the intense focus on the fighter evokes a fascination with the actions themselves and the extension of such actions onto the viewer's own body.[37]

Deren's concept of verticality is useful for approaching contemporary screen dance examples, which are frequently characterized by their vertical film structure. They are generally distinguished from other short films by their lack of narrative and spoken word—exploring the quality of a moment, an idea, or an emotion through the film's visual and aural movements. Many also contain an element of fantasy or the fantastic, departing from the familiar and occurring outside the logic of everyday activities. *Touched*

---

[37] Dancefilm spectatorship and a gestural model for corporeal engagement will be discussed in more detail in Chapter 7.

(1994), a film by David Hinton and choreographer and performer Wendy Houstoun, provides a more recent example of verticality in dancefilm (see fig. 4.4, video 4.4ⓓ).

Touched opens in a busy pub with a close-up of a handshake. The camera moves up the body of a man until a woman comes into frame whispering in his ear. He caresses her face and the camera pans down to their interlocked hands before she moves away; the camera holds still on their lingering grasp. A woman preens in front of a mirror in the quiet of the restroom, her delicate touches to her face performed slowly and deliberately. As she moves into and away from the mirror, figures are glimpsed behind her in an intimate embrace, but distance and a lack of focus obscure them. A woman whispers in another's ear. She slowly spins her stool and tilts her head and the whispering mouth chases her ear, repeating the action as it speeds up until the whisperer stops; the camera joins in with its own dizzying perspectives. Heads are thrown back in exaggerated laughter; figures stagger, swoon, and collapse, finding comfort on the floor. Faces move close to each other, mouths close but not touching, and hands caress. The faces dance around each other, pulling quickly away and returning until they end in a kiss. And the camera dances around *them*, providing different perspectives on the action.

Touched is dominated by close-ups on everyday gestures of communication and utility, usually between two people amongst the large cast. There is no audible dialogue—the relationships between characters are depicted through the camera's view on physical actions, which is either intimate and mobile, or static and obscured, by walls or crowds. These relationships do not progress in any clear way; the actions become more intimate, unrestrained, and passionate as the film progresses, suggesting an increasing degree of intoxication, but there is little continuity between specific couples. The film reads as a meditation on the activity of drinking and socializing, with movement at various levels of the filmic performance filling out the theme. The proximity of the camera to the action and its constant mobility certainly take the viewer close to *what it feels like* in such situations. The swooning, swilling actions of the performers and camera create a kinaesthetic pattern that leads into the discussion of movement across figures in the following section, drawing the audience into a field of movement that has no firm anchor, replicating the floating, fuzzy sensations of intoxication.

4.2 Depersonalization and Movement as an "Event" across Figural Forms

> *There is a potential filmic dance form, in which the choreography and movements would be designed, precisely, for the mobility and other attributes of the camera.*
>
> Maya Deren[38]

In his introduction to the first book of collected essays on Deren, *Maya Deren and the American Avant-Garde*, Bill Nichols sees the filmmaker's preoccupation with dance,

---

[38] Clark et al. (1988), 318.

Figure 4.4 *Touched* (1994, d. David Hinton). Photo: Dan O'Neill. Courtesy Dan O'Neill.

play, games, and ritual as being connected to the concept of *depersonalization* that Deren describes in her essay, "An Anagram of Ideas on Art, Form and Film":[39]

> The ritualistic form…creates fear, for example, by creating an imaginative, often mythological experience which, by containing its own logic within itself, has no reference to any specific time or place, and is forever valid for all time and place.…Above all, the ritualistic form treats the human being not as the source of the dramatic action, but as *a somewhat depersonalized element in a dramatic whole.*[40]

The performers in Deren's vertical films are not *characters* or *agents* defined by, or requiring development through, dialogue and story. They are closer to an *image*: "the person, the body, in its conversion into the luminous sense of its film presence, its cinema," although here we have a particularly motile luminous presence.[41] In Deren's films involving numerous cast members, corporeal performance is one filmic movement among many—a privileged and central element informed by a variety of dance practices but one that is independent of any specific performer, spreading out across people and things. Performance in such films serves the vertical film form by releasing figures from the demands of storytelling, allowing them to become part of a transference of movement across bodies and to resonate in moments that are freed in space and time. Such a use of depersonalization in film has become a common element in a variety of dancefilm examples and illustrates another way in which Deren's films instituted new modes of choreography for film.

The idea that dance plays a role in the depersonalization of performance in Deren's films is discussed by Maria Pramaggiore in relation to the films *Meshes of the Afternoon*, *At Land*, and *Ritual in Transfigured Time*. Pramaggiore writes:

> Deren's persistent interest in dance and ritual…manifests itself in these films as an obsession with images of bodies in motion and an exploration of the implications of movement for the individual body.[42]

Pramaggiore describes how movements of and across bodies and objects, facilitated by the operations of the camera and editing, become central to meaning production in these particular films. The qualities of the movements themselves will be explored further in the following section as it is the choreographic nature of matches on action and their role in another order of movement that is of interest here: "movement as a force…as an event which is not independent of bodies but is independent of any one person's body," and which complicates spatial and temporal relations.[43] This results in the destabilization of coherent physicalities and identities,

[39] Bill Nichols, "Introduction," in Nichols (2001), 10.
[40] Deren (2001), 20. My emphasis.
[41] Stephen Heath, *Questions of Cinema* (London: Macmillan Press, 1981), 178–81.
[42] Maria Pramaggiore, "Performance and Persona in the US Avant-Garde: The Case of Maya Deren," *Cinema Journal*, 36, 2 (1997): 26.
[43] Ibid, 27. Lauren Rabinovitz had previously commented on this order of movement in Deren's films, *Meshes of the Afternoon* and *Ritual in Transfigured Time*. Of the former, she writes that Deren's fragmented body is "linked together only by the continuity of movement," and that any suggestion of "fluid activity" in the party scene in *Ritual in Transfigured Time* comes, not from stable identities or narrative, but from the gestural movements shifting across performers (Lauren Rabinovitz, *Point of Resistance: Women, Power and Politics in the New York Avant-Garde Cinema, 1943–71* [Urbana: University of Illinois Press, 1991], 62–63).

producing "multiplied and fragmented film protagonists": Deren's depersonalization.[44] The individual is transfigured in the service of the work as a whole and the action is "held together," as Deren writes, "almost exclusively by the consistent *mode of movement* common to a variety of individuals who are identified as singular and are used as interchangeable variables within a consistent pattern created by the film instrument."[45] In this way, Deren believes she created a "homogeneous entity in which the inner patterns of relationships between the elements create, together, *a larger movement of the body as a whole.*"[46]

The depersonalization of performers through a continuity of motion across bodies (and objects) so that they become "interchangeable variables" within a larger choreographic movement, a "force" or "event," is a cine-choreographic strategy common within dancefilm. The focus is on the filmic "body as a whole," maintaining a consistency in the order of movement across the constituent mobile elements that will, to a greater or lesser degree, sacrifice their singularity. Dance as a performance mode is of course ideal for such a strategy, providing the choreographic tools and rehearsal methodologies for developing, articulating, and repeating gestures and movements throughout the course of a particular scene. Deren's use of dance and choreography as the primary organizing methodology for her films is never clearer than in her orchestration of sequences where a movement phrase or quality moves across frames, edit cuts, bodies, and spaces, making the body of the film a choreographed whole.

An example of this depersonalization is the movement of action across the bodies of Rita Christiani and Maya Deren in *Ritual in Transfigured Time*.[47] This silent, short film begins in a domestic environment, moves to a party scene, and includes modern dance performed in an outdoor setting. All the sections of the film feature cinematic manipulations of space and time, and continuity is established by the strong use of gesture and/or dance throughout. In the film, Christiani and Deren appear as separate entities in the opening shots, but, as the film progresses, matches on action are used to depict the women as interchangeable. They are dressed similarly; both wear scarves around their shoulders and have dark, tightly curled hair framing their faces.

At the end of the central party scene, a match on action shifts Christiani and Frank Westbrook to a garden location. Three other women are there, sometimes appearing as a trio. Westbrook spins the women around one by one, each spin ending with a freeze-frame that transforms the women into copies of the statues in the garden. Christiani walks away from the scene and, as she turns back, a match on action replaces her with Deren. Christiani then continues walking away throughout a parallel edit sequence, returning to find Westbrook also a statue. Westbrook leaps off the pedestal and pursues Christiani, reaching to grab her out of shot when a final match on action replaces her with Deren. Deren runs under a pier and into the

[44] Ibid, 19.

[45] Clark et al. (1988), 456. Here Deren is referring to the party scene in *Ritual in Transfigured Time*.

[46] Ibid, 456–57. My emphasis.

[47] Sitney sees this film as the one where "Deren openly grappled with the problem of using dancers in a film" and the problem of "the prestylization of the dance in film." He uses Erwin Panofsky's term "prestylization" to account for the radically aestheticized corporeal performance, a term close to Deren's own "stylization" (Sitney [1979], 24–32).

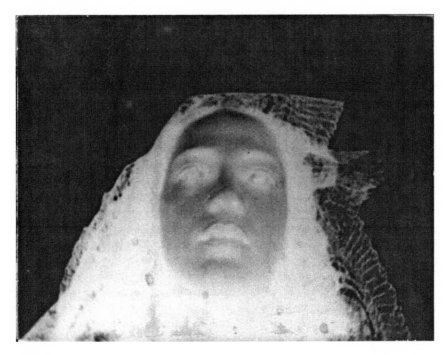

Figure 4.5 *Ritual in Transfigured Time* (1945–6, d. Maya Deren). Courtesy of the Maya Deren Collection, Howard Gotlieb Archival Research Center, Boston University.

water, the final negative shots of a floating bride nullifying identification until we finally see that it is Christiani's face (see fig. 4.5).

The authors of *The Legend of Maya Deren* argue that Deren identified strongly with Christiani, who grew up in Trinidad and had some knowledge of that country's equivalent of Voudou, Obeah.[48] Deren's explanation of their roles in the film is simple enough: "In this film Rita and I appear interchangeable, as if we were merely different aspects of a single personality."[49] Deren states that at the heart of the film is the idea of ritual as an "action" that "seeks the realization of its purpose through the exercise of form."[50] The vertical form of the film is marked by the action of the performers and the continuity of that action *across* those performers, particularly Christiani and Deren. The subsuming of the individual into the collective and the fluid subjectivity afforded by ritual possession is mimicked in the actual form of the film; the players sacrifice individuation to the action or movement across the film as a whole.

Another example of this type of treatment of the dancing body occurs within the dancefilms of David Hinton. In my discussion of *Touched*, I described how the swooning movements of the characters and camera continue across figures and

[48] Clark et al. (1988), 450.
[49] Ibid, 472.
[50] Ibid, 629.

scenes. In Hinton's film versions of Lloyd Newson's stage works, *Dead Dreams of Monochrome Men* (1990) and *Strange Fish* (1992), movement sometimes operates as a force shifting across and between bodies that become exchangeable, with continuity maintained through choreographic and filmic operations. Both films feature a shift from the individual to the collective through figural and filmic movement and a destabilization of subjects and time-space, in this case to make sociocultural observations that go beyond individual stories or situations.

Strange Fish takes place in a multiroomed set resembling a seedy hotel. Characters regroup and repartner around two central protagonists (played by Nigel Charnock and Wendy Houstoun) in a series of scenarios based on social interaction and intimacy. Degrees of individualization vary, but one scene uses disguise and the choreography of camera and bodies to confuse distinctions between two women in a mute satire of seduction. The women (one of them Houstoun), similarly dressed and wearing blonde wigs, enter a room where a young man is entertaining himself by balancing tea candles on his shoulders. Operating as a team, the women begin to vie for his attention, moving rapidly to disorient him. A point-of-view shot represents his static field of vision as the women circle him, the two blonde wigs bobbing across the frame, faces obscured, and the masses of hair mutating into a disembodied white puppet. The precisely choreographed trio that follows continues the theme with the two women constantly replacing each other midmovement in proximity to the man. The camera cuts in tight to smooth out the transitions, or, alternatively, they occur out of frame. The scene ends with the man choosing one of these "interchangeable" women and Houstoun is ultimately left alone, as she is repeatedly throughout the film.

Dead Dreams of Monochrome Men is set in a similarly ambiguous space that resembles alternatively a nightclub, a gallery, and an empty apartment (see fig. 4.6). The opening scene establishes the interchangeable value of the four male performers' bodies (played by Lloyd Newson, Russell Maliphant, Nigel Charnock, and Douglas Wright) as they lean against a bare wall in an indefinable space, obscured by shadows and flashing lights. All are dressed in shirts and pants, two of them with shaved heads, and glances are passed from one to another until Newson moves in to seduce Maliphant. Newson covers the other man's unresponsive body, writhing against him, and continues to do so against the wall after Maliphant has withdrawn to repeat Newson's movements of seduction with Wright. Meanwhile, Charnock slowly crumbles down the wall in the distance, mouth frozen in a scream. The set is divided by walls that separate the "players" from each other, and while constant shifts in filmic perspective maintain a malleable sense of space, the isolated figures are organized spatially within the mise en scène and through editing to create a continuity of movement across figures. This recalls Deren's comments regarding *A Study in Choreography for the Camera*:

> This principle—that the dynamic of movement in film is stronger than anything else—than any changes of matter…I mean that movement or energy is more important, or powerful, than space or matter—that in fact it creates matter.[51]

---

[51] Ibid, 263. Deren elaborates this idea in practical terms in her essay on editing, "Creative Cutting": "It is impossible to overestimate the compelling continuity of duration which movement carried across the splice can create…even identifiable backgrounds become subordinate to it when assisted by a manipulation of angles" (Ibid, 618–19).

Figure 4.6 *Dead Dreams of Monochrome Men* (1990, d. David Hinton). Photo: Eleni Leoussi. Courtesy DV8 Physical Theatre.

The continuity of movement creates a new space that is illogical yet material. The shifting spatial configurations of the opening scene continue throughout the film to take in other locations that magically materialize with the assistance of dramatic changes in light, which suggests that continuity of movement does indeed create its own cinematic matter in the form of virtual spatial relations.

Spatial and figural transfigurations occur in another scene where Charnock and Wright appear to watch Maliphant through a window with their backs to the camera. As the camera pans out, the "real" Maliphant is revealed behind them, and the original image is shown to be a reflection on the window glass. When a venetian blind is switched, the reflected image turns into another man. In the following rapid dance sequence in which the choreography appears to pass between figures, the camera cuts from fleeting, indiscernible bodies to focus on a couple in an intimate tangle, the partners constantly changing. The camera moves right around the action, shooting from all perspectives, further confusing the delineation of individuals. Throughout the film, bodies are constantly struggling with, climbing on, and clinging to bodies, forming single units of confused limbs and torsos.

The final sequence of *Dead Dreams of Monochrome Men* begins in a black, undefined space with Charnock wrapped around Wright's head. Wright goes limp and is manipulated by Charnock. Covering Wright's mouth with his own, Charnock transmits movement/life into Wright, who finally drives Charnock against a wall until he goes limp. Somehow we have been transported into a new space—a bare and miserable apartment. With the situation now reversed, Wright animates the limp body by pushing, pulling, twisting, and throwing it. Both now wearing only underpants, the discernible differences between the two become inconsequential. The parts of their bodies become thoroughly entwined and the source and consequence of force becomes indistinguishable across the two bodies, which together enact movement as an *event*. Wright exchanges underpants with Charnock and drags him into a half-filled bath before Wright also goes limp. Meanwhile, Newson has played out a similar animation of the unresponsive Maliphant—also wearing only white underpants—and hung him up by the ankles like a piece of meat. A shot from inside the roof where Charnock is suddenly looking down on Maliphant creates a final disorienting space-time shift before Charnock slides down the hanging body and the film ends with three prostrate, half-naked figures sprawled throughout an empty apartment. The male figures in this film may exhibit certain consistent tendencies, but nothing as unambiguous as characterization emerges. The continuities regarding appearance, movements, and motives (lust, comfort, control, submission, objectification, fear) are spread across the moving bodies, adding a collective or social dimension to issues of sexuality, mortality, violence, isolation, and identification. The moving elements within the film are subsumed into the larger choreographed body of the whole work, the ambiguities reconciled through a continuity of motion to create cogency.

In these films, scenes such as the "animation" of Charnock by Wright constitute a type of *verticality*. What is occurring is a sort of movement conundrum, an extended study of a single directive that is playing out only to draw our attention to its quality or meaning. The disassociation from distinct characterizations is extreme but the interest in the movement is not of the order of "movement for movement's sake" that we saw in the early avant-garde examples, being more aligned to the theme-based actions of Touched. Verticality, depersonalization, and movement as an event often work together in dancefilm as the choreography of filmic movement takes the place of the narrative drive, providing the material that fills out the thematic content. In Dead Dreams of Monochrome Men, the process of depersonalization and the quality of the movements themselves take thematic exploration to a deeper level: in this case, notions of sexual desire, dependency, and mortality. While the dance itself has a logical continuity regarding cause and effect—that is, a force of energy instigates a movement that plays out the intensity of the force—the non-descript location, dissolution of movement across bodies, and deemphasis of characterization and motivation produce an ambivalent situation shifting between violence and tenderness, death and life, immobility and motion. In such examples, the possible coexistence of dramatic, narrative, or horizontal drives and verticality is made clear.

4.3 Gestural Stylization and Filmic Manipulation of the Performing Body

> Movements should be rather an extension and perfection of a normal movement . . .
>
> Maya Deren[52]

In my discussion of Maya Deren's film practice, I began with structures or movements that involve the filmic whole, showing how these strategies can be found in dancefilm both preceding and following Deren's work. Drawing closer to the detail of performance that constitutes these inner patterns I will now focus on Deren's ideas about screen acting—how they too have been informed by dance and how they, in turn, inform current dancefilm practices. This particular dancefilm innovation of Deren's is another episode in the deeply interdisciplinary practice of gestural cinema that stretches from early narrative cinema to the present and is tracked across this book.

Deren's discussion of acting is connected to her critique of those films that are premised on literary models. She suggests that the interiority inherent to the novel form, when applied to the screen, led to the development of "symptom-action" gestural clichés or "visual clichés" that summarize, through the performance of a reductive physical action, emotions or responses that would be developed over pages in a novel. According to Deren, such clichés mask the "effort of transcription" for an audience familiar with this mode of screen performance by standing-in for, or symbolizing, "the literary terms in which the film is actually conceived."[53] The connection with the histrionic mode of acting described in the previous chapter is clear, although Deren is certainly not directing her critique at performance in early cinema but at the

---

[52] Clark et al. (1988), 268.
[53] Deren (2001), 40–41.

contemporary, mid-century film industry. For Deren, screen performance should break free of literary references and the reductive gestural language that this produces.

Deren also states that the gestures of everyday life may not provide a viable alternative for developing a mode of performance suitable for the screen:

> In creating a new form, the elements must be selected according to their ability to function in the new, "unnatural" context. A gesture which may have been very effective in the course of some natural, spontaneous conversation, may fail to have impact in a dance or film.[54]

Like the artists of the early silent film form that she so admired, Deren was seeking a new gestural language specifically devised for the screen. For Deren, dance and film share issues regarding physical performance; they both create "unnatural" contexts removed from reality and require gestures appropriate for such a context. Deren rejects both overcoded or cliché gestural performance and the everyday body as, in one way or another, inappropriate for her ideal cinema. Deren's use of both untrained and trained dancers demonstrates perfectly Paul Valéry's tension between the dancerly and the everyday: the idea that dance is a physical discipline constantly engaged with the pedestrian. For *Ritual in Transfigured Time*, Deren encouraged Christiani and Westbrook "to free themselves from the habits of their long stage experience in order to enter a new idiom of dance creation."[55] She wrote in her shooting notes for *Study in Choreography for the Camera*:

> Movements should be rather an extension and perfection of a normal movement so that audience [sic] is kinesthetically identified with them, under illusion [sic] that they too are capable of it.[56]

Deren saw dance and choreography as a means of leading physical movements toward "stylization," "extension and perfection." In her article on *Ritual in Transfigured Time* for *Dance* magazine, Deren writes that she calls the film "a dance film, or a film dance" because "stylized or casual, full-figured or detailed" movements work across the film "according to a choreographic concept."[57] She aimed to manipulate movement through performance *and* through filming and editing to create a larger, coherent choreographic whole. In fact, Deren's application of stylization to the movements of her performers was in keeping with her understanding of film movement itself as stylized:

> I feel that film is related more closely to dance than any other form because, like dance, it is conveyed in time.... [I]t conveys primarily by visual projection and...it operates on a level of stylization—it is the quality of the movement that renders the meaning.[58]

In turning to stylization of movement for her cine-choreographic process, Deren was drawing on the same ideas as the by then well-established American modern dance tradition. Before *Ritual in Transfigured Time* was finished, Deren was writing to the *New York Times* dance critic John Martin (who had reviewed her films):

[54] Ibid, 23.
[55] Clark et al. (1988), 459.
[56] Ibid, 268.
[57] Ibid, 458.
[58] Maya Deren, "Cine-Dance," *Dance Perspectives*, 30 (1967): 10.

...I find myself more and more thinking in terms of using natural, untrained movement...as the elements which, rhythmically manipulated in filming and in editing, can be woven into the stylization of a dance. This is a sort of extension of the film-dance theory...the utilization of informal, candid-type movement, to create a formalized whole.[59]

Deren's communication with Martin provides some insight into the terms of reference for her choreographic manipulation of everyday actions. Deren refers to rhythmic manipulation, stylization, and formalization of "natural" movement as methodologies in her direction of action and performance for the screen. These strategies, along with her choice to write to Martin in particular, reveal the influence of modern theater dance on her movement aesthetic.

As the dance critic at the New York Times from 1928 until 1962, Martin chronicled, championed, and defined American "modern dance" in the city where it thrived. By 1945, Martin had identified the key tenets of the new American dance in a series of lectures published as The Modern Dance: the form recognizes movement as its basic substance, rejects the imitative function of dance, explores the body's full physical range and dynamics in expressing psychological or emotional states (what he calls metakinesis), and lacks unessential ornamentation.[60] Martin's description of movement as choreographic "substance" and as "a constant thing" in modern dance would have been read in opposition to the ballet's emphasis on pose where "the movement that united them was unimportant," also demonstrating the long reach of Loïe Fuller's movement revolution.[61] His description of a stripped-back, essential, yet experimental approach to movement that explores interior states without reverting to mime or mimicry is applicable to the movement content in Deren's films. Her total rejection of mime and gestural equivalents for language signals her departure from the choreographic explorations of Ruth St. Denis earlier in the century that resonated with silent cinema performance, aligning her choreographic sensibility firmly with the new generation of modern dance artists such as Martha Graham and Doris Humphrey.

Martin was also a vocal admirer of Katherine Dunham's work and the choreographer's influence on Deren's dance aesthetic should not be underestimated. Growing directly from her anthropological fieldwork in the Carribean, the Dunham Technique emphasized a hypermobility in the pelvic girdle, a flexible and articulated spine, isolation of body parts, and percussive, polyrhythmic phrasing.[62] Frank Westbrook's movements in the garden sequence of Ritual in Transfigured Time consist of leaps, stamps, and sharp head and torso movements that are rhythmic and percussive in attack, suggesting the influence of the Dunham technique. But perhaps of even more significance for Deren was the holistic approach to dance practice taken by Dunham,

---

[59] Ibid, 455. Jackson details reviews of Deren's work in dance magazines and columns (Jackson [2002], 5).

[60] John Martin, "Part I: Characteristics of the Modern Dance," in The Modern Dance (New York: Dance Horizons, 1972), 1–33.

[61] Ibid, 6–7.

[62] Academics and researchers such as Vicky Risner, Brenda Dixon-Stowell, Paula Durbin, Julie Kerr-Berry, and Constance Valis Hill have argued for a revision of the history of American modern dance that would reclaim Dunham's contributions. Valis Hill states, "Dunham technique has infused modern technique; we need to give it its due—all those knee drops, ways of isolating the body, using the body fluidly, all those Afro-Carribean translations....Look at Mambo [1954]...then go back and reread the entire modern repertoire in terms of the technique she materialized and codified" (quoted in Thomas F. DeFrantz, "Due Unto Dunham," Village Voice, June 6, 2006).

who not only introduced Afrocentric aesthetics into American concert dance but also insisted upon the connection of dance with everyday life and religion, as was the practice in her spiritual home of Haiti. Having firsthand experience of Dunham's creative process as her secretary, starting in 1941, soon after Dunham's breakthrough full-length work *L'Ag 'Ya* was premiered in 1938, it would have made sense to turn to dancerly actions to enhance domestic and social scenarios in order to create ritually charged performances in films such as *Ritual in Transfigured Time*.[63] In this film, we can see the influence of modern dance technique in the framing and direction of the performers in the party scene, which also provides an exemplary study of Deren's use of depersonalization.

Shot at close-range to the cramped action in a domestic interior, the camera takes in only the torso and heads of the guests. It contains a climactic sequence of beckoning gestures that are repeated, stylized, and transferred among the close crush of the crowd. The welcoming, ingratiating, engaging movements are so familiar and so much what a gesture is thought to be: sociable, functional, meaningful. But an intense and carefully detailed rendering of hand gestures and broader arm movements is excessive and relentless—defamiliarizing the movements through graphic isolation and repetition. This formalization of natural movement translates the gestures of communication into careful, obscure shapes formed by hands in space. An extended arm comes into frame again and again, finds its mark, drawing someone in, becoming the prelude to a delicate partnering as arms close in to create an intimate space, hanging momentarily in the air before dissolving in the *gestural exchange*. Movement is the basic substance of the performance here with a shift away from mimesis and toward an extension and repetition of gestures that blur the bodies' physical limits. The recurrence of shapes and choreographed sequences across bodies, along with the reiteration of particular shots and increasingly frequent edits, builds an escalating rhythmic pace across the scene.

In *Ritual in Transfigured Time* we see both abstracted gestures with a dancerly quality (the welcoming gestures of the party-goers) and candid actions (Christiani walks solemnly through the crowd), and in most cases rhythmic editing completes the process of stylization. Rather than quoting familiar, signifying actions or trying to represent everyday, utilitarian behavior, the physical performances in Deren's films (particularly those with less explicit dance content such as *Meshes of the Afternoon*, *At Land*, and *Ritual in Transfigured Time*) trace movement trajectories and loiter along gestural routes that escape into verticality through strategies that preempt Bausch: repetition, exaggeration, abstraction, or rhythmic manipulation. Such processes facilitate the transference of movements across bodies by converting action to set "moves" that could be taught to various cast members. These are processes commonly used by choreographers today, particularly in dance theater where other performance disciplines such as film and theater inform the development of a physical language. The success that dance theater artists such as DV8 Physical Theatre, Pina Bausch, Wim

---

[63] Butler comments on the connection between ritual, dance, and community or culture in Deren's work: "The emphasis on the ensemble in *Ritual* can be seen to relate not only to Deren's interest in the depersonalising effects of ritual but also to her understanding of the importance of community in dance" (Butler [2007], 12).

Vandekeybus, and Hans Hof Ensemble have had with dancefilm owes much to these early experiments with dancefilm performance modalities undertaken by Deren.

In *Meshes of the Afternoon*, the physical performance of Deren, who plays the main protagonist, is characterized by exaggerated everyday movements, stylized, dancerly gestures, and the effects of slow-motion, fragmentation, repetition, multiplication, shadow-play, and overlapping editing. In the opening shots, where Deren picks up a flower, notices a figure ahead, and walks down a street and into a home, her presence is established through shots of her hands and feet and her shadow thrown onto the pavement and wall. This technique of fragmenting the performer's body continues throughout and we do not see Deren's entire face until well into the film. The opening section ends with a close-up on Deren's eye closing and a point-of-view shot through a window and onto the street where she had just been, fading to black as her eye shuts. The following repetitions of the opening actions gradually increase regarding stylization, with new movement sequences added. Deren now chases the figure with graceful leaps—the run extended through overlapping editing. The various sequences of her movements on the stairs are manipulated in several ways. In one, she exaggerates her run upstairs, kicking up her heels. In another her progression is played in slow-motion and shot from several angles. In a particularly motile sequence her ascent is shot from above with a swinging camera, Deren lunging from side-to-side as if the staircase is rocking (see fig. 4.7). In her final ascent she appears frozen at various positions on the stairs through a series of shots from a still camera.

Figure 4.7 *Meshes of the Afternoon* (1943, d. Maya Deren). Courtesy of the Maya Deren Collection, Howard Gotlieb Archival Research Center, Boston University.

Expansive and dramatic gestures such as her lunge through a curtain at the top of the stairs and her later tumble backward down the stairs in a series of back arches constitute a new order of movement that goes beyond the everyday, resembling the generous movements of the Dunham technique. Small, eccentric gestures like taking a key from her mouth or raising her hand to her face are performed slowly and dreamily, often in tight close-up. The everyday, domestic setting is rendered uncanny through the actions of the protagonist and the spatial and temporal manipulation of those actions through cinematic means. In fact, in this film the manipulation of figural movement into something dance-like even extends to objects as knives and keys are made to "dance" through framing, physical manipulation, and editing, creating "magical" animation and transformation. The movement "event" of the film passes from Deren through her fragmented and multiplied selves to inanimate objects through stylization and filmic manipulation.

In Hinton and Newson's *Dead Dreams of Monochrome Men*, gestural stylization occurs in an "unnatural" filmic scenario, comparable to the type of performance in Deren's films. The movements performed by the cast are mostly utilitarian pushing, pulling, catching and climbing on each other, attempting to scale a wall, or dropping off a ladder. But there is another order of movement: social or communicative actions, such as an embrace or a grab for attention, that are quickly evolved into highly choreographed variations on the central gestural theme. In one case, Charnock and Maliphant face each other, tight close-ups intensifying the proximity of the two men. Maliphant moves to caress Charnock, who dodges away from his touch. Soon Charnock is dodging away violently before Maliphant even moves, falling to the floor. Maliphant then tries to catch him before he impacts, and this leads into another sequence where Charnock throws himself from a ladder and expects Maliphant to break his fall. This long and intense exchange shifts from informal movements into a pattern through repetition, building upon a broader pattern across the film of intimate gestures of contact gone awry. These movements depart from the everyday through exaggeration, repetition, force of action, and the flow and precision of movements.

Examples of stylization can also be found in Hinton and Houstoun's *Touched*, where the camera joins in with the choreographed movements. The action of reaching for a glass is repeated and systematically interrupted by other movements to become a choreographed sequence. Heads thrown back in laughter or to toss down a drink are exaggerated and repeated across characters and shots to create movement patterns. Gestures of intimacy become a dance, such as the prelude to a kiss already described, and another sequence where similar actions are performed as the couple hum a simple musical phrase, hands and faces dancing in and out of proximity with each other. The sensuality of whispering, a head rolling around with a mouth chasing close to an ear, is repeated several times, becoming a circular dance of complicity and seduction.

Deren's ideas and practices relating to dancefilm have much to offer our understanding of the filmic operations specific to the form, as demonstrated through my discussion of both recent and early dancefilm examples. Her cinematic concepts are written through with movement orders and choreographic concepts that reveal the centrality of the moving body and dance to her cinema. Deren's significance regarding both the historical development of dancefilm and the definition of specific cinechoreographic orders makes her an essential figure in any discussion of screen dance.

5

Anarchic Moves, Experimental Cinema

...one day I went to scout Trisha [Brown's] solo at her loft, curious about the new work. She had named the solo Water Motor *and it was short at about four minutes. I was stunned when I saw it. Not only was it absolutely thrilling.... Somehow you could hardly see the movement because it just went too fast. It was totally new.*

Babette Mangolte[1]

Babette Mangolte's film of Trisha Brown's choreographic work *Watermotor*, titled *Water Motor* (1978) (see fig. 5.1), together with a 1980 film of the same work by video artist Peter Campus tell us much about the type of dance that challenges the parameters of human perception.[2] This type of dancing is exemplified in the choreography of Brown, particularly during the period in which these films were made, and can be found across periods, genres, and contexts. The two films of *Watermotor* also reveal something of the nature of dance as a filmic subject: more specifically, where the movements of the dancing subject demand something more of the filmmaker, beyond the standard techniques developed for rendering movement on film. This is the point at which certain categories of dance outstrip the reproductive technologies of the moving image, leading to an experimentation with film techniques. This chapter thus draws out ideas about both dancing and the moving image and the experimental cine-choreographic practices that can result when the two meet.

The films of *Watermotor* are exemplary models of cine-choreographies resulting from the filmic registration of challenging dancerly movement. They also represent a particular moment in the history of dance and technology when experimental video and film in the United States—particularly the New York-based collectives of the sixties and seventies that included filmmakers such as Mangolte, Charles Atlas, Amy Greenfield, and Shirley Clark—were influenced by new genres of theater dance. This period takes its place in a lineage of experimental dancefilm charted in this book from early cinema; through Surrealist and Dadist filmmakers such as

---

[1] Babette Mangolte, "On the Making of *Water Motor*, a Dance by Trisha Brown Filmed by Babette Mangolte," unpublished paper, September 2003. She was also the cinematographer for Yvonne Rainer on the films *Lives of Performers* (1972) and *Film about a Woman Who . . .* (1974) and has made films of Rainer's recent choreographies, *Yvonne Rainer AG Indexical* (2007) and *Yvonne Rainer RoS Indexical* (2008). Mangolte has also done more recent work with Brown: a short film for a rework of *Homemade* (2000) for White Oak Dance and an installation in the Tate Modern in London, *Trisha Brown's Roof Piece, 1973* (2001).

[2] *Watermotor for Dancer and Camera* (1980, d. Peter Campus) is one of three Trisha Brown dancefilms making up *Dancing on the Edge*. The slow-motion part of Campus's film also appears in *Solos, Duets and Pizza* (1984, various directors), and is possibly derivative of Mangolte's earlier film.

Figure 5.1 *Water Motor* (1978, d. Babette Mangolte). Photo copyright 1973 Babette Mangolte. All Rights of Reproduction Reserved.

Ferdinand Léger, Man Ray, and René Clair; singular revolutionaries such as Maya Deren; to contemporary short dancefilms. I have argued that, as a film subject, dance has a tendency toward unrestrained, hyperbolic motility and unexplained stasis, which challenges film's tendency to order, restrain, frame, and cut. Dance has thus sustained a special relationship with the cinematic avant-garde across the years.

Yvonne Rainer's development of a movement model in both her writing and practice that is characterized by continual, uninflected, and consistently varying motion contests the regular patterns and rhythms of human action associated with dramatic performance and the everyday, producing what I will call *anarchic phrasing*. Brown further developed the idea of phraseless, neutral, unpredictable movement in her choreographic research of the late 1970s, continuing the postmodern charter of creating movement beyond preexisting modes of production and execution. Hubert Godard, whose ideas on gestural production have already been introduced, links his concept of the *gestural anacrusis* to this particular period of Brown's work. Following his definition, *gestural anacrusis* refers to the "source" of movement, the "pre-movement zone" where the quality and nature of the following gesture takes form. I will argue that Rainer's model of *anarchic phrasing* is connected to the *gestural anacrusis*, as such phrasing absorbs the anacrusis into the choreographic flow. In doing so it produces a dance without privileged moments—dancing that challenges both human perception and reproductive technologies.

By *cinematic registration* I mean the process whereby the mechanical recording apparatus, both in shooting and postproduction, *renders* the filmed subject. In the films under discussion, the exceptional pace and/or phrasing of the profilmic activity challenges cinematic reproduction by creating problems of visibility or legibility. This leads filmmakers to experiment with various rendering techniques such as slow motion, multiple-exposure, repetition, reverse-motion, and digital postproduction techniques such as image "scratching." These can all serve to produce new forms of choreographic practice and new modes of cine-choreography. The rendering process goes beyond reproduction, bringing the choreographic elements into a new state or condition; the film/filmmaker enters into an intense dialogue with the subject matter so that the point where the dance begins and ends becomes redundant, the film itself becoming dance-like. Within the broader field of dancefilm, such work represents an extreme dealing with both radical dance *and* film practices and includes some of the most progressive and experimental examples of the form. Such approaches to dance-film can be found across cinematic history, from Jean Renoir's *Sur un air de Charleston* (1926) to recent experiments by Antonin De Bemels and Gina Czarnecki.

In the case of the films of *Watermotor*, the dancer constitutes a cinematic subject that challenges registration, almost fulfilling Godard's premonition of Brown "disarmed to the point of disappearance."[3] In the opening quote, Mangolte is describing her first encounter in 1978 with a new choreographic work by Brown. She was to photograph the dance but, after seeing it performed, Mangolte decided she would like to film it. In Mangolte's account, this desire was driven by the radical departure the dance made from Brown's previous work along with concerns regarding Brown's continuing ability to perform the challenging choreography.[4] However, during the process of filming, issues beyond advocacy and preservation came into play for the filmmaker. The nature of the movement—its speed and complexity—presented something new to Mangolte and challenged her original plan of a straightforward, "unbroken camera movement." Once Mangolte had her planned takes, she decided to shoot the dance again in slow motion. She states:

> I took the gamble to shoot in slow motion just to discover the movement in a less impersonal and more interpretative way. I just wanted to see the movement slower in order to understand it better, but also to see something in it that you can't see any other way.[5]

Here Mangolte articulates an impulse to engage with and unravel Brown's performance through filming, but also to create something altogether new. Mangolte had already shifted from still photography to the moving image to accommodate this desire and the choice to shoot in slow-motion marked another shift in her artistic relationship with the profilmic material. Mangolte enters into a subjective dialogue with the performance, choosing a cinematic effect that would transform the performance into a new cine-choreography. The discourse between camera and dance, resulting from a desire for knowledge through visual apprehension, produces a new aesthetic object. Commenting on the dance *Watermotor*, Brown's peer Rainer says that she did not really "appreciate" it until she saw Mangolte's film.[6] The film,

[3] Hubert Godard quoted in Laurence Louppe, "Corporeal Sources: A Journey through the Work of Trisha Brown," *Writings on Dance: The French Issue*, 15 (Winter 1996a): 8.
[4] Mangolte (2003).
[5] Idem.
[6] Yvonne Rainer, "Engineering Calamity: Trisha Brown," *Writings on Dance: Constellations of Things*, 18–19 (Winter 1999a): 177.

like Brown's performance in the loft studio, produces something new that cannot be seen "any other way," and in this respect it goes beyond the profilmic object.

5.1 Yvonne Rainer: Anarchic Phrasing and the Challenge to Reproductive Technologies

> ... *we are culturally not trained to observe dance.*
>
> William Fetterman on Merce Cunningham[7]

> *Dance is hard to see. It must either be made less fancy, or the fact of that intrinsic difficulty must be emphasized to the point that it becomes almost impossible to see.*
>
> Yvonne Rainer[8]

Yvonne Rainer, who began choreographing in 1960 and made her first film in 1966, is a key figure in the story of the New York avant-garde in terms of both her writing and practice, and in relation to dancefilm as I am conceiving it in this chapter. Despite Rainer's influential work in the field of cinema, I will focus on Rainer's writing and choreographic practice. Although Rainer maintains an interest in the performing body and choreography in her film work, the general quality of the corporeal and filmic movement and the increasingly sociopolitical nature of the content places this aspect of her work beyond my discussion here.

Rainer was the most prolific writer within the group of practitioners surrounding the Judson Dance Theatre, authoring several documents that have come to speak for that period in dance history, including the much quoted manifesto, "'No' to Spectacle...."[9] The essay that is most relevant to the unravelling of central strategies in Rainer's aesthetic project here is "A Quasi Survey of Some 'Minimalist' Tendencies in the Quantitatively Minimal Dance Activity Amidst the Plethora, or an Analysis of *Trio A*." This essay concerns *Trio A*, a dance from a larger work that was Rainer's last with Judson, *The Mind Is a Muscle*. It is here that Rainer most clearly describes the quality of movement that she aspired to in her choreographic work—a quality that informs my reading of a particular type of dancefilm.

---

[7] William Fetterman, "Merce Cunningham and John Cage: Choreographic Cross-currents," *Choreography and Dance*, 4, 3 (1997): 60.

[8] Yvonne Rainer, "A Quasi Survey of Some 'Minimalist' Tendencies in the Quantitatively Minimal Dance Activity Amidst the Plethora, or an Analysis of *Trio A*," in *What is Dance?* ed. Roger Copeland and Marshall Cohen (Oxford: Oxford University Press, 1983), 331.

[9] Yvonne Rainer, "'No' to Spectacle...," in *The Routledge Dance Studies Reader*, ed. Alexandra Carter (London: Routledge, 1998), 35. See Sally Banes on Rainer as dance theorist: "An Open Field: Yvonne Rainer as Dance Theorist," *Yvonne Rainer: Radical Juxtapositions 1961–2002*, ed. Sid Sachs (Philadelphia: The University of the Arts, 2003), 21–39). Sections of this chapter were included in an earlier article written in 2003, "Great Directors: Yvonne Rainer," (*Senses of Cinema* 27, July-Aug 2003, http://www.sensesofcinema.com/contents/directors/03/rainer.html). Since then there has been a flurry of new publications on Rainer, including: Sachs (2003); Yvonne Rainer, *Feelings Are Facts: A Life* (Cambridge: MIT Press, 2006); Catherine Wood, *Yvonne Rainer: The Mind Is a Muscle* (London: Afterall Books, 2007); and Carrie Lambert-Beatty, *Being Watched: Yvonne Rainer and the 1960s* (Cambridge: The MIT Press, 2008), as well as writing by Noël Carroll, Rose-Lee Goldberg, Susan Leigh Foster, and Ramsay Burt, among others.

If Merce Cunningham had worked to loosen the relation between movement and meaning through random choreographic structures, Rainer added to this a critique of the conventional *tone* of performance. By *tone* I mean the modulation or inflection of a movement phrase or sequence. Beyond the actual steps of the choreography, it is an element of performance that can alter or modify the quality of a phrase. Rainer states, "it was an attitude about performance.... The organisational battle had been fought for the most part by Cunningham and Cage, as far as I was concerned."[10] In her pursuit of a new attitude, Rainer was one of the first dance practitioners to make a wholesale return to the *everyday body* as an alternative to the *performing body*, which displays skills and virtuosity. If the movements were to digress from the functional or purposeful (movements that were the basis for another strand of work within the field), then the tone would contest this by falling just as completely into line with an everyday attitude.

By manipulating the tone or attitude of performance Rainer could control another aspect: phrasing. Rainer argues that traditional dance phrasing creates units of movement that mimic the larger theatrical structure: They have a beginning, a climax or moment of "registration," and an end. Here the term *registration* has a photographic aspect: There is an ideal point within its course at which the movement could be rendered. This model of phrasing corresponds with the virtuosic display of skills and tricks and the tone of theatricality Rainer was working against.[11] Rainer's critique of conventional phrasing may have been influenced by ideas in John Cage's *Grace and Clarity*, where he writes:

> Good or bad, with or without meaning, well dressed or not, the ballet is always clear in its rhythmic structure. Phrases begin and end in such a way that *anyone* in the audience knows when they begin and end, and breathes accordingly.[12]

Rainer worked toward an "unmodulated" quality in her dancing on all levels, from individual phrases to the choreographic whole. The choreographer wanted to give the impression that the body is "constantly engaged in transitions," a "continuity of separate phrases" that did not repeat and "does not allow for pauses, accents, or stillness."[13] Through this "evening out" Rainer developed a movement aesthetic that broke with the familiar syntax of movement described by Cage, creating dance sequences that interrupted patterns and rhythms that were easily recognized by an audience, developing action that amounted to "one long phrase."[14] In the case of *Trio A* there was also a conscious effort to work against "kinetic development."[15] In the following description I am referring to the film *Trio A* (1978), made twelve years after its original stage performance in 1966, directed by and featuring Rainer herself.

[10] Yvonne Rainer quoted by Willoughby Sharp and Liza Bear, "The Performer As Persona: An Interview with Yvonne Rainer," *Avalanche*, 5 (Summer 1972): 52.

[11] Rainer (1983), 328.

[12] John Cage, "Grace and Clarity," in *Merce Cunningham: Dancing in Space and Time*, ed. Richard Kostelanetz (Chicago: A Cappella Books, 1992), 22. Cunningham's movement can by no means be considered in direct opposition to Rainer's model of phrasing, although his choreography does feature defined figural forms. Cunningham states, "Climax is for those who are swept away by New Year's Eve" (Kostelanetz [1992], 39).

[13] Rainer (1983), 329–30.

[14] Yvonne Rainer, *A Woman Who . . . Chapters, Interviews, Scripts*, (Baltimore: The Johns Hopkins University Press, 1999a), 64.

[15] Ibid, 62.

In *Trio A*, one movement moves into the next with no pauses or stillness, the transitions being indiscernible from the steps themselves. For instance, walking to the back of the stage seems to end one phrase but also becomes the beginning of the next. A moderate pace is maintained with the exertion of just enough energy to complete the move—the performer's body appearing weighty and relaxed. The actions have the quality of everyday physical tasks, often looking uncoordinated and awkward. Basic movements—somersaults, squats, rolls, walking, marching, running, handstands, toe taps, skipping—are combined with disparate arm, head, and torso activities that complicate the movement and challenge notions of integrated choreographic phrasing. Toe taps in a semicircle on each leg are combined with rolling chest contractions. Wide circling arms are continued as each leg is carried forward, high off the ground, head and eyes to the side. The head and arms continue as the dancer sinks into a lunge. During a running and squatting sequence, the head is looking to the ceiling and the left arm is held straight and forward off the body. Rainer creates an uncanny dance that neutralizes both dramatic phrasing and the performative posture of the dancer, challenging the audience to see choreographic activity anew. Susan Leigh Foster writes that the dance "unsettled the eye, making the sequence difficult to follow."[16] This leads us back to the question of filmic registration. A continuity of movement that is "constantly engaged in transitions" presents the filmmaker with a new model of phrasing requiring specific cinematic approaches.

The nature of Rainer's dance with its lack of privileged moments would appear to place it in direct opposition to the mechanisms of still photography. Carrie Lambert uses photographs of *Trio A* to describe "a categorical conflict of dance and photography" that is "embodied, set in motion, reworked" in *Trio A*.[17] Lambert bases her thesis on Rainer's use of photographic terminology in the choreographer's description of the traditional phrasing that she was working against. Rainer describes how such phrasing is geared toward moments of "registration" that assist in the photographic documentation of such work, writing in a letter to Lambert, "the dance photographer is conditioned to watch for those moments of suspension that will best 'register like a photograph'."[18] From the description above, it is clear how the movements in *Trio A* are certainly hard to isolate from the transitions, creating what Lambert refers to as "one continuous photogenic moment."[19]

[16] Susan Leigh Foster, *Reading Dancing: Bodies and Subjects in Contemporary American Dance* (Berkeley: University of California Press, 1986), 175.

[17] Carrie Lambert, "Moving Still: Mediating Yvonne Rainer's *Trio A*," *October*, 89 (1999): 92. Lambert goes so far as to say that, "Rainer specifically designed this [work] to oppose photographic effects." Lambert then goes on to rework this opposition. Her argument, and Rainer's concession, that *Trio A* does not fully achieve its opposition to photographic registration, is noted. However, I believe Rainer's aim to achieve unmodulated phrasing in her radical reworking of dance performance is evidenced in *Trio A* and led directly to the realization of such a movement quality in other dance work. This points to the significance of Rainer's work and ideas for the analysis of the dancefilms under discussion here.

[18] Ibid, footnote 65, 110. Rainer's account of the dance photographer's task is supported by these comments from photographer Lois Greenfield, who revolutionized the art form with her 1/2000 second exposures: "...with ballet the moments are either right or wrong.... What attracted me to modern or post-modern—let's call it experimental—dance, was that it was composed of equally valid moments" (quoted in Virginia Brooks, "Dance and Film," *Ballett International*, 2 [1993]: 24).

[19] Idem.

If Rainer's dances of this period do, as Lambert suggests, oppose photography in their actual construction, the way in which *Trio A* achieves this would appear to align it directly with the cinematic. This connection links Rainer to the examples of Trisha Brown's dancing in the two films of *Watermotor* that follow regarding the way certain subjects seem to call for the reproductive technology of the moving image. Rainer's dancing exceeds Lambert's idea that it offers one long "continuous photogenic moment." As Giorgio Agamben argues, it can be said that the cinematic apparatus returns the still or frozen gesture or pose back to the flow from which it has been isolated. Rainer's movement cannot be captured by a series of stills but seems to call for the particular reproductive processes of the cinematographic apparatus in order to capture the flux of motion as a movement image. One could conclude that Rainer's dancing, and movements of a comparable order, are particularly suited to the production of dancefilm.

An account by Mangolte of her experience photographing Brown's work adds weight to this idea. In her article on photography, Mangolte makes a point relating to the affinity between ballet and the pose and the tendency for modern dance to avoid any such decisive moments—an observation clearly informed by her work photographing numerous choreographies by Brown and Rainer. She makes the general observation that, "[i]f for an average dance you shot at f/2 and 1/250 shutter speed, for Trisha you needed 1/500, unless you didn't mind the blur of fast movement."[20] This problem with "registering" Brown's movement eventually put Mangolte off photographing dance altogether and further explains Mangolte's choice to film *Watermotor*.

Given the rigorous levelling strategies of Rainer's choreographic methodologies, the question could be asked: Would such dancing register at all? The excessive movement and unfamiliar phrasing involved in such dancing produces a cinematic subject so heterogeneous, so challenging to ideas of filmic production, that it demands constant invention from the filmmaker. I will address this issue in the following discussion of the films of *Watermotor* and other examples from the avant-garde where, to return to my opening quote from Rainer, we perhaps witness how the "intrinsic difficulty" of "seeing" such dance can be "emphasized to the point that it becomes almost impossible to see."

5.2 Trisha Brown: Registering the Gestural Anacrusis

> *It was a very elusive form of movement. I couldn't grasp it. I didn't know how to bank it.*
>
> Trisha Brown on *Watermotor*[21]

Trisha Brown's *Watermotor* is an exemplary model of dancing that challenges the viewer's ability to *see* the movement. Brown's description of her own dancing in

[20] Babette Mangolte, "My History (The Intractable)," *October*, 86 (1998): 106.
[21] Trisha Brown quoted in Rainer (1999b), 173.

Watermotor as something so "elusive" that even she could not "grasp" it reiterates Mangolte's observation regarding the difficulty of "seeing" the movement quoted in the introduction to this chapter. Rainer also describes the challenge the dance presented to the viewer:

> But even that first time [seeing Brown perform *Watermotor* live] I knew there was something that was truly new. And I luxuriated in the novel feeling of being confronted with the necessity of educating myself. The pressure was clearly on me—on all of us in the audience—to "see again," to catch up with a spirit that was leading the way.[22]

The provocative nature of the choreography, confronting the spectator with something new, creates a necessity or pressure that is productive. New modes of perception are encouraged as the audience follows the dance's lead. Filmmakers also had to surrender to the terms of this new type of movement, utilizing modes of filmic registration that both interrogate and complicate the choreography, highlighting the difficulties it presents to perception.

As has been well-documented, Brown's movement research has gone through many stages, but I am focusing here on a particular phase of her work that first appeared in the Accumulations series, is fully articulated with *Watermotor*, and continues into her present work. This cycle of choreography is described by Marianne Goldberg as "a breakthrough in non-scored intuitive work" consisting of "multilayered, multidirectional movements." Based on improvisations, Brown set about locking down these complex and intricate phrases "to capture spontaneity."[23] Rainer remembers the effect of *Watermotor* and its follow-up group work, *Glacial Decoy* (1979):

> These two dances knocked me out.... The unpredictable rhythms, about-faces, counterpointing gestures rippling across extremities, the lightening-quick images that coalesced and evaporated in the fluid movement...[24]

This movement can be read as a continuation of the research into phrasing begun in Rainer's dancing and writing as outlined above, building on the idea of an aesthetic of continual, uninflected motion.

In a series of articles translated in *Writings on Dance #15: The French Issue*, a particular reading of Brown's dance practice attempts to account for the exceptional status of her movement quality, beginning with a reflection on the nature of dance itself. Godard describes the radical charter of contemporary dance: a project "not in search of a model, but *a profoundly original gesture*, breaking with the previous cognitive order and semantics."[25] In fact, this idea of an original gesture has shaped the entire history of twentieth-century dance. Godard describes this evasive source of movement in his description of movement "starters":

[22] Ibid, 177.
[23] Marianne Goldberg, "Trisha Brown, U.S. Dance, and the Visual Arts: Composing Structure," in *Trisha Brown: Dance and Art in Dialogue, 1961–2001*, ed. Hendel Teicher (Cambridge: MIT Press, 2002), 39.
[24] Yvonne Rainer, "A Fond Memoir of Sundry Reflections on a Friend and Her Art," in Teicher (2002), 48.
[25] Laurence Louppe, "Singular, Moving Geographies: An Interview with Hubert Godard," *Writings on Dance: The French Issue*, 15 (Winter, 1996b): 17. My emphasis.

One inevitably goes back to the mystery of what happens before the movement: what body image? what geography? what history? and above all, what intentionality? The pre-movement is an empty zone…and yet everything is already played out there, the entire poetic charge and tonal colouring of the action. A brief passage, a low pressure trough corresponding to this wholly founding moment: *the gestural anacrusis*.[26]

Godard's description here provides us with a term for the moment immediately prior to dance that is rich with potential—what he calls the "pre-movement zone." The *gestural anacrusis* will become my term for the activity that occurs between stimulus and movement, or one movement and another. In Godard's account it is being used specifically to describe the "founding moment" in the creation of an "original gesture," the activity that occurs in the body prior to actual movement. According to Godard, this activity is informed by the individual's body image, their sense of corporeal geography and history, and an intentionality that can have a variety of sources (such as words, images, and music). This concept in Godard's writing connects with his ideas on gesture rehearsed elsewhere in this book. The complex network of variables—body image, geography, history, intentionality—that shape the founding gestural moment, explain the mediality of gesture but also determine the originality.of the gesture: its tone, "color," and poetic.

The in-between zone of the gestural anacrusis is absorbed into the continuity of Brown's movement during this phase in her choreographic research, following Rainer's movement, which was "constantly engaged in transitions."[27] Brown's elusive, quick, fluid, and multidirectional dancing is "ungraspable," to use the choreographer's own term, offering no fixed forms and dissolving any possible privileged moments, producing *anarchic phrasing*. Brown herself describes the process that achieves this effect: "I put all these movements together without transitions and, therefore, I do not build up to something. If I do build up, I might end it with another build up."[28] Brown thus thwarts dramatic expectations from the level of the basic dance unit to the choreographic whole. Louppe compares Brown's movement in her performance series, *Accumulations* (1971–1973, 1979), to Brownian motion, which is a term from physics relating to "any of various physical phenomena in which some quantity is constantly undergoing small, random fluctuations." These movements have the following characteristics: "a given particle appeared equally likely to move in any direction, further motion seemed totally unrelated to past motion, and the motion never stopped."[29] Here is movement that exists entirely in the in-between state, never formulating into a moment that is privileged, a moment of registration. Phraseless and uninflected, here is Rainer's neutral phrasing taken to the extreme. Brown's dancing and its privileging of the gestural anacrusis exemplifies the radical movement that challenges filmic registration and inspires my understanding of the cine-choreographies in the dancefilms described in this chapter.

[26] Idem. My emphasis.
[27] Rainer (1983), 329–30.
[28] Trisha Brown, "Locus, 1975," in Teicher (2002), 87.
[29] Louppe (1996a), editor's footnote 4, 11. Louppe's use of this term in relation to Brown is attributed in a later article by Louppe to "chapterist, art critic, and philosopher Guy Scarpetta" writing in 1979 (Laurence Louppe, "Brownian Motion and France: Cartography of an Impression," in Teicher [2002], 68).

Babette Mangolte's *Water Motor* is an uninterrupted long-shot in an open performance space. Brown performs the solo dance, moving around the space dramatically, which takes her right to the edge of the fairly static frame. The movement is airy and ineffable: tiny runs and flicks of the feet, swooning balances, detailed arm gestures above swinging legs and torso. There are extremely rapid direction changes and adjustments of effort to create an intricate corporeal mapping of the space. The body moves on so quickly that the only steps that can be recalled are those that are repeated—a flicking hand and scooting leg. The question of how to capture Brown's mercurial and elusive movement is addressed by the repetition of the sequence in slow-motion in the second half of the film, satisfying a desire to see what is barely perceptible in "real" time. Now there are energy trajectories, whole phrases spun out of action and counteraction or triggered by deliberate manipulations of the effects of gravity. The connection to the title of the work also seems to be enforced in this cinematic rendering. The movements do appear as if underwater, the body dragging against its environment, while the phraseless fluidity that absorbs transitions produces the consistency of flowing water. And the motor could refer both to the unrelenting and steady locomotive energy and the cinematic mechanism that the explicit film techniques point to.

Peter Campus's *Watermotor for Dancer and Camera*, made two years after Mangolte's film, takes the production of cine-choreographies through experimental film techniques a little further. Filmed as a basically stable midshot, Brown's figure is superimposed with a second image of her shot from a different angle and running just behind the first temporally. In a reversal of Mangolte's film, the action proceeds in slow-motion first, then is repeated in real time. In both film versions, the continual movement fills out the space of the frame in an undifferentiated flow, amplifying the quality of the unmodulated choreographic phrasing; each movement is given the same treatment and carries the same weight.

The corporeal machinations of the profilmic performance are both exposed and concealed in this complex cinematic rendering. Slow motion allows for some revelation regarding the direction of locomotive energy, and the repetition of the actions close behind the first enact an instant replay that reiterates the unfamiliar actions. But the superimposition and the use of repetition also create a trailing effect that complicates any accurate perception of the profilmic, creating a new cine-choreography. Furthermore, the double exposure gives an effect of transparency to the bodies, and the ghostliness is intensified by the doubling. This is indeed a body "disarmed to the point of disappearance" through the use of slow motion and ghosting effects.[30] These two films of *Watermotor* and the following dancefilm examples share an effort to not only render, but elaborate on a poetics of motion that outstrips conventional cinematographic methods, creating new modes of cine-choreography. All of the films involve a registration of the anacrusis, revealing the transitions or the "pre-movement" as part of a fluid motility, or drawing attention to these usually insignificant "low-pressure troughs."

---

[30] One wonders if it is a mere coincidence that Rainer had Brown "disappear" from her film, *The Man Who Envied Women* (1985), made five years after this short. In Rainer's film Brown is an invisible protagonist existing only in voice-over as an omnipresent narrator.

Gina Czarnecki's *Infected* (2001) mainly consists of a figure shot from a turning camera some distance above, moving around on her hands and feet. The film begins with a small organic form that increases in size and complexity until a human body (performer Iona Kewney) is recognizable. The filmmaker uses field editing (the effect of having fifty frames per second and multilayering the editing to create a ghost trail of movement), "glitches" in the editing, superimposition, and a digital enhancement of the elasticity of the dancer's body to create the constantly moving and fluid cine-choreography. The odd angle of the camera adds to this effect with the spine, head, and limbs constantly reconfiguring and challenging the viewer's ability to discern either the body or details of the movement. At times Kewney resembles something more animal than human, her physical facility and the filmic treatment transforming her into something hyperreal. Kewney's movements are fluid, unmodulated, and rapid, sometimes sped up, at other times slowed down, and while the quality and range of the motion is consistent the choreography does not repeat itself. The filmmaker takes the dancer as her subject, focusing on her mercurial choreography, but also plays with the viewer's ability to discern the form and *see* the body's movements. Czarnecki creates a new cine-choreography that incorporates a dialogue between dance and the most experimental possibilities of her reproductive apparatus (see fig. 5.2, video 5.2⬤). She continued this investigation in her more recent films, *Nascent* (2005) in particular, but it is in this example that we can discern a profilmic performance that appears to provoke Czarnecki's radical creative response.

Another filmmaker that shares Campus and Czarnecki's approach in both rendering and obscuring demanding choreographic action is Belgian video and sound artist, Antonin De Bemels. The three films in his early *Scrub Solo Series* (1999–2001), which feature dancer and choreographer Bud Blumenthal, involve digital manipulation of the moving figure through a process of "scrubbing"—the audiovisual equivalent of "scratching." The process mixes the footage so that physical movements are repeated, sped up, stretched out, and skipped; the technique sometimes creates a trailing effect behind the movement that maps the trajectories of the actions. These traces reveal something of the activity of the action through space, but the final effect is abstraction that clearly goes beyond the demands of the original choreography, demonstrating how dancefilm can be both responsive to, but also productive of, anarchic phrasing. Hands cupped together rotate to create a translucent, stuttering sphere, as does a shaking head (see fig. 5.3, video 5.3⬤). Intricate hand gestures are broken down and their components revealed through isolation and repetition, simple movements made complex through filmic manipulation. Hands coming together in a cutting movement are held at the point where they make contact, amplifying a tiny detail within a movement trajectory. Any original phrasing or distinctions between discrete movements and in-between moments are overwhelmed in postproduction with the institution of new rhythms and phrases that constitute a filmic reworking of the choreography. And the body becomes more and more evasive, the film freezing on a blurred figure, superimpositions creating extra limbs, a face obscured beyond recognition. As Stamatia Portanova's writes of De Bemels's later *Stroboscopic Trilogy* (2003–2005):

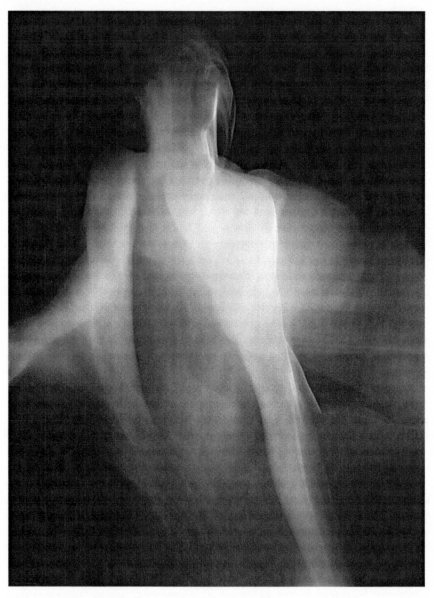

Figure 5.2 *Infected* (2001, d. Gina Czarnecki). Film still courtesy FORMA
Arts & Media Ltd.

Figure 5.3 *Scrub Solo Series* (1999–2001, d. Antonin De Bemels). Film still courtesy and copyright Antonin De Bemels.

…De Bemels knows that the viewer will never be able to actually see everything that is super-imposed in the technical processing of his videos: perception and imagination are overcome, overflown, pushed towards their own quantitative/qualitative limit.[31]

The "impossibility of seeing" dance becomes the subject, pushing the idea to create a study in corporeal elusiveness. De Bemels has taken this line of investigation further in his impressive body of work that includes *Se Fondre* (2006). In this film, which is based entirely on everyday movements and gestures, the tension between stasis and movement is intensified through digital manipulation to the point where any sense of a movement trajectory becomes defunct, let alone the traditional arc of a movement phrase. Here, the "in-between" is simultaneously compressed into nothing through a barely perceptible impulse to break into movement and extended infinitely in that same stuttering duration. A resistance to any recognizable concept of movement phrasing is entirely the product of the filmic treatment.

---

[31] Antonin De Bemels and Stamatia Portanova, "Stroboscopic Trilogy," *Inflexions*, 2 (2008) (Online. Available at: www.inflexions.org, July 9, 2009). Portanova's "philosophical reflection" on the "artistic question posed to technology" by De Bemels's work includes, among other things, a description of "microscopic video-choreographic cinema" created via the digital cut. This reading of "micro-movement" in De Bemels's work has some affinities with the microchoreographies described in relation to the close-up in dancefilm, coinciding with the "poetry of things" produced by the pure movement of tiny shifting and moving parts.

Certain social dance forms can be compared with the phraseless continuum of the choreographic work exemplified by Brown in their use of innovative or deeply traditional rhythms that depart from conventional western norms and involve a degree of improvisation and/or risk. The Charleston was a popular subject in early cinema. Jerome Delamater calls it the "quintessential image of the 'jazz age'," suggesting that the dance was in perfect synchronicity with the modern rhythms that grew out of contemporary urban American culture.[32] The dance form appears in films such as *Our Dancing Daughters* (1928, d. Hunt Stromberg) and *So This Is Paris* (1926, d. Ernst Lubitsch). Two experimental films of the time feature slow-motion sequences of the dance, indicating that these modern human rhythms were a challenge to filmmakers. The Charleston scene in Jean Renoir's *Sur un air de Charleston*, discussed previously, features a prolonged, slow-motion sequence of the Charleston that amounts to a movement study. And Charlestoning feet in slow-motion appear in Man Ray's *Emak Bakia* (1927). The repetition of the actions and phraseless continuum connect such movement to the anarchic phrasing described above, making this type of movement, and other repetitive social dance styles, a precedent for the research and aesthetics of the postmodernists.

The complex rhythms and continuity of certain ritual dance make this another obvious connection to the type of movement under discussion and also appear to challenge the filmmaker technically. In Hillel Schwartz's discussion of what he terms a "new kinaesthetic" that emerged between 1840 and 1930, he describes a movement order akin to Henri Bergson's "modern movement" and the continuous and uninflected movement I associate with postmodern dance in this chapter. He also states, "...that kinaesthetic did not have exclusively Western roots."[33] Schwartz lists West African, Sufi, Balinese, and Japanese movement forms as sharing affinities with this "new kinaesthetic" and being influential on Western performance training during this early period when the foundations of theater dance were laid. I have also mentioned elsewhere the undeniable significance of Afrocentric aesthetics in the development of twentieth-century theater dance, contributing to the cultural ascendance of continuity of movement evidenced in this new form. These connections between ritual or traditional dance and twentieth-century theater dance are evidenced in dancefilm examples that take the anarchic moves of the former as their subject.

Maya Deren shot her Haitian footage of Voodoun rituals (1947–1954) mainly in slow motion, and a recent film featuring African dance, *Black Spring* (2002, d. Benoit Dervaux), has been treated in postproduction with a slow-motion/blurring effect that obscures the feverish, pounding, repetitive rhythms of the dancing bodies to the point of disappearance. Michelle Mahrer's documentary on trance dancing in various cultures, *Dances of Ecstasy* (2002), also treats the profilmic material with similar

[32] Jerome Delamater, *Dance in the Hollywood Musical* (Michigan: UMI Research Press, 1981), 15. Choreographic and cinematic rhythm loitered at the periphery of this project but have recently been taken up eloquently by Laurent Guido, whose work reveals a rich discourse on the topic in French film theory and offers much potential for further development. See Laurent Guido, "Rhythmic Bodies/Movies: Dance As Attraction in Early Film Culture," *The Cinema of Attractions Reloaded*, ed. Wanda Strauven (Amsterdam: Amsterdam University Press, 2007), 140–56.

[33] Hillel Schwartz, "Torque: The New Kinaesthetic of the Twentieth Century," in *Incorporations*, eds. Jonathan Crary and Sanford Kwinter, (New York: Zone, 1992), 110.

special effects, suggesting that this type of radical, often improvised continuum of motion defies traditional filming techniques. Ecstatic dancing at rituals in Brazil (Candomble), Korea (Kut), Morocco (Hadra), Turkey (Sufi), and Nigeria (Orisha), and Western practices including raves, are all treated with mostly in-camera effects such as slow motion, superimposition, and extreme close-up, along with fast-editing and animation in postproduction in an attempt to render the unpredictable and excessive movements of the performers. But an effort to perhaps mimic the trance state in this film, and others such as Deren's Haitian footage, makes for frustrating viewing, the impetus to make dance "even harder to see" complicating the significant documentary function of these films.

The gestural anacrusis has been used in this chapter as a means of explaining the way that radical dance practices can inspire radical cine-choreographies. In dancing where the phrasing is complex and the in-between is highlighted, sustained, and dispersed (instead of being reduced to the status of "transition" between ideal movements and forms), *anarchic phrasing* results. Such phrasing can be found in postmodern dance practices as well as social and ritual dance and challenges both the habits of human perception and the process of cinematic registration. This results in dancefilms where the filmmaker is drawn into an intense dialogue with the profilmic material, adapting his or her tools to the subject. Such films constitute a specific cine-choreographic form that deals with movement on the level of visibility and legibility, mapping the limits of our ability to truly *see* dance and drawing the viewer into a new sensorial and affective relationship with the moving body.

6

The Musical

Moving into the Dance

In the 1953 Vincente Minnelli musical *The Bandwagon*, featuring Fred Astaire and Cyd Charisse, the lead characters experience artistic difficulties in the rehearsals for their new show. Charisse/Gabrielle Gerard asks Astaire/Tony Hunter, "Can you and I really dance together?" and they head to Central Park to find out.[1] In this scene in the park, the point where a stroll ends and a dance begins opens out to become a place where questions of genre, corporeal performance, and the relationship between choreography and everyday movements can be played out and explored both on film and in analysis. The couple walk in unison, creating a rhythm that preempts the dance to come and allowing room for another modality or register to take over. As they move onto the dance floor, the time seems right for them to move into dance and take the spotlight as the other dancers become spectators, a familiar device in the film musical. But Minnelli moves through this possibility, keeping us hanging in there with the awkward couple who are hoping to find a way to become dance partners.

If the move into the dance is delayed here it is because, in this scene, a walk becomes a dance well before the dance begins, serving not only as an introduction but taking on a life of its own.[2] That difficult moment when the performers move into the dance is prolonged to an excruciating degree, highlighting what Alain Masson calls a gestural "degree zero." Gilles Deleuze quotes Masson in his discussion of the musical number and screen performance:

> Between the motor step and the dance step there is sometimes what Alain Masson calls a "degree zero," like a hesitation, a discrepancy, a making late, a series of preparatory blunders (Sandrich's *Follow the Fleet*), or on the contrary a sudden birth (*Top Hat*).[3]

These are situations where the characters' movements undergo a transformation into dance, moving beyond what Deleuze calls "the motor situation."[4] What they "give birth to" is a new mode of corporeal performance.

---

[1] For readings of this scene in relation to genre and narrative see Richard Dyer and John Mueller, "Two Analyses of 'Dancing in the Dark' (*The Bandwagon*, 1953)," in *The Routledge Dance Studies Reader*, ed. Alexandra Carter (London: Routledge, 1998), 288–93, and Mueller, "Fred Astaire and the Integrated Musical," *Cinema Journal*, 24, 1 (1984): 28–40.

[2] Mueller comments on the way "walking" in this scene crosses over between the dancerly and the everyday, describing it as a "reflective, musically intricate dance-walk" (Dyer and Mueller [1998], 292).

[3] Gilles Deleuze, *Cinema 2: The Time-Image*, trans. Hugh Tomlinson and Robert Galeta (Minneapolis: University of Minnesota Press, 1989), 61.

[4] Ibid, 62.

The examples Deleuze gives in the quote above are from earlier Astaire films where the characters that he and Ginger Rogers play stumble into a dance competition, perform an "unrehearsed" dance where Rogers keeps missing cues, or dance as a reflex action whenever they hear a certain melody. In these scenes, the characters' movements occupy a nebulous middle-ground—a stuttering shift from the everyday to the extraordinary, the glitch at the interface between walking and dancing. It is the film's attempt to negotiate the gap between the dance number and the plot and it is a moment that we the spectators can sometimes "feel," like the crunching gear-shift in a manual car just before the engine increases its revolutions.

I have already introduced the term *gestural anacrusis* to refer to the founding moment of an original gesture—the "up-beat" that preempts the first strong beat of the movement phrase. I explained how the anacrusis becomes absorbed in the continual flux of the dance described in the writing of Yvonne Rainer and exemplified in the dances of Trisha Brown, indefinitely suspending the shift into fixed or privileged gestures. In this chapter the gestural anacrusis as the pre-movement zone refers to Masson's "degree zero." It is the moment between one mode of performance and another—the space where the shift occurs between walking and dancing, utilitarian movements and choreography, between recognizable behavior and dance-like deviations. The anacrusis thus occurs through the body of the performer who actualizes the suspension between modalities, creating a state of anticipation that can be carried across an entire film. The gestural anacrusis in the film musical thus differs from the pre-movement zone in the works discussed in Chapter 5 which never actualize into new and discrete forms but maintain the in-between status of the movement. The unstressed movements prior to the actual dance number in the musical lead into transformations between distinct performance modalities.

The anacrusis is central to the dancefilm musical because it is the film genre that most successfully negotiates moments where performative modalities coexist: dramatic, melodramatic, or comedic acting leads into dance, sometimes bridged by a song. The point of conversion between everyday gestures and dance is the key to understanding the role and importance of the dance star in the film musical—a surprisingly neglected element in theories of the film musical. The common approach to understanding the relationship between the dance number and the narrative in film is to see the dancing as a colorful interruption that is either beside the narrative point altogether, or at best reiterating or developing the desire that drives the film (sex, money, creativity). The success of the number—and the film overall—is generally measured by the degree to which the dance number is integrated into the film; the dance should fall into line with the other elements in support of the linear drive.[5] Attention has been given to a dancer's style or choreographic invention within the production number, but it is the way the musical

---

[5] See for example Jane Feuer's *The Hollywood Musical*, 2nd ed. (Bloomington: Indiana University Press, 1993); Rick Altman's *The American Film Musical* (Bloomington: Indiana University Press, 1987); and Jerome Delamater's *Dance in the Hollywood Musical* (Michigan: Ann Arbor, 1981). For a recent example continuing in this tradition see Lauren Pattullo, "Narrative and Spectacle in the Hollywood Musical: Contrasting the Choreography of Busby Berkeley and Gene Kelly," *Research in Dance Education*, 8, 1 (2007): 73–85.

star moves through the film, the way they smoke, walk, sit, and flirt, that leads us into the dance. By considering the dancer first and foremost, one can reverse the relationship between the production number and the film as a whole, making the number the central and influential element rather than the foreign or disruptive one. In this way we can recuperate the role of the dancer—and particularly the female dancer—as a pivotal element in the larger machine that is narrative filmmaking. And following this, we can consider contemporary narrative short dancefilms as the most recent development in a rich historical film genre that privileges the dancing star.

So the dance star will be revealed as the film musical's primary, unifying element, and the gestural parameters of a given performer become a kind of performative domain that unifies a character, a film, and bodies of work. The gestural parameters, performative domain, or corporeal specificity of the dance star will be referred to as the performer's *idiogest*: their gestural idiolect. The audience is familiarized with the star's idiogest through a focused attention on the star's moving body in the production numbers and throughout the film as we follow the performer through their plot-driven paces. Ginger Rogers, Rita Hayworth, and Marilyn Monroe will be analyzed in relation to these ideas, showing how the body of the star provides the link between the various elements of the filmic performance. Rogers, Hayworth, and Monroe provide contrasting types of musical stars, both in relation to their role and function within the films they appear in, and the quality of their individual idiogests. They also differ regarding their relation to dance as a performance mode. Rogers is primarily recognized as a singing and dancing musical comedy star and secondarily as a dramatic actress. Hayworth is positioned as a screen siren, dramatic actress, and dancer. And Monroe is remembered as a siren, comedic and dramatic actress, and musical star. Their differing skills provide comparative examples when looking at corporeal performance both within and beyond the musical number.

The foremost characteristic of the dance musical star is a capacity for excess motor expenditure, which facilitates their ability to move through the anacrusis and into the dance.[6] This capacity is directly linked to their ability as a dancer. Paul Valéry's definition of *dance*—as "an action that *derives* from ordinary, useful action, but *breaks away* from it, and finally *opposes* it"—puts this physical activity into a direct and oppositional relation to the everyday, which has significance in relation to screen performance in the musical.[7] In order for the performer to negotiate the transition from the acting styles employed in the classic Hollywood fiction film to the corporeal excesses of the dance number, a kinaesthetic potential to outstrip the utilitarian demands of a given scenario is required.[8] As we saw in my discussion of the *gesture-dance*, the dancer offers a performing body ready and equipped to transgress familiar gestural behavior. In the film musical, a cinematic order was developed

---

[6] This is suggested in Deleuze's comments above regarding the musical number shifting the character beyond the motor situation.

[7] Paul Valéry, "Philosophy of the Dance," in *The Collected Works of Paul Valéry, Volume 13*, ed. Jackson Mathews, trans. Ralph Manheim (London: Routledge and Kegan Paul, 1964), 207.

[8] Theorists of the film musical have aligned the acting techniques of musical stars with the conventions of classic narrative fiction film in general. I discussed the diverse origins of this style of acting in Chapter 3.

that took these performances as their template, performances that were in excess of narrative, function, and utility, perhaps constituting a history of mainstream exposure to deeply acinematic film practices.[9] Following this, we can consider the affinities between the film musical and the other types of dancefilm, both historical and contemporary, that have been aligned with acinematic and avant-garde film practices.

The anacrusis is not limited to the specific moment of interface between gestural modalities but extends to the coexistence of different performative registers across entire films. Potential to shift performative gears becomes attached to a dancefilm star, spreading out across entire film performances. In the "Dancing in the Dark" number, the walk leaks into the dance, so that something pedestrian or "unrehearsed" stays with the performance and creates a degree of tension between the obviously staged nature of the scene and the improvisational mood of the dance (see fig. 6.1). Alternatively, when Astaire/Tony Hunter walks down the street in the same film and into an entertainment arcade on 42nd Street, his jaunty steps lead naturally and easily into his spectacular "shoeshine" routine. Movements of everyday life and dance spill into and across each other. The inevitability of "spontaneous" shifts from pedestrian behavior to the exceptional physical actions of dance follow these figures through their narrative paces and I will show how the city, which most often acts as the setting for such films, can appear to facilitate such shifts.

The general physical manner of these stars becomes fascinating as they appear to carry this potential with them. This, in turn, creates a state of expectation that informs the film structure as a whole so that the musical can be considered a *larger format vertical film form*. This term draws on Maya Deren's definition of *vertical film form*, an alternative to the narrative drive of classic fiction film that has a horizontal, linear course. The *larger format vertical film form* refers to the influence of the gestural anacrusis on the overall musical film, particularly noticeable in—but not limited to—examples following the classic period and exemplified in the films of Bob Fosse.[10] In such films, the often extreme idiogest of the usually female star dominates the film to such a degree that the anacrusis is always present, creating a fluidity between "life" and "performance." Key examples here are Liza Minnelli's performance in *Cabaret* (1972, d. Bob Fosse) and Shirley MacLaine in *Sweet Charity* (1969, d. Bob Fosse).

Throughout this chapter I will show how in dancefilm, from the Hollywood musical on, the dance often begins with and returns to the gestures of the everyday body. In the final section, the use of a particular style of physical performance in contemporary dancefilm, found in the work of directors Pascal Magnin and Clara

[9] Such an approach to the film musical form is aligned with alternative views of the genre from theorists like Tom Gunning and Deleuze who see the musical as a site where radical tendencies in film practice survive and flourish. These theorists focus on specific operations within the genre such as an abstract mise en scène and the use of intense color, stressing the very cinematic nature of the form which liberates their analyses from narrative to a great extent. See Tom Gunning, "The Cinema of Attractions," in *Early Cinema: Space, Frame, Narrative,* ed. Thomas Elsaesser with Adam Barker (London: BFI, 1990), 55, and Deleuze's cinema books.

[10] The classic Hollywood musical era has its origins with Busby Berkeley's work in the mid-thirties, carries through the Rogers-Astaire series into the forties, where it peaks with the work of directors such as Vincente Minnelli, Stanley Donen and Roy Del Ruth, George Sidney, and William A. Seiter before the beginning of a decrease in production and the genre's transformation in the late-fifties.

Figure 6.1 *The Bandwagon* (1953, d. Vincente Minnelli). Courtesy Photofest.

van Gool, will be read against a history of this type of play, this mobility in the register of gestural modalities. This history encompasses the elegantly choreographed "e-motions" in melodrama, peaking in the musicals of Stanley Donen and colleagues, and later in the work of Fosse, where dance and the everyday move into step with each other. It will thus become clear how the short dancefilms of the last two or three decades, which have been discussed as revolutionary, are only recent arrivals to—and draw directly from—this heritage.

6.1 The Musical Star, Corporeal Familiarity, and Potential: *"The way you wear your hat . . ."*

. . . you can't describe a dance without talking about the dancer.

Merce Cunningham[11]

At the center of the musical is the star; of all the classic film genres, fans and academics alike focus their attention firmly on the leading performers. But as George Kouvaros points out, analysis of the star persona in film studies in general has "tended to deflect considerations of how being is constructed in and through the cinema," focusing more on "economic and institutional factors—that is, issues external to the film.[12] The focus on musical stars within film theory has been attributed to the problematic question of auteurism in such a formulaic genre.[13] With a perceived absence of director-driven aesthetics in the film musical, the star has been promoted as the overriding creative element linking bodies of work together. In turning attention back to "considerations of how being is constructed in and through cinema," it becomes clear that the tendency to make a primary association between musicals and specific performers is actually due to two key elements: first, the specificity and interdependency of particular choreographic styles and a dancer's gestural parameters, which runs across films, dance directors, and film directors; and second, the impact of the musical star's corporeal performance on the overall character of the films in which they appear. In the following I consider this influence of the musical star, which is determined by their corporeal specificity—their gestural idiolect or idiogest—and the operations of the gestural anacrusis.

Merce Cunningham's variation on William B. Yeats's famous dictum quoted above could not apply more than to the dance stars of the classic Hollywood musical period. In such films, and many more contemporary musicals, music videos, and shorts drawing from this tradition, choreography does not exist as something that could be performed by just anyone but is intimately tied to specific dancing bodies. While choreographers such as Hermes Pan worked across films, directors, and musical stars, ultimately the style of particular performers overrides any other choreographic input. "Show dancing" of this period certainly involved a degree of stock sequences and standardized steps, but the corporeal specificity of musical stars resulting from various techniques and cultural influences, along with their individual physical characteristics, unequivocally ties each dance number to the performer(s). Both Cyd Charisse and Eleanor Powell perform dazzling turns at breakneck speed in

---

[11] Merce Cunningham and Jacqueline Lesschaeve, *The Dancer and the Dance* (New York: Marion Boyars, 1991), 27. This is a variation on the Yeats quote:

O body swayed to music, O brightening glance,
How can we know the dancer from the dance?
(William. B. Yeats 'Among School Children' [VIII])

[12] George Kouvaros, "Where Does It Happen? The Place of Performance in the Work of John Cassavetes," *Screen*, 39, 3 (1998): 245.

[13] Gene Kelly states, "there is no such thing as an auteur in the musical film.... I am not an auteur, and nobody else is an auteur..." (quoted in David Parkinson, "Dancing in the Streets," *Sight and Sound*, 3, 1 [1993]: 33). See also Pam Cook on the issue of auteurism in the musical and the overriding "star" element in *The Cinema Book* (London: BFI, 1985), 108. Cook makes an exception for Vincente Minnelli and Howard Hawks.

various production numbers, but the expansive balletic quality of Charisse and Powell's compact and relaxed spins are signatures within kinaesthetic fields that are recognizably different and become reassuringly familiar.

Such an approach to understanding star performance in the musical has been informed by André Bazin's discussion of Charlie Chaplin from 1948 where he writes, "the continuity and coherence of Charlie's aesthetic existence can only be experienced by way of the films that he inhabits."[14] Bazin cites Chaplin's physical appearance, the qualities of his movements, and his psychological motivations as the elements providing recognition to his audience.[15] This led me to focus on the details of corporeal behavior in the following analysis of three female film musical stars. As stated, the star's physicality and particular way of moving is a central focus of the musical film, and this focus is, of course, most pronounced in the dance numbers where the camera, mise en scène, and editing all conspire to place the performer literally center stage, where her skills can be showcased. Such attention to the moving figure highlights the particular style of the featured artist and provides space for the audience to either become acquainted with a new dancer or refamiliarize themselves with a known performer.

In Ginger Rogers's sixth star turn in her partnership with Fred Astaire, *Shall We Dance* (1937, d. Mark Sandrich), the female lead first appears as a flip-book image that the love-struck Astaire (playing ballet dancer Pete Peters aka Petrov) is showing his manager (played by Edward Everett Horton). The jumpy image mimics the quality of early cinema and transforms into the "real" woman performing with a male partner in a club. Rogers's character, dance star Linda Keene, is funny, feisty, and nonplussed by her fame. Keene is a star in her own right and she excels professionally in a popular dance style that Petrov envies. In most of the RKO "Fred and Ginger films," Rogers's character is a professional entertainer before she encounters Astaire, and this corresponds with her biographical history. Rogers won the Texas State Charleston Championship at fourteen and worked consistently, first on vaudeville and then Broadway stages, with big bands, and on the screen (from the age of nineteen).[16] She had twenty films under her belt to Astaire's one when they joined forces in *Flying Down to Rio* (1933, d. Thornton Freeland).[17] However, our sense of her dance style is inextricably bound to her partnership with Astaire and it is an interesting exercise extricating the specifics of her idiogest from his.

Rogers appeared in several musicals prior to *Flying Down to Rio*, including *42nd Street* in which she played the wise-cracking, cynical chorus-dancer, Anytime Annie, and *Gold Diggers of 1933* (1933, d. Mervyn LeRoy), which she opened with a pig-Latin rendition of "We're in the Money." Her personal style is also spotlighted

---

[14] André Bazin, "Charlie Chaplin," in *What Is Cinema? Volume 1*, ed. and trans. Hugh Gray (Berkeley: University of California Press, 1967), 144.

[15] Ibid, 144–45.

[16] Rogers made her screen debut in *Young Man of Manhattan* (1930, d. Monta Bell).

[17] Astaire had made his screen debut with Joan Crawford and Clark Gable in *Dancing Lady* (1933, d. David O. Selznick), on loan to MGM from RKO, where *Flying Down to Rio* would have been his first film except for production delays (Ginger Rogers, *Ginger: My Story* [London: Headline, 1991], 111). As Rogers herself states, "for every film I did with Fred Astaire, I did three or four without him. Our partnership was a limited one only in his case, not in mine" (114). Rogers worked with a wide variety of directors and was critically acclaimed as a dramatic actress, winning a Best Actress Oscar for her role in *Kitty Foyle* (1940, d. Sam Wood). In contrast, Astaire never worked outside the musical comedy genre. Rogers felt her work was never really appreciated by director Mark Sandrich, who worked closely with Astaire and directed most of the Rogers and Astaire films.

in the musical comedy *In Person* (1935, d. William A. Seiter), made after four films with Astaire. Rogers plays opposite George Brent as a musical star who has a nervous breakdown and travels to the country incognito to recover. Rogers performs two solo song-and-dance numbers created by Hermes Pan, with whom she had a working relationship predating Astaire: one to her own voice on the radio, the other on a film set. The first, "Lease on Life," begins with her tapping and walking in time to the radio (see fig. 6.2). She performs to prove to Brent's character that

Figure 6.2 *In Person* (1935, d. William A. Seiter). Courtesy BFI Stills.

she is indeed the star, Carol Corliss, in the process satisfying our desire to see Ginger Rogers dance. In the instrumental break she takes up the song first and then dances an up-beat tap dance, picking up her feet and creating clear beats and rhythms while maintaining a relaxed posture and "improvising" with the furniture in the room. For the dance she is shot in long-shot and kept in the center of the frame. The number on the film set, "Out of Sight, Out of Mind," begins with Rogers/Carol singing, cigarette in hand and walking on a moving circular bar with the male chorus sitting around looking up at her. She wears a long gold dress and is lit with a spotlight while the chorus is in shadow. They lift her down and she performs a slow dance with stylized shapes and poses dominating, remaining at the center of the symmetrical patterns of the chorus. Then the chorus surrounds and obscures her and she emerges in a short tunic, her slim muscular legs a surprise given the rarity of such outfits for Rogers. She leads the men in a tap number that is snappy and clear but simple, neat, and spatially contained. The arm movements are minimal and there is little movement in her hips, torso, and head. Her feet are kept low to the ground.

In partnering Astaire, Rogers's physical profile corresponds with that derived from her solo appearances. In the upbeat tap numbers, Rogers is light and keeps her weight up and out of her lower body. This gives her movements an appearance of effortlessness and makes her easy for Astaire to manoeuvre. She appears relaxed despite her poise, supporting the apparent lack of effort in her movements. Her feet stay low to the ground unless the choreography requires her to pick her knees up, and her tapping is contained and delicate. There is also a relative lack of animation in her face. The more dramatic, ballroom-based numbers exhibit the same overall quality: Rogers's movements are light, graceful and relaxed, contained and delicate. Dancing "cheek to cheek," Rogers shadows Astaire, staying very close and never breaking away into her own steps as Astaire often does. Her chest is not particularly open with her shoulders often pulled forward and her chin tucked down. Rogers's torso and head remain stable and connected so that back-bends and swinging head movements can appear a little awkward at times. She rarely raises her arms, keeping them low and simple, and she often stops to let Astaire leap around her. Fast turns and dramatic shapes feature in such numbers and the couple cover space propelled by Astaire, who always appears to exert more energy than Rogers. In this way, Rogers is the perfect compliment to the virtuosic Astaire, deflecting attention toward him in a way that other partners could not.[18] The characteristics of Rogers's dance style outlined here will be shown as central to her overall screen performance and its impact on the films in which she appeared.

Rita Hayworth, whose father was dance director and performer Eduardo Cansino, has been described by a typically overwhelmed film commentator as "just about the

---

[18] Astaire's solos far outnumber Rogers's two across the ten films they made together. Rogers performs a solo song and dance routine, "The Yam," in *Carefree* (1938, d. Mark Sandrich) and "Yama Yama Man" in *The Story of Vernon and Irene Castle* (1939, d. H. C. Potter). These were both passed on to her by Astaire, who did not want them. In her autobiography, Rogers does not mention her song, "Let Yourself Go," in *Follow the Fleet* (1936, d. Mark Sandrich) or her solo song and dance audition in the same film when listing her solo performances in the RKO series.

Figure 6.3 *You'll Never Get Rich* (1941, d. Sidney Lanfield). Courtesy Photofest.

most stunning event in the history of Hollywood's woman dancers."[19] She had her first success in musicals and her first starring role in one was opposite Astaire in *You'll Never Get Rich* (1941, d. Sidney Lanfield).[20] The first scene including Astaire/Robert Curtis shows him taking a rehearsal with Hayworth/Sheila Winthrop in the front row of the chorus. He pulls her up for a mistake and they dance together as teacher and student, but she equals him in a snappy, sharp, and rhythmic tap routine that preempts their mutual romantic interest and compatibility on the nightclub dance floor later that night (see fig. 6.3). Skillful and energetic, Hayworth's dance style is sampled in this brief initial scene, but we have to wait until Astaire has performed two tap solos and the plot throws them together in a performance at an army camp to see Hayworth in full flight. The ballroom number they perform, "So Near and Yet So Far," is in Astaire's signature style (the dances are staged by Robert Alton) and shows off Hayworth's expansive quality; her head swings freely where

---

[19] Ethan Mordden, *The Hollywood Musical* (New York: St. Martin's Press, 1981), 116. Mordden points out that Hayworth could not specialize in her forte—dancing—as she was "Columbia's Big Lady," while MGM had multiple female stars allowing performers like Powell to stick to what they did best (210). For this reason, he says Hayworth "typifies the Hollywood star as commodity" (212).

[20] Hayworth was a Hollywood survivor, making thirty-six films prior to her breakthrough film, *The Strawberry Blonde* (1941, d. Raoul Walsh), co-starring James Cagney. She danced in her family act from childhood, appearing in *The Dancing Pirate* (1936, d. Lloyd Corrigan) as a member of "The Royal Cansinos." She was billed as Rita Cansino up until a new contract at Columbia in 1937 when Harry Cohn changed her name to Rita Hayworth.

many musical stars keep their upper bodies and head well-controlled and focused to the front, and she performs large arm movements and travelling steps quickly and with full extension. Her long limbs do not inhibit her dexterity and she manoeuvres easily around Astaire. In a second number, "Wedding Cake Walk," the choreography (again staged by Alton) reveals her range with multiple quick turns, swing-style sequences, and a reference to another African American vernacular dance, the cake-walk.

Hayworth was one of the few female musical stars to take the lead in numbers that emphasized dance over song, often accompanied by a male chorus.[21] In the musicals following those she made with Astaire she performs more solos than duets. *Cover Girl* (1944, d. Charles Vidor), the film that gave Gene Kelly his screen break, begins with a chorus number that is brash and messy; the theater director Danny McGuire (Kelly) shakes his head in the wings. Long-limbed Hayworth/Rusty Parker pulls focus with her expressive face and extra mobility in actions such as the violent head tossing and hip pumping that mark the number as excessive and "wrong." One of the highlights of this film is a stage number, "Cover Girl," featuring Hayworth/ Rusty with a male chorus. The number begins with a medium shot of Hayworth's face, panning out to a long-shot as she runs down a long, winding ramp that exceeds the diegetic stage space. The choreography features large arm movements and bold leaps performed quickly and covering a lot of space. Hayworth wears a long gold gown that is striking against the blue set and men's costumes, with the skirt further extending her movements—a device that reappears in other Hayworth solos. We will see how Hayworth's idiogest, which is established in these numbers, carries across the films she appears in and creates a general state of expectation for the viewer.

Marilyn Monroe is an interesting case due to the iconic status of her physical image, which exceeds even Hayworth's. Her association with the dance musical is through her early career films *Ladies of the Chorus* (1949, d. Phil Karlson) and *Ticket to Tomahawk* (1950, d. Richard Sale), and her major films *Gentlemen Prefer Blondes* (1953, d. Howard Hawks), *There's No Business Like Show Business* (1954, d. Walter Lang), and *Let's Make Love* (1960, d. George Cukor).[22] As Dyer points out, she plays an entertainer in ten out of her thirty-one screen appearances and in six of those her character is a chorus dancer. Unlike Rogers and Hayworth, her characters are not always successful professionals and are often struggling for recognition and respect (*There's No Business Like Show Business*) or stuck in jobs that are going nowhere (*River of No Return*, *Bus Stop*, and *Some Like It Hot*). This difference is reflected in Monroe's extremely motile and relaxed idiogest that lacks the control displayed by Rogers and Hayworth and is suggestive of responsiveness, sensuality, and instability.

Gentlemen Prefer Blondes opens with a song-and-dance number choreographed by Jack Cole and performed by Jane Russell/Dorothy Shaw and Monroe/Lorelei Lee,

[21] Hayworth was not a singer and her voice was dubbed by various artists. This perhaps shifted the focus further to her dancing skills. Other female dancers to take a lead role in numbers that emphasized choreography over song included Ann Miller, Eleanor Powell, Shirley MacLaine, Juliette Prowse, Leslie Caron, and Cyd Charisse.

[22] Monroe also dances in vocal numbers in *River of No Return* (1954, d. Otto Preminger), *Bus Stop* (1956, d. Joshua Logan), and *Some Like It Hot* (1959, d. Billy Wilder).

Figure 6.4 *Gentlemen Prefer Blondes* (1953, d. Howard Hawks). Courtesy Photofest.

"Two Little Girls from Little Rock"[23] (see fig. 6.4). The two women are framed as the stars of the film in their bright red, sparkling dresses set against a muted blue backdrop. Monroe and Russell perform mostly in synchronicity in this opening number so that the different movement styles of the two performers are apparent. Monroe is looser in the hips and shoulders than Russell and so appears more at ease with the choreography. She has more range in the pumping hip actions and various shoulder movements, drawing attention to her performance, which is comparatively more mobile and detailed. The choreographed actions have a staccato rhythm with accents on beats and lyrics, but Monroe softens the movements with no full extensions and the constant small movements that fill out her actions in general. This sense of softness is aided by Monroe's rounded figure, which differs from the more lithe and muscular bodies of performers specializing in dance such as Rogers and Hayworth. Rather than the sense of lift and verticality associated with professional dancers, Monroe's movements have weight and are grounded in her pelvic area. Cole keeps the movements simple but rhythmically snappy with most of the choreography created for arms, shoulders, and hips. (The number is filmed mainly in midshot.) Rapid arm shapes draw attention to the performers' faces (Monroe has two close-ups during the number while Russell has none) and Monroe's features are

[23] Howard Hawks's film followed Monroe's first starring role, which was in the thriller *Niagara* (1953, d. Henry Hathaway) and was the first musical comedy in which she starred. (Monroe had second billing to Adele Jergens in *Ladies of the Chorus* four years earlier.)

constantly animated in her trademark manner, even more so when she is not singing. For this reason the mid-shot and close-up become more and more dominant in the shooting of her production numbers, particularly in films such as *River of No Return*, *Bus Stop*, and *Let's Make Love*. Like Hayworth, the more Monroe's screen persona became tied to the role of sex object, the less movement she was required to do in her feature numbers. The quality of Monroe's close-ups can also be compared to *micro-choreographies*, where the choreographic action is taken up by small movements diffused across a corporeal surface.[24] Monroe's idiogest is directly linked to the gestural anacrusis in her films, which, as we shall see, is sustained in the "excitable" and highly motile body of this film star.

This focused attention on the film musical star's moving body, which is privileged by the mise en scène, camera, and editing, cannot, in fact, be limited to discrete "numbers" especially as dance sequences move in and out of scenes demanding other corporeal modalities. The intense focus and associated pleasures of familiarity promoted in the dance numbers are carried across to our way of viewing the performer throughout the entire film. This focus is magnified by the possibility that, at any minute, the performer will move through the gestural anacrusis and into a dance. We see the musical star walk down the street, move around her home, enter a party or nightclub, and do all the things that performers do in other types of films. What is specific to the everyday on-screen activities of these performers is the pleasure we derive from watching a physicality we are so familiar with and that has the potential to shift performance modalities at any moment, creating a state of sustained expectation.

The potential in these performances can be considered in relation to the model of dance taken from Valéry: a corporeal mode growing out of everyday movements that accommodates the fact we possess "more vigour, more suppleness, more articular, and muscular possibilities" than we need.[25] Dance is the mobilization of an excess motor capacity that can remain latent in nondancers, but in the musical star this capacity enables the shift across the gestural anacrusis.[26] The corporeal capacity of the musical star can be connected to the fact that such performers are commonly characterized as possessing a remarkable joie de vivre. Adrienne McLean describes the dancing in the classic American musical as invoking "attributes of energy, freedom, joy, and happiness," an observation repeated numerous times across writings on the genre.[27] A capacity for embodying heightened

---

[24] In Dyer's chapter on Monroe and sexuality, he equates this mobile quality in Monroe's facial close-ups, especially the quivering mouth, with a formlessness he associates with the vaginal orgasm (*Heavenly Bodies* [London: BFI and Macmillan, 1986], 57–58).

[25] Valéry (1964), 198.

[26] Two musical theorists who touch on this aspect of the musical star are Dyer and Leo Braudy. In his essay "Entertainment and Utopia," Dyer lists "energy" as one of the "ideals" of entertainment, capitalism, and utopia found in the musical, and defines it as the "capacity to act vigorously; human power, activity, potential..." ("Entertainment and Utopia," in *Movies and Methods Volume II*, ed. Bill Nichols [Berkeley: University of California Press, 1985], 224). He describes how in a film like *On the Town* (1949, d. Stanley Donen and Gene Kelly), an energy "runs through the whole film, *including the narrative*," and there is a "sense of the sailors as a transforming energy" (231–32). In a similar way, Braudy's chapter on the musical, "Musicals and the Energy from Within," describes the genre as displaying a "positive appreciation of private energy" through a celebration of dance (Leo Braudy, *The World in a Frame: What We See in Films* [New York: Anchor Press/Doubleday, 1977], 139). Braudy writes that, "the musical looks ahead to a utopian world born of individual energy. In the musical, success is achieved through the assertion of personal force" (140). For an account of the role of energy in contemporary dance see Dee Reynolds, *Rhythmic Subjects* (Alton, Hampshire: Dance Books, 2007).

[27] Adrienne McLean, "Feeling and the Filmed Body: Judy Garland and the Kinesics of Suffering," *Film Quarterly*, 55, 3 (2002): 7. See also Delamater (1981), 105; Feuer (1993), 162; and Altman (1987), 54.

emotional states and an easy departure from the corporeal constraints of utilitarian life are key characteristics of the musical star. In *A Star Is Born* (1954, d. Sidney Luft), James Mason/Norman Maine describes star quality as "that little something extra," and the "little jabs" and "jolts of pleasure" that Judy Garland/Esther Blodgett's singing gives him.

It is this human potential for physical vigour, power, energy, and force beyond the utilitarian, exemplified in the performances of the musical star, that the spectator intuitively recognizes or feels. The excess somatic energy in such performances transfers kinetically to the audience through an affective force. In viewing such a star, the spectator moves into the rhythm of a performance that is always ready to negotiate the anacrusis, to exceed the mundane, and break into an enactment of the human potential for physical virtuosity and play. The moment when the characters move into the dance, shifting from everyday actions to another performative register, can make the viewer squirm with what feels like a kind of embarrassment, the spectator relating to a bodily potential or capacity that is rarely realized in real life. The opening example of the "Dancing in the Dark" number exemplifies such "difficult" moments. Our anticipation of—and often discomfort during—the gestural anacrusis on screen could reflect our ambiguous feelings about the performers' physical potential. To see the mobilization of a corporeal capacity that is suppressed in everyday life and limited to sport, the dance studio, nightclub, or bedroom can be both exhilarating and confronting.

There is perhaps a connection between this recognition on the part of the audience of a corporeal life beyond the everyday, and the common—and often reductive—observations relating to the popularity of the musical genre: its particularly enthusiastic fan base and the perceived link to escapism.[28] These associations have meant that, as a subject for critical appraisal, the film musical has had a questionable status until taken up by film theorists in the late seventies and eighties. In 1981, Altman observed that the genre attracts more fans than scholars and suggests that the films call for an exceptional degree of spectatorial involvement.[29] Studies of the film musical have often overlooked the importance of the corporeal activity on screen and the body of the musical spectator. With the general focus on issues of narrative and film structure, there has been little attention given to the dance content outside of such concerns.[30] It is perhaps our ambiguous relation to the film

---

[28] For a summary tracing the emergence and analysis of the popularity of the musical film genre from early critical writings up to more recent approaches, see Cook (1985), 106; and Dyer (1985), 220–32.

[29] Rick Altman, introduction to Jim Collins, "Toward Defining a Matrix of the Musical Comedy: The Place of the Spectator Within the Textual Mechanisms," in Altman (1987), 135.

[30] Articles that do include some discussion of corporeal performance in the film musical include: Jodi Brooks, "Ghosting the Machine: The Sounds of Tap and the Sounds of Film," *Screen*, 44, 4 (2003): 355–78; Dyer and Mueller (1998); Dyer, "A Star Is Born and the Construction of Authenticity," in *Stardom: Industry of Desire*, ed. Christine Gledhill (London: Routledge, 1991), 132–40; Steven Cohan, "'Feminizing' the Song-and-Dance Man: Fred Astaire and the Spectacle of Masculinity in the Hollywood Musical," in *Screening the Male: Exploring Masculinities in Hollywood Cinema*, ed. Steven Cohan and Ina Rae Hark (London: Routledge, 1993), 46–69; and McLean (2002). Books include: Dyer (1986); Deleuze (1989), on the physical characteristic of the shift from everyday movement to dance in the musical (61); Delamater (1981), regarding choreographic genres and styles and the corporeal performance of particular musical stars including Eleanor Powell and James Cagney (with a description of Cagney's physical performance in non-musicals); Siegfried Kracauer, *Theory of Film: The Redemption of Physical Reality* (Princeton: Princeton University Press, 1997), which includes general statements on the shift from everyday movement to dance in the musical and other dancefilms (42–44); and McLean (2004).

musical's enactment of excessive corporeal activities that led to this characteristic in critical writing on the genre.

Hayworth is a particularly interesting example regarding the dance star's corporeal potential and spectatorial anticipation. The narrative of the musical-thriller, *Affair in Trinidad* (1952, d. Vincent Sherman), contrasts Hayworth/Chris Emery's behavior in performance with her demure off-stage personality, a plot device to throw her character's actions into doubt. In fact, across all of Hayworth's films, her dance style—with its extreme extension, energy, range, and spatial coverage—is contrasted with an everyday posture or carriage that is controlled and upright. Hayworth's characters in these films are mostly professional dancers who are career-minded and independent. Her screen persona's professionalism and ability, and a no-nonsense approach to men, reads through her posture and walk; she moves brusquely and stands tall with her shoulders back and head high. Hayworth's carriage also renders her ready to move into a dance at any time. In films such as *Affair in Trinidad*, her "everyday" corporeality seems to be restraining this potential throughout the narrative, which fuels our expectations. Hayworth's dance numbers are a literal explosion of this control into excessive movements that test the parameters of the choreographed steps, pulling focus in duets and carrying whole numbers with her bold presence.

The most extreme example of this release occurs in *Gilda* (1946, d. Charles Vidor). Hayworth plays an ex-dancer who has married to spite an ex-lover, played by Glenn Ford. She dances "cheek to cheek" three times with a variety of partners and has physically hysterical reactions to several situations, but the "explosion" in performance comes very late in the film with her rendition of "Put the Blame on Mame"; she teases the audience through anticipation. This number is Hayworth's most vampish with uncharacteristic hip grinds and a restricted choreographic range, including elements of burlesque strip, so that at the end of the number she has to be restrained from completely disrobing (see fig. 6.5). Hayworth's star image is often at odds with plotlines that have her tricked into marriage, denied her ambitions, or dominated by an overbearing male (father, husband, or lover). The idiogest of some female musical stars reads beyond, and in spite of, the often repressive storylines, creating performances where the moving body contradicts the ideologies they are meant to enact. Hayworth's talent, ability, and immense control over her performing body throughout her films challenges her characters' ultimate dependence on men.[31] Monroe's framing as a dumb blonde in most of her musical comedies is similarly challenged by her comedic and performance skills and a physical excess that prods at the parameters of such a stereotype.

In *Gentlemen Prefer Blondes*, Monroe/Lorelei and Russell/Dorothy walk into crowded spaces together three times in long-shot—the busy ship dock, the ship's dining room, and their double-wedding—stepping in time with each other and pulling the crowd's focus. Their pace is relaxed but rhythmic and the swing in Monroe's walk in particular draws further attention to the action. These entrances link to a

---

[31] The notion that dance in particular can challenge the ideological function of the image is one of McLean's central arguments in her revision of Hayworth's star image (McLean [2004], 196).

Figure 6.5 *Gilda* (1946, d. Charles Vidor). Courtesy Photofest.

series of promenades made by Monroe across several films that demonstrate her exceptional physicality through the performance of everyday movement. In *Some Like It Hot*, Monroe/Sugar is watched by Jack Lemon/Jerry and Tony Curtis/Joe as she walks down a train platform, Lemon/Jerry commenting, "Look at how she moves! It's like jello on springs.... Must have some sort of built-in motor or something." Monroe/Sugar's performance of "Runnin' Wild" in the train shortly after this reiterates the centrality of Monroe's moving body to the film from this point on; her

Figure 6.6 *Some Like It Hot* (1959, d. Billy Wilder). Courtesy BFI Stills.

shoulder shimmies and hip shaking showcase the small movements so apparent in *Gentlemen Prefer Blondes* (see fig. 6.6). (In *Some Like It Hot*, despite two strong male leads, Monroe "*is* the film," as Ethan Mordden writes.[32]) This is followed through with numerous long-shots of Monroe/Sugar running and walking around the hotel, beach, and pier, where the majority of the film's action is set. Monroe's walk in

---

[32] Ethan Mordden, *Movie Star: A Look at the Women Who Made Hollywood* (New York: St. Martin's Press, 1983), 227.

long-shot also features to excess in *The Prince and the Showgirl* (1957, d. Laurence Olivier).[33] The action, which is mostly contained within a private room of an embassy, consists almost entirely of an interplay between seducer and seduced, enacted first with Olivier/the Prince as the seducer, then Monroe/Elsie Mariner in a reversal of the scenario. The camera's attention is intensely upon Monroe/Elsie in a fitted white dress set against the dark background of the sombre room, manoeuvring constantly and excitedly, drunk and sober. The narrow skirt limits her to small, quick steps that increase the effect of her extreme motility, especially in the long-takes of her moving about the embassy's foyer.

Part of the function of such shots is to showcase the often spectacular dresses Monroe wears and to frame the star's body as an object of desire. But these images of Monroe moving through everyday life, getting from A to B in the service of the storyline, are also performative moments when the audience becomes familiar with the actress's idiogest and her potential for movement beyond utility. Monroe's corporeal excess is characterized by the small movements that register all over her body, including her face. As already noted, her extremely mobile, soft, and loose corporeality also has an excitable element that renders her ready to respond to, or kinaesthetically usurp, any given situation. In *The Prince and the Showgirl*, Monroe/Elsie's physical range, excess, and limitless stamina seem to be matched by a force of will that changes the course of the royal family's lives. In *Some Like It Hot*, Monroe/Sugar's behavior when playing catch with the girls on the beach is like an overexcited child, jumping and kicking her feet in a hysterical manner, leading into her seduction of Curtis/Joe's pseudomillionaire character and signalling her ability to achieve her ambitious goals. When Russell/Dorothy and Monroe/Lorelei shift into "When Love Goes Wrong" in *Gentlemen Prefer Blondes* at a Paris café as their troubles intensify, Monroe/Lorelei performs an impromptu dance that is all shimmies and hips—moves that pay for the bill and lead them on to get a job in a Parisian club.

Rogers differs from Hayworth and Monroe in her musicals with Astaire regarding the impact these leading ladies have on the films in which they appear, although her impact on the overall quality of these films is no less powerful.[34] Rogers's low-key, contained dance style remains consistent across the RKO films in which her characters are usually being pursued by a resourceful and enthusiastic Astaire. She carries herself in a relaxed manner, shoulders slightly slumped, and taking broad strides with a slight swagger. There is an air of professionalism and a street-wise savviness in all her actions, and her humorous lines are delivered dry and sharp. Rogers usually maintains a decorum throughout that is the perfect foil to

---

[33] Dyer comments on the focus on Monroe's body in *The Prince and the Showgirl* as well as Monroe's walk in *Niagara*, commenting on its extreme motility, which escapes definition and form, "has no edges and boundaries" (Dyer [1986], 22 and 57).

[34] Delamater writes, "The Astaire-Rogers series is an example of a possible theory of the *performer* as auteur, for each of the films is dominated by the style of its stars" (Delamater [1981], 51). Although he uses the plural, Delamater reserves all artistic power and influence for Astaire, describing his relationship with Rogers both on- and off-screen as that of a "mentor"—"a Pygmalion-Galatea/Svengali-Trilby relationship" (56). Mordden offers a more interesting view, suggesting that Rogers was one of many savvy collaborations entered into by Astaire, as she was his perfect partner: "Astaire needed Rogers more than she needed him" (Mordden 1981, 120).

Astaire's goofy posturing. If, as Delamater writes, Rogers inevitably falls under Astaire's spell and becomes "subject to his whims and desires," it is surely Rogers who casts the first spell.[35] While Astaire is clearly the choreographic talent behind the duo, somehow on-screen Astaire appears to covet more than Rogers's affections. As in the plot of *Shall We Dance*, Rogers/Linda has access to a style Astaire/Peter admires—her restraint and whiff of cynicism keeping her one-step ahead of her pursuer.

The idiogests of these musical dance stars are what enable the operations of the gestural anacrusis that bridges the shift between performance modalities that is so particular to the musical genre. It is the performers' ability to move easily across the anacrusis—their unique corporeal capacity or potential—that draws the musical together under their influence. The gestural anacrusis thus exceeds the discrete musical number, shifting across modalities in the body of the star and creating a sense of suspension and anticipation that effects the film form as a whole.

6.2 Verticality in the Film Musical and the Gestural Anacrusis

. . . in dancing one achieves a more magic relationship to space than one does in the course of ordinary walking.

Maya Deren[36]

Bob Fosse's *Cabaret* frames its star, Liza Minnelli (playing cabaret performer Sally Bowles), as the central and influential force within the film musical to an unprecedented and powerful degree. Minnelli/Sally's first appearance in the film is in an on-stage line-up at the end of a show at the Kit Kat Club. At this point she is one amongst many fascinating figures and faces on screen and, beyond audience foreknowledge of her star status, there is little hint of the imminent significance of her particular screen presence throughout the film. In the next scene, Minnelli/Sally is at the door of her boarding house; her clown-like mask of make-up, huge dark green nails, and exaggerated voice and gestures are shocking in the light of day. Limiting his locations almost exclusively to the Kit Kat Club, rooms in the boarding house, and a millionaire's mansion, Fosse builds a world around his star that works for her and makes sense of this outrageous figure who hauls the narrative along in her wake. The excessive quality in every aspect of Minnelli/Sally's physicality—her make-up, sculptured hair, overwhelming fashions, extraordinary singing voice, and what can be described as her hyperextended idiogest, her limbs appearing to extend beyond the usual limits—prefigures the challenging journey her character will take.

Minnelli's performance in *Cabaret* in 1972 epitomizes a new kind of musical star whose gestural sphere and excess motor capacity dominate and drive a new vision of

[35] Delamater (1981), 59.

[36] Maya Deren quoted in *The Legend of Maya Deren: A Documentary Biography and Collected Works. Volume 1 Part Two: Chambers (1942–47)*, ed. VèVè A. Clark, Millicent Hodson, and Catrina Neiman (New York City: Anthology Film Archives, 1988), 613.

being in the film musical genre.[37] This is not a woman whose professionalism and physical adeptness take the film to a satisfying and happy conclusion. Continuing on from Monroe's screen persona, Minnelli along with other female musical stars of the late sixties and seventies (Barbara Striesand, Shirley MacLaine, Bette Midler) provide a new kind of virtuosic performance whose optimism is not quite so convincing, allowing for a more ambiguous and less rosy view of our world.[38] Fosse is able to successfully change the terms of the musical genre by attaching his star's corporeal specificity closer than ever to the overall quality of his film, working the gestural anacrusis more deftly throughout the narrative and letting the performance "speak for," or rather "embody," the film.

In Cabaret, Minnelli's production numbers stage her physicality almost in caricature. Fosse's choreography—with its sharp angles, awkward and unnatural postures, and extremes of mobility, minimalism, and stasis—appears as if custom-made for his star. In "Mein Herr," Minnelli/Sally's first stage number, she moves quickly onstage and strikes a pose with a chair. Small pulses of her hips or other body parts while maintaining extreme postures (foot up high in a lunge, hips forward, chin to front shoulder, arms held back off her body) contrast with quick movements across space and overextended arm gestures, her head back and mouth wide as she belts out the song. The small movements appear intensely minimal on Minnelli's body with its long and loose limbs. She is built for the enormous, broad arm gestures that punctuate her songs and seem to extend the sound.

Minnelli/Sally's corporeal profile on stage is, however, only marginally intensified from her everyday behavior and it is the insistence of the gestural anacrusis throughout her performance that leads to my next point. In Cabaret, the performance of life and performance as profession are intricately interwoven, from the opening address to the camera by the MC (played by Joel Grey), through the plot manoeuvres to the final montage, which sets Minnelli/Sally's personal life against the excesses of the Kit Kat Club. Her musical numbers, which are all performed on the club stage, do not explode with the same impact as Hayworth's; they register only as reiterations of a corporeality that exceeds every scenario it appears in. In her interactions with Michael York/Brian Roberts, Minnelli/Sally is constantly striking cliché poses and performing the femme fatale or tragic heroine for him. She screams under a bridge as a train goes over releasing some of her excess motor capacity, lugs a gramophone to York/Brian's room for a failed seduction, bursts in on a private class looking for alcohol, and holds her hands up under a lamp as if in prayer ("Look

---

[37] Strangely, Cabaret is the only screen musical in which Minnelli dances as if she exhausts her excess physical capacity in one extraordinary film.

[38] The case of Judy Garland and the tone of A Star is Born pre-empts the darker mood in musicals from the late sixties on, with Feuer referring to the film as "the first of the antimusicals" (Feuer [1981], footnote 6, 173). New York Times film critic Jennifer Dunning articulates a sentimental attitude regarding this shift: "the movie dance numbers that once expressed emotions too joyous to be put into words have now gone the way of plots about the kind of uncomplicated romance that prompted most of that joy" (quoted in Walter Kendrick, "Dancing in the Dark," Salmagundi, 118–19 [Spring–Summer 1998]: 19). One of the most significant films since Fosse's innovations regarding a revision of the film musical form is Lars von Trier's Dancer in the Dark (2000). Björk, a popular music star, plays the lead in this her first film role and her physical performance is central to the film. Reaching a new level of darkness, José Arroyo states that "Dancer is a musical about alienation" ("How Do You Solve a Problem like von Trier?" Sight and Sound, 10, 9 [2000]: 14).

Figure 6.7 *Cabaret* (1972, d. Bob Fosse). Courtesy Photofest.

everybody—positively a nun's hands aren't they?"; see fig. 6.7). Minnelli/Sally poses gratuitously in underwear to seduce York/Brian, impersonates the postures of Clara Bow in a boat and an aristocratic party girl at dinner, dances around the millionaire's lounge room to entertain her host, and plays dress-up in preparation for an African safari.

Minnelli's screen performance in *Cabaret* is not so much engaging our anticipation of dancerly excess as constantly mobilizing this potential. I have argued that the Hollywood dance musical is dominated and characterized by the gestural parameters of the star's idiogest. That idiogest is marked by the star's dancerly capacity to exceed the demands of utility, mobilizing the excess "vigour," "suppleness," and "articular and muscular possibilities" that we as humans possess. This capacity or potential enables the star to negotiate the anacrusis—the often awkward point between performance modalities—and move the action from the everyday to the exceptional corporeal behavior that dancing entails. But we have also seen that the musical star carries this potential with them throughout their performance in a given film so that the anacrusis is never far away; actions carried out in the service of the plot often pulse with a barely contained urge to move into the dance. In later musicals such as *Cabaret*, this barely contained impulse breaks into almost every scenario in the film through the body of the star, creating entire films that ride along the cusp of the anacrusis, sliding from the everyday to performance and vice versa.

This concept of the musical has a bearing on the overall structure of the form and provides an alternative to the two models of the musical that have dominated film

theory to date: the idea that the musical number is a discrete unit that either operates as a disruptive spectacle or must be integrated into the classical narrative flow.
It is not adequate to limit analysis to a comparison between the musical and the par-
adigm of classic narrative fiction form—a model built on exclusivity regarding variable filmic "movements" (as Jean-François Lyotard argues in his essay, "Acinema").[39]
If the idiogest of the musical star dominates film performance, the musical numbers
dominate the film as a whole. The film proceeds as if in anticipation of the dance
sequences, which gives the films an overall quality of *suspended verticality*. The gestural anacrusis haunts every scene, just as corporeal potential marks every action.
Rather than working from the narrative toward the number, working the other way
reveals dance as a performative modality that calls acinematic operations into play,
insisting upon experimentation and innovation in the fiction film form. At this
point we need to think through the structure of the Hollywood musical outside the
monolith of the classic narrative fiction film, turning back to Maya Deren's model of
vertical film form for inspiration.

Deren's notion of verticality has been described as an alternative to the narrative
drive of classic fiction film—a film form that is more concerned with "qualities,"
"concerned, in a sense, not with what is occurring but with what it feels like or with
what it means."[40] Deren provides the examples of opening and dream sequences, along
with her own shorts.[41] Verticality is not cinematic inertia, but it is made up of visible
and auditory *film movements* that elaborate upon the *how* of a filmic moment, taking
on a particularly choreographic quality in Deren's own films. In its mobilization of film
movements beyond narrative exigencies, vertical film form shares a number of features
with Lyotard's Acinema. The dominance of dance as a corporeal modality and the
dance number as a performative register over the dance musical as a whole, and the
relatively minor status of plot and character motivation, amounts to a film form that
privileges verticality. Whether indulging in a prolonged dance sequence such as "The
Continental" in *The Gay Divorcee* (1934, d. Mark Sandrich), which runs to 17 minutes, or suspended in the conundrum of mistaken identity with Astaire chasing Rogers
through a surreal deco "Neapolitan" hotel, verticality overrides the linear drive of the
musical film at almost every level of filmic performance. Quality rather than content
becomes primary in these *larger format vertical film forms*.

Another film directed and choreographed by Fosse typifies the musical's change in
mood. It also has a female star who dominates the performative field of the film and an
opening sequence and overall film structure that exemplifies the idea of the film
musical as a larger format vertical film form. *Sweet Charity* opens with Shirley MacLaine/
Charity Hope Valentine leaving her house, running down the steps of her brownstone
and onto the street with a little kick of her foot. The opening sequence of the film
follows MacLaine/Charity around the streets of New York as she visits a furniture shop,
goes to the bank, and buys lingerie. Her physical performance in these everyday, urban
scenarios raises the sequence to the equivalent of a production number, turning objects

[39] Jean-François Lyotard, "Acinema," *Wide Angle*, 2, 3 (1978): 53–59.
[40] Maya Deren quoted in "Poetry and the Film: A Symposium," in *The Film Culture Reader*, ed. P. Adams Sitney
(New York: Prager Publishers Inc., 1971), 173–74.
[41] Ibid, 185.

Figure 6.8 *Sweet Charity* (1969, d. Bob Fosse). Courtesy Photofest.

such as beds and revolving doors into play things and walking and gesticulating in an excessive fashion. The city becomes her stage as she overrides gestural categories, but the city also ignores her. Throughout the film, MacLaine/Charity's optimism that her luck will change fuels her fairly continuous torrent of kinetic surplus that culminates in charged production numbers such as "If They Could See Me Now," "There's Got to Be Something Better than This," and "I'm a Brass Band" (see fig. 6.8). The star's corporeal profile has an element of desperation in its excess that seems to preempt the tragedy of her character's tale. The extreme extension of her lanky limbs, her almost violent arm and head gestures that throw energy away from her body so freely and carelessly, mark her as failed before it happens. This is a film that celebrates the mediocre, hopeful, and lonely, and MacLaine is the perfect star with her overwhelming physical performance. This is not a professional controlling her world; Charity lacks any kind of skill, as demonstrated in the job interview scene. The tension between this diegetic "fact" and the virtuosic performance by MacLaine of a body "out of control" makes for a fascinating spectatorial experience.

Made three years before *Cabaret*, with its impressive form structured so perfectly around Minnelli's performance both on- and off-stage, *Sweet Charity* gives a privileged function to the anacrusis, which is rarely held in check, usually being converted into a number of some sort. The opening sequence is an example of how MacLaine's performance, along with a series of color-washed freeze-frames, shapes an everyday scenario into a "number" before MacLaine/Charity's song, "Personal Property," even begins. There is an insistence on the verticality of the production numbers throughout the film that matches the element of desperation in MacLaine/Charity's idiogest. Other everyday scenarios such as Charity's first date with John McMartin/Oscar and her aimless wandering after her final rejection are staged to the score through montage and still shots: a choreography of images to music.[42] Almost every other scenario transforms into a number: the hysteria in the lift ("It's a Nice Face"), the drama of the proposal ("I'm a Brass Band"), her "date" with Vittorio Vitale ("If They Could See Me Now"), and another date with McMartin/Oscar ("Rhythm of Life"). The potential in MacLaine's performance does not merely inform the overall film but turns its whole world into a performance. Even MacLaine's job interview is read by the clerk as a performed gag.

In the films of Bob Fosse we can see how the performance of dance and dancers on screen is revealed yet again as an oppositional tendency—this time in the narrative fiction film form. The body of the dance star cannot be contained by the narrative and exceeds any sense of "functionality" in every scene in which the star appears. Movement on every level of filmic production is effected, producing what I have called *larger format vertical film forms* dominated by choreographic terms.

6.3 The City As Accelerator of Excess Motor Capacity in the Musical Star

> *The city is of course one of the great elements of the musical . . . and as a result the musicals are among the rare poetic works so far to accept big city life without using it simply as decorative detail or a satirical target.*
>
> D. Newton[43]

The status of the musical film as a large vertical format is related to the specific nature of the mise en scène in this genre. Two general models of the mise en scène

---

[42] I do not have time here to discuss the often substantial role played by music regarding the shift between performance modalities in the musical.
[43] D. Newton quoted in Cohan (1993), 69.

in musical films can be identified. These are the "everyday" scenarios from which everyday movements are developed into a dance number, and the fantasy scenario where the artificial nature of the design elements are highlighted.[44] In this discussion I am focusing on the former, which brings the musical star into more direct contact with the gestural anacrusis and also has had more influence on the contemporary dancefilms that draw on the genre.

The film musical put dance back into everyday scenarios—a point clearly demonstrated above in the example of the postclassical musical *Sweet Charity*. From the vaudeville stages and opera theaters of the nineteenth century, the outdoor gatherings where Isadora Duncan performed for a privileged few, and the early film renderings of dance against a black proscenium space, the film musical transplanted dance into everyday environments in a huge operation of restaging that has had irreversible repercussions for both dance and dancefilm. The impact on show dancing saw inventive negotiations of everyday objects and real environments, which became part of the choreographic project. Theater dance would also be inspired by this choreographic incorporation of the contemporary world beyond the stage in its development of what has been called "American ballet," particularly through the work of George Balanchine, Jerome Robbins, and Eugene Loring, who created ballets based on colloquial environments and activities. Some would dabble in choreography for the musical stage and all went on to work in films.[45]

The everyday environment of the Hollywood musical is, more often than not, the city. If musicals made in eastern block countries or India often feature dance numbers in agricultural/rural environments, the classic American musical rarely takes place outside a major metropolis.[46] City streets and elegant apartment interiors along with theaters, nightclubs, and movie lots are the setting for these musical stars who sashay, strut, and lounge in perfect sync with the city's rhythms, or rush, trip, and gape in awe as they stumble off boats, trains, and planes. But, as Newton observes in the opening quote, they are not merely settings in the decorative sense of the word; they become

[44] There is a comparable distinction in Gilles Deleuze's discussion of the musical: (a) "where the characters find themselves in situations to which they will respond through their actions, but that more or less progressively their personal actions and movements are transformed by dance into movement of world which goes beyond the motor situation"; and (b) where "the point of departure only gave the appearance of being a sensory-motor situation... it was a pure description" (Deleuze [1989], 62). The latter offers an alternative function of the musical star that applies where the mise en scène takes on a formative function. In such a case, the film itself operates as "pure description," abandoning the reproduction of the real. The dance sequences then amplify or make sense of the film by completing the transition to the "movement of the world," just as in Deleuze's examples of the flat, colorful studio sets that Stanley Donen brought to life through choreography in The *Pajama Game* (1957) and *Singin' in the Rain* (1952) (Deleuze [1989], 62–63).

[45] The influence of popular choreography created for film on contemporaneous theater dance has not been fully interrogated with most accounts, stressing the reverse effect. See Delamater (1981), 88 and 140; and Lisa Jo Sagolla, "The Influence of Modern Dance on American Musical Theatre Choreography of the 1940s," in *Dance: Current Selected Research*, Volume 2, ed. Lynnette Y. Overby and James H. Humphrey (New York: AMS Press, 1989), 50–52. Peter Wollen lists a series of ballets premiered in America in the late 1930s and early 1940s that represented contemporary life in America, including works by Erick Hawkins (*Show Piece* 1938), Eugene Loring (*Yankee Clipper* 1938 and *Billy the Kid* 1938), and Agnes de Mille (*Rodeo* 1942) (*Singin' in the Rain* [London: BFI, 1992], 13). Two important crossover works of this period were George Balanchine's 1936 choreography for the stage musical, *On Your Toes*, and Robert Alton's choreography for the stage production of *Pal Joey* (1940), starring Gene Kelly. The influx of choreographic artists to Hollywood from the metropolis of New York from the 1930s—Albertina Rasch, Sammy Lee, Seymour Felix, and Larry Ceballos—may have also impacted on the importance of the city in the film musical genre.

[46] Exceptions such as The *Sound of Music* (1965, d. Robert Wise), *Brigadoon* (1954, d. Vincente Minnelli), *South Pacific* (1958, d. Joshua Logan), *Seven Brides for Seven Brothers* (1954, d. Stanley Donen), and *Oklahoma* (1955, d. Fred Zinnemann) appear toward the end or after the classic period and have plotlines set in Europe or in an historic period/locale associated with an agricultural economy.

an active element in the film as a whole. Scott Bukatman adds that film musical sequences set in New York City suggest "some fundamental causal relation between urban stimulus and embodied response."[47] Besides providing dance with a new proximity to the everyday, the possibilities lurking in the big city seem to ignite the potential for excessive motor expenditure as the characters throw themselves into the heady mixture of ambition, desire, play, and wealth that is on offer.

The urban setting of the Hollywood musical provides the ideal location for the shift through the gestural anacrusis. Steven Cohan presents the "Dancing in the Dark" number from *The Bandwagon*, set in Central Park in New York city, as "a frequently cited example of the perfect integration of narrative and number."[48] Earlier I challenged the ideal of integration in relation to this number by demonstrating how complex the transition from walking to dancing is in this scene where the demands of city life and metropolitan ambitions drive two apparently opposing forces together. Any idea of smoothness is counteracted by the excessive duration of the anacrusis and the various tensions related to generic expectations and star potential. In the following discussion of the role of the city in accelerating the star's negotiation of the anacrusis (and thus, the influence of the dance number over the musical film form), we return to the point of conversion between everyday gestures and dance. These pivotal screen moments become a key to both the function of the dance star as the film's primary, unifying element and the genre's successful appropriation of Acinematic film elements.

The Rogers and Astaire films for RKO are almost exclusively set in sophisticated, urbane environments. If Rogers's kinaesthetic profile is easy, neat, and delicate, Astaire's defining physical characteristics are his casual, worldly grace and loose-limbed flair. Together, their styles are perfectly in step with the elegant nightclubs, apartments, hotel rooms, and theaters that they inhabit. Astaire is often shot walking along city streets. Signifying the iconic status of the star's corporeal screen presence, *Silk Stockings* (1957, d. Rouben Mamoulian) opens with a close-up of Astaire's feet walking down the street, into a theater, and back-stage, his pink socks, short trouser legs, and bouncy gait immediately recognizable. *The Gay Divorcee* includes a montage sequence as Astaire/Guy Holden walks the streets of London looking for Rogers/Mimi Glossop. Playing the gambler Lucky Garnett in *Swing Time*, Astaire first meets Rogers/Penny Carol at a cigarette machine on a Manhattan street, which begins a series of tricks and ploys with Astaire/Lucky chasing her into a dance school. His pretence that he lacks dancing skills is marked by alarming exaggeration and frightening prat-falls, and his revelation of his skill is just as thrilling as he leads Rogers/Penny in one of their most dazzling routines to "Pick Yourself Up." Astaire's corporeal range and skill carry him through the film toward finally getting his girl. In *Shall We Dance*, Astaire/Pete again exhibits the savvy opportunism of a successful city-dweller, manipulating events to suit his purposes. Dog-walking on board a luxury cruise ship provides the space for Astaire/Pete to enact a choreographed seduction

[47] Scott Bukatman, *Matters of Gravity: Special Effects and Supermen in the 20th Century* (Durham: Duke University Press, 2003), 159.
[48] Cohan (1993), 49.

of Rogers/Keene. She owns a dog and he borrows one to join in the pacing activity. She is walking in time to nondiegetic music and he falls into the rhythm, teasing the audience with a familiar prologue to their routines. Initial rejection by Rogers/Linda is followed by a montage sequence covering several days in which Astaire/Pete gets more dogs, her dog follows him, until finally there is a cut to them walking arm-in-arm in spritely double-time. Rogers's/Linda's dog stops and watches as they keep going, signalling the excess kinetic energy of the two stars. This performance of seduction works the space of the gestural anacrusis to perfect effect, providing a walking sequence that shifts their physical relationship increasingly closer to their inevitable dance duet. The characters' movement toward this inevitability is propelled by desire not only for each other, but for creative success within the milieu of metropolitan life that they inhabit.

There are many other instances where walking shifts into dance in the Rogers/Astaire films, also informed by an urbane lifestyle and often taking place in public spaces. In *The Gay Divorcee*, the "Night and Day" number takes place in a ballroom of a stylish hotel with Astaire/Guy singing to Rogers/Mimi who keeps walking away, Astaire/Guy blocking her path in a prolonged series of physical negotiations until he grabs her as she passes and turns her around and into the dance. In *Top Hat* (1935, d. Mark Sandrich), Astaire/Jerry Travis begins singing "Isn't This a Lovely Day" to Rogers/Dale Tremont in a rotunda in a park, and walks in time with the song, Rogers/Dale slipping in behind him before they begin a call-and-response sequence that segues from "improvisation" to a full-blown routine. "Never Gonna Dance" in *Swing Time* features another drawn-out introduction to a routine beginning with a song. Starting on a curved staircase, Rogers/Penny passes Astaire/Lucky walking in time with the music. He follows and they walk around the dance floor side by side before moving into a slow sad dance. Although the follow through from song to dance is rarely denied in their films together, the period of anticipation marked by a walk seems to serve another function besides negotiating two gestural registers. This walking and the pedestrian walking featured elsewhere throughout their films create a connection or overlap between performative modalities that ultimately draws the dance number out beyond the containment of the choreographed sequence. Walking becomes dancing and can be read as such outside the parameters of the "routine" in films where the actual dancing generally takes up only one-sixth of the screen time.[49]

6.4 The Influence of the Musical Genre on Contemporary Dancefilm

> . . . *film images have been and continue to be the repositories for many, if not most, of our notions of what bodies are supposed to do and to look like.*
>
> Adrienne McLean[50]

---

[49] Mordden estimates that there is an average of approximately twelve minutes of dancing in the Astaire-Rogers RKO films, which run to 110 minutes, but states that the films "set a tempo for dance, so every time Astaire and Rogers appear...the film...does what we want it to" (Mordden [1981], 114–15). Mordden gets close here to describing the influence of the musical number over the film as a whole.

[50] McLean (2002), 13.

McLean's words here resonate with the gesture-dance of Chapter 3 and Hubert Godard's ideas regarding how screen performance is one element amongst many (individual, social, cultural, historical, environmental) that impact upon the development of our gestural sphere. For many dance filmmakers, who perhaps relate more closely to the culture of the cinema than the stage, the familiar bodily behavior featured in classic narrative cinema, and the way such behavior inhabits the musical scenario as "potential," provides movement material ripe for reworking. The film musical has promoted particular gestures of the body, specific performance modalities, and cues for shifts between modalities. When contemporary dance enters this territory, it takes on this history. Equally, what contemporary dance can often bring to the encounter with cinematic performance conventions associated with the musical is an interrogative, experimental approach, a new perspective that shuffles around our coordinates for viewing dance as screen performance.

There are a number of continuities that can be traced between the musical and certain contemporary short dancefilms. In the following examples of films by directors Pascal Magnin and Clara van Gool, narrative takes on a role where it has been absent from most of the shorts discussed to this point. But while narrative makes an appearance, verticality still dominates so that any linearity is subverted or becomes secondary to the filmic performance. As in the specific use of mise en scène discussed above in relation to the musical, in these recent short dancefilms the action moves beyond the stage and studio, occurring in everyday scenarios and often in urban settings that "ignite" the physical action. Corporeal performance is central and is tied to specific performers/characters who unify the films through their negotiation of the gestural anacrusis, being marked by a capacity for excessive motor activity that enables such negotiations. Although these performers are not film stars in the traditional sense (although they are all well-respected dance artists), the audience cultivates a familiarity with their specific corporeal performance through the film's sustained focus on the same. Finally, in all of these examples, spoken dialogue is minimal or absent so that these films operate as a development of the wordless production numbers of the classic Hollywood musical.

Two narrative shorts by Swiss director Pascal Magnin use the skills of the choreographers/dancers to develop new intensified or transformed meanings out of common gestures to tell stories through the body rather than dialogue. Dancefilms such as these share with gesture-dance an interest in expression, increased physical range, and a connection with the everyday body, but they have a degree of affinity with the narrative imperative of the film musical and share the musical's attachment to the corporeal performance of certain artists. The fine line between gesture and dance in Magnin's collaborative works results in a newly formulated "musical" in which we can observe channels of exchange between bodily gesture, dance, narrative, and cinema. *Reines d'un Jour* (1996) is set in a rural environment and features a group of performers, male and female.[51] They use the landscape—grassy hills and the village buildings—to develop movements that describe personal relations and,

---

[51] The choreographers/performers are Marie Nespolo, Christine Kung, Véronique Ferrero, Mikel Aristegui, Antonio Buil, and Roberto Molo.

Figure 6.9 *Reines d'un Jour* (1996, d. Pascal Magnin). Film still courtesy and copyright Pascal Magnin.

more simply, respond to the surroundings. They roll down the hill and race back up again, turning agricultural terrain into a place of play. The men lock heads and shoulders in imitation of the local fighting bulls (see fig. 6.9). A woman creeps along a row of leather boots that creak under her weight. Along with these mimetic gestures, small dramas are enacted as couples grab at each other, manipulating and clinging to each other's bodies. They pass along breath, the invisible force impacting on each body down the line. And they dance with the villagers at a celebration, twirling partners around the small outdoor dance floor.

There is no tension between the everyday and the performers' potential in these bodies; throughout the film we begin to expect novel and exploratory behavior. The bodies of the performers are staged as exceptional amongst the village inhabitants although there is some interaction particularly with children. In this setting, which is reminiscent of the folk musical, these bodies have a capacity that outstrips the social and utilitarian functions of the villagers—a capacity that seems to be ignited by the beauty and novelty of the terrain. The dancers' excess motor capacity moves them from everyday gestures through the gestural anacrusis to choreographies that respond to a lifestyle and way of being that is far removed from most of our experience. A certain idealism and sentimentality charges the performance of the dancers who carry out an intense exploration of the everyday as it exists in this particular place and a coercion of social and intimate actions into a dance.

Contrecoup (1997), choreographed by Guillermo Botelho and performed by Alias Compagnie, begins on a busy city street with the gestures of a sharply dressed man becoming a dance of yelled abuse. The shift from emotionally charged everyday behavior to dance is subtle, setting up the terms for the dominating corporeal performance that plays with the anacrusis. A story about relationships and loneliness is told in this film through a series of somewhat random scenarios performed in urban public and domestic spaces, creating a primarily vertical film form. The spaces of the musical become the spaces for everyday gestures to be developed into choreography, and the skills of the performers allow for an extreme embodiment of psychological states well beyond the everyday.

The performances of the lead male and female couple drive the film and dominate screen time. The central love story is not dissimilar from the romantic tug-of-war at the heart of the classic musical, but the ambiguous and dark tone of the film along with the quality of the dancing create something new. Gestures of intimacy or play quickly evolve into confrontational tussles and the domestic interior morphs in nightmarish changes of scale that physically isolate the characters. The outsider character who opens the film engages in a scenario with the woman who has walked out on her partner. The two dance together, playfully slapping each other, which gradually evolves into a dance. The slaps performed by the man become increasingly more violent and abusive until the woman runs away in fear. The urban setting seems to drive these exceptional bodies from acceptable to unacceptable behavior, giving free reign to their capacity for excessive corporeal actions.

Another dancefilm director, Clara van Gool, works within the same territory as the musical, intensifying social and domestic dramas through the use of gesture and dance. *Nussin* (1998) is a work that exemplifies this filmmaker's remarkable use of an everyday mise en scène and dance. The film opens with a distant female figure standing in the snow by a railroad track. She lifts her arms slightly and moves into a solo tango performed without music. There is a cut to a close-up of her feet and then her face before she moves out of frame and the scene ends. The next scene is set in a kitchen with two couples (played by Bennie Bartels, Martine Berghuijs, Claudia Codega, and Dries van der Post) dancing to tango music under pulsing, colored party lights. The camera is close and very mobile; the characters are drunk and the looks that are thrown between them establish tensions that are played out throughout the film. A mystery is also set up as we follow an unidentified character's stiletto-clad feet through the snow, the final murder revealing the wearer's identity and the film ending as it begins with the solo female dancer.

Nussin consists almost entirely of tango dancing—either in couples or solo—and a few quiet domestic moments such as bathing, doing push-ups, or sitting quietly on a bed. These two modalities of activity often overlap: The brushing of teeth is incorporated into a dance in a bathroom or a quiet moment of reflection is interrupted as a dancer passes the doorway. The performers hardly ever stop dancing and are driven by their excess motor capacity through jealousy, desire, murder, and grief. Beyond Fosse's strategies, here the drama emerges through the dance. Actions are heavy with the potential for dance or, more often, dance transforms the everyday environment. Tango, a style that is weighted with sexuality and drama, is the perfect performative vehicle for this story of sexual duplicity and revenge. The cold and isolated setting, established through panning shots of the city and the dilapidated condition of the domestic interiors, fuels the claustrophobic and desperate mood. This is a true antimusical, a meditation on the dark side of desire, "concerned, in a sense, not with what is occurring but with what it feels like or with what it means."[52] The narrative

---

[52] Maya Deren quoted in Sitney (1971), 173–74.

Figure 6.10 *Lucky* (2001, d. Clara van Gool). Film still courtesy and copyright Clara van Gool.

exists only through the performers' bodies and the movements of doomed love that provide continuity across the various spaces—interior and exterior—of the film.

In another film of van Gool's, *Lucky* (2001), featuring dancer and choreographer Jordi Cortès Molina, the action moves from a cemetery to the busy streets of Barcelona, to an apartment and its gardens. With its central, solo performance this film exemplifies, more than those mentioned above, the role of the dance star as a unifying force, providing continuity across the vertical film structure just as the stars of the film musical did. The film begins with a slow pan across catacomb-like tombs in a cemetery followed by a zoom into an empty tomb with Molina appearing inside, illuminated by a cigarette lighter. He crawls through the tunnel, which is intercut with scenes of an old man, bent over and shuffling around his apartment. Molina emerges with a suitcase through a grating in the pavement on a busy street. Walking along and crossing a road, he begins to slow down and hunch over, mimicking the physical character of the old man.

This begins a series of parallels and matching actions between the younger and older characters (both played by Molina), which, together with a letter from father to son, establish the central relationship around which the film is based. The initial everyday actions of crawling and walking are interrupted by a slip through the anacrusis into another mode, and this potential is taken up when Molina behaves like a child while playing with an orange in the garden outside the apartment. Tossing the fruit he then traces it around his body, jumps with it, and throws it from hand to hand in front of his face, his head following the action and then shaking furiously. The shift in this scene from play to choreographed actions prepares us for the following solo dance that is cued by music and begins with Molina seated at a piano with his head down. He lifts his head, runs his hand along the wooden surface of the piano, and then moves into the dance with expansive and dramatic movements (see fig. 6.10).

Although there has been some introduction to Molina's corporeal presence before this point in the film, nothing prepares the spectator for this performance. Molina is a solidly built man so that his generous and swooning movements have a forceful impact. Dramatic falls to the floor and a moment on his bed in foetal position give the solo a mood of anguish and longing. Once the performance has shifted the film into this mode there is no going back, and a return to the gestures of everyday comes only at the very end. Two more solos follow and the mood shifts through romantic and delirious joy with big flying gestures, a swirling camera, and confetti, to convulsive frustration with Molina's body struggling on the apartment floor. The force of Molina's performance carries this film; we are introduced to his idiogest gradually beginning with basic, utilitarian movements. His impressive motor capacity and ability to articulate complex emotions is a surprise, but we become fully absorbed in his performance, which "embodies" the themes of the film.

The way these contemporary shorts take form around central, dance-based performance(s), together with their play along the gestural anacrusis, owes much to the film musical. These short, "vertical" films that incorporate character, narrative, and dramatic elements draw on the characteristics of the musical genre that enable a shift from everyday behavior and gestures to extraordinary corporeal actions through an attention to the skilled bodies of the central performers. That filmmakers such as Magnin and van Gool have so successfully combined story and dance indicates a familiarity with the cinematic model of the musical and its capacity to not only accommodate dance, but build a cinema of movement around it.

7

Dancefilm as Gestural Exchange

Jean-François Lyotard's body of writing charts "the story of our disenchantment with grand narratives" in the postmodern era. This project has engaged consistently with aesthetics and the artistic avant-garde, involved a critique of the "order of production" in cinema, and draws the body into the equation as an alternative, non-linear model for thought.[1] In his 1993 essay, "Gesture and Commentary," Lyotard explores the problematic relation between works of art and philosophical discourse—a project that arrives at a reinvestment in a gestural, performative, and affective mode of aesthetic experience.[2] As a template for the transmission of art and ideas, such an approach is particularly productive for addressing dancefilm, which privileges the moving body as subject.

Lyotard's use of the term *gesture* in "Gesture and Commentary" and in his earlier essay, "The Unconscious As Mise-en-Scène," should be defined and distinguished from the use of the term elsewhere in this book.[3] Lyotard uses the terms *gesture* and *gestus* to describe the various elements of aesthetic production and reception which together constitute a model of *gestural exchange*, from the work of the artist, to the components of the work of art, to the immediate response of the viewer and the labor of the philosopher's discourse. These ideas suggest a gestural contagion and fluidity between performers, between performers and spectators, between films, and between disciplinary boundaries. Such an understanding of gesture opens up the idea of what a gesture can be and what kinds of things can thereby be gestural in dancefilm.

So for Lyotard, *gesture* or *gestus* refers not only to the work of the artist. It also refers to the attempt by the philosopher to respond to the work of art, a response Lyotard describes as "a crossing or passage: a translocation, a transcription, a transposition, a transition, a translation," using "the most sophisticated gestures of which our discourse is capable":[4]

> ...the strange words that philosophy uses when it distorts its learned vocabulary, its vocabulary of knowledge, in order to come into contact with what it does not

---

[1] David Macey, "Obituary: Jean-François Lyotard 1924–1998," *Radical Philosophy: A Journal of Socialist and Feminist Philosophy*, September/October (1990): 53; and John Rajchman, "Jean-François Lyotard's Underground Aesthetics," *October*, 86 (1998): 3.

[2] Jean-François Lyotard, "Gesture and Commentary," *Iyyun, The Jerusalem Philosophical Quarterly*, 42, 1 (1993): 37–48.

[3] Jean-François Lyotard, "The Unconscious As Mise-en-Scène," in *Performance in Post-Modern Culture*, ed. Michel Benamou and Charles Caramello (Madison: Coda Press, 1977), 87–98.

[4] Lyotard (1993), 39–41. These ideas are aligned with another of Lyotard's major concepts: "presenting the unrepresentable" (Rajchman [1998], 4).

know…paying its debt to the *gesture* of color, volume, tone, and line, without the intention of peacefully *di-gesting* it within the organism of a system…[5]

For Lyotard, gesture is first a term denotative of operations beyond the realm of the language of knowledge—operations resistant to assimilation by pre-existing systems of representation. Second, these gestures, once set in motion, demand responding gestures that share this quality. So we have three strata of "gesture" in this encounter: the gesture of the work of art itself, the gestures that constitute the work of art ("color, volume, line, and tone"), and the gesture of response. The ruling gesture remains the *originary gesture*—the work of art itself—which draws both its components and its respondent into the realm of its authority.[6] He provides other lists of what I will call *component-gestures* that are even more comprehensive: "rhythms, virtual sonorities, lines, angles, curves, semantic colors";[7] "curve, chromatism, rhythm, tonality, or envelopment."[8]

It is clear how Lyotard's definition of gesture as it relates to the work of art corresponds to those gestures that Paul Valéry ascribes to the realm of dance, those movements of the body that oppose "ordinary, useful action," operating outside the rules of logic and functionality.[9] Throughout this book I have shown that dance, as a mode of screen performance, tests the parameters of cinematic production, resulting in new types of filmic performance, which I have termed *cine-choreographies*. Lyotard's investigation of the challenge that the gesture of the work of art presents to philosophical thought can be of assistance in developing a conceptual framework that can accommodate the variety of dancefilms discussed in this book, some of which are revisited here, where the primary focus is on corporeal action operating beyond the familiar. Lyotard's concepts are applied to the gestural activity of/in dancefilm in order to develop a model of gestural exchange that encompasses all aspects of the *filmic performance* as it manifests on screen and as it is experienced by the spectator. In my examples, gestures are not limited to movements of the body but include movements constituted by the camera, light, editing, objects, design, and also the gestures of spectatorship and analysis. However, the originary gesture is the originating movement that constitutes the primary subject of the cine-choreographic work. This originating movement is thus found to be at the heart of the gestural exchange in dancefilm. To approach dancefilm as gesture is to acknowledge that they are themselves gestures of art, operating within a circuit of gestures that occur, transmit, and respond. This gestural field is, itself, characterized by the heterogenous matter of the orginating gesture.

In "Gesture and Commentary," Lyotard refers specifically to Valéry's ideas in explaining the particular condition of the work of art as gesture—a condition that sets it beyond our language processes and structures of knowledge, ascribing to art its

    [5] Ibid, 38.
    [6] It should be noted here that Lyotard never refers to the elements he lists as components of a larger gesture, but it seems inherent in his description of the work of art as an "event," and the "singularity" he ascribes to this event, that the components form a unity of sorts.
    [7] Ibid, 42–43.
    [8] Ibid, 46.
    [9] Paul Valéry, "Philosophy of the Dance," in *The Collected Works of Paul Valéry, Volume 13*, ed. Jackson Mathews, trans. Ralph Manheim (London: Routledge and Kegan Paul, 1964), 207.

own form of productivity. Lyotard quotes Valéry, equating his own term *gesture* with Valéry's term "productive spirit":

> Everything that we can define is immediately detached from the productive spirit... and opposed to it. The mind at once turns it into the equivalent either of a matter... on which it may operate or of an instrument with which it may operate.[10]

According to Lyotard it is the "productive spirit" of art as a "space-time-matter event" that accounts for its difficulty and impenetrability for philosophical thought, and this condition of the work of art should not be compromised by the drive to define or utilize the work by applying referential, cognitive, or objectifying processes to it.[11] For Lyotard, the work of art divests these processes of philosophy of their legitimacy and disarms them. In its "singularity" or "*effect*," in its "occurring" or "*actus*" (the latter is defined as "the gesture of a matter in, with, and toward space-time," which it "immediately re-organizes") the work of art is a "movement," a "*thrust*."[12] It requires responding gestures from the philosopher that are akin to its own "spatial gestures, temporal gestures, linear gestures, chromatic gestures." The responding gestures do not mimic those of the work of art but come up to meet them—they are what he calls "discursive gestures."[13]

Lyotard's gestures are thus characterized by a sort of *motility* made explicit in terms such as "movement" and "thrust," but hinted at in the term *gesture* itself and the various descriptive terms above prefixed "trans-" (*translocation, transcription, transposition, transition, translation*). *Gesture*, or the Latin *gestus*, historically refers to the "bearing" or "carriage" of an individual and only more recently to "movement of the body" for "effect" or "as an expression of feeling."[14] The prefix trans- is from the Latin preposition meaning "across."[15] These gestures move across from their origin, through the space-time in which they manifest, to their reception or "effect." They are constituted by this movement and it is not just their motility that is of significance but the attention they call to their progress—the "bearing" of the crossing itself. These definitions of gesture/gestus imply a spectatorial dimension, as does Lyotard's gesture. Lyotard writes of how the artist "needs" and "calls" for a response to their work and how the work of art "insists and persists within philosophical thought itself."[16]

But, it should be noted, the account of the actual point of reception is missing from this first part of "Gesture and Commentary." Lyotard jumps directly from the gesture of the work of art to the struggle of the philosopher to articulate a response—a struggle I have compared to the task of analyzing dancefilm. What precedes the attempt to translate? If the gesture of the work of art eludes philosophical thought, where does it go? These questions are significant for my consideration of dancefilm and spectatorship,

---

[10] Paul Valéry quoted in Lyotard (1993), 44.
[11] Ibid, 40–41.
[12] Ibid, 39–40.
[13] Ibid, 42. Discursive: "Passing rapidly or irregularly from subject to subject; rambling; digressive" (*The Shorter Oxford English Dictionary: On Historical Principles*, 3rd ed., ed. C. T. Onions [Oxford: Clarendon Press, 1992]).
[14] Ibid.
[15] Ibid.
[16] Lyotard (1993), 38 and 48.

particularly in relation to the kinaesthetic responses alluded to throughout this book. They form the basis for the last section of this chapter, which deals with, on the one hand, the gestural exchange between dancefilm elements and the task of critical gestures of analysis, and, on the other hand, an account of affective spectatorship in relation to dancefilm. This corresponds with Lyotard's distinction in the second half of "Gesture and Commentary" between (a) the work of the philosopher *in relation to the operations of thought,* and (b) the problem of accounting for responses to a work of art *prior to thought.* The spectatorship solicited by dancefilm is thus divided in this chapter into the labor of critical analysis and a more immediate, affective response that "constructs" a spectatorial body that can meet the call of the originary gestures of dance.

At the risk of damaging the *productive spirit* of Lyotard's critical gesture, the gesture of the work of art proposed in his essay can be summarized as consisting of component gestures and as inspiring responding gestures, all of which operate under its influence. Importantly, the nature of this "gestural rule" has no relation to existing structures of thought and cannot be contained by the language of knowledge. It manifests as a singular movement—a *space-time-matter event*—and calls particular attention to the bearing or manner of this movement as that which constitutes it; in coming into space-time it reorganizes that same space-time, drawing this too under its influence. In calling attention to itself in its "performance" and inspiring a response from those attending, it requires that that response remains true to its productive spirit and that it comes across, moves into its unknown terrain.

Lyotard offers a particularly performative model of the gesture of the work of art that has a clear affinity with the cinema of movement that is dancefilm. The most obvious correspondence is the dimensionality and movement in and across space and time of both Lyotard's gesture and the originary gestures in dancefilm. The latter draw component-gestures and responding gestures into a performative "play" or gestural exchange. Rather than actions forming a logical movement within a larger trajectory from A to B, Lyotard's gestures and the gestures in many dancefilms oppose such containment. What is specific to the movement of bodies or objects in dancefilm is the way in which they trace trajectories, loitering along gestural routes, *calling attention to themselves,* and resisting any impulse to be digested into existing orders, establishing an *autonomy* to which the entire film must "bend" or "accede."[17] It is the autonomy of the originary gestures, and consequently the gestural exchange in dancefilm, that will be explored and explicated in this chapter. Lyotard's description of the task of the philosopher can be compared to my own work here as both spectator and writer. What I need to consider in the following analysis is how the calling-to-attention operates in the dancefilm and what kind of *labor* can meet its call.

7.1 Gestural Autonomy in Dancefilm

Dancefilm can be considered in relation to three *gestural operations* described by Lyotard. The first of these is the *call-and-response imperative* of the gestural exchange—

---

[17] Ibid, 39 and 41.

the performativity of the originating gesture and the inherent demand for a response—and will be discussed in relation to Maya Deren's *Ritual in Transfigured Time* (1946). The second is the *improvisational tendency* of the gestural encounter, which refers to the nature of the response provoked by the challenging work of art. This is discussed in relation to dancefilm through the contemporary examples of Anna de Manincor's *da nero a nero. Tempo per pensare* (1999) and Mahalya Middlemist's *Falling* (1991). The final gestural operation to be examined is the merging of *actus* and *situs* in the gestural order, the assimilation of the two sides of the gestural encounter, so that in the dancefilm we find that the mise en scène bends to the originating gesture. For my example I return to *Hands* (1995, d. Adam Roberts).

The dancefilms discussed throughout this book demonstrate a particular type of gestural proffering and are like Lyotard's gestures of art in that they operate outside the known. This is in contrast to more familiar cinematic gestures such as a slap across a face, a hand hovering over a gun holster, a finger running around the rim of a glass, or a body cringing away from danger. All these gestures have functions, tell us things, and carry a weight of meaning within a film. In Lyotard's "Acinema" essay, he refers to the types of movements or gestures that would depart from such familiar and functional actions. Lyotard suggests that the director of a "cinema of order" would eliminate: "*all impulsional movement, real or unreal, which will not lend itself to reduplication*, all movement which would escape identification, recognition, and the mnesic fixation."[18] In dancefilm, unfamiliar bodily behavior operating as originary gestures is aligned with such "impulsional movement," challenging both other filmic elements and the respondent to leave behind the recognizable and enter into what could most appropriately be described as a dance: an encounter where succumbing to who leads is the only assurance of any success. And the success of the call-and-response encounter is perhaps characterized by the care with which it proceeds and not by the amount of knowledge accumulated. The careful and attentive negotiation is the thing, not what can be taken away when the music has ended. No force is required, just a lack of resistance and a willingness to be moved by what is not known but makes its presence apparent.

In Maya Deren's *Ritual in Transfigured Time*, we have a perfect example of gestures that invite us to move into step with them, abandoning the comfort of the known and giving ourselves over to so many strange partners. A process of call and response is initiated by the originary gestures and is played out within the filmic performance in the central party scene. Like Gene Kelly's typical open-armed finishing pose, both sending out *and* hauling us into his gestural world, an extended arm in any context is a gesture calling for a response.

We are led into the film through a series of gestures in a domestic environment that shift between conforming to and abandoning this definable context, thus initiating a passage into the unknown. A woman can be seen through a doorway; she is seated and feeding a hank of yarn to someone out of sight. Another woman sees her and raises an arm as if to attract her attention, but then we see she is directing this gesture elsewhere. There is no response and she moves toward the seated woman

---

[18] Jean-François Lyotard, "Acinema," *Wide Angle*, 2, 2 (1978): 57.

through a different doorway, arm still raised, the awkward gesture shot from several angles and slipping away, almost between shots, from any determined function. There is a cut to the seated woman who is frozen in position and who consequently proceeds with her gestures of labor, now in slow motion and under the pressure of a strong wind that blows the last wool from her hands. She is then held for a long time in a gesture of release, her arms up and eyes closed as if in surrender.

These opening gestures both present themselves in and across space-time and call attention to themselves in the way they inhabit the same. The screen time given them, the different perspectives, the temporal distortions applied to them, and the way they are performed emphasize their non-functional nature and establish their place at the center of the action. As the central focus of the film, these gestures begin the process of calling all that they come into contact with into their order, which is constantly in production. They depart from any recognizable function and draw us out of familiar cinematic territory, compelling us with their potential.

In this film, it is the party scene that seems so compatible with the crucial aspect of Lyotard's gesture: the crossing-movement or *space-time-matter event* that manifests the productive spirit of the originating gesture and insists that we move into step (see fig. 7.1). And the beckoning quality of the gestures in this sequence exemplifies—literally illustrates—the model of gesture informing this chapter. In the thrust of the performers' arms through the space of the mise en scène, in the openness they illustrate, in the way that they call one another into their physical space and then release them from that encounter without any actual exchange beyond a momentary proximity, it is as if we are watching Lyotard's discursive gestures in action. These are gestures that pursue their mark but never realize an impact—the performers draw each other near as if to speak or embrace, only to meet face to face and move on without resolution. The movement of the gestures through space and time overwhelms the moments of proximity that defuse and transform into new trajectories. The thrust of the space-time-matter event manifests as a movement and sets up its autonomy as that which has no impact, resolution, or reason within our systems of knowledge, but instead draws us into a fascination with the movement or passage itself. We enter into the dance through a lack of resistance, indulging in a proximity or contact with the unknown.

If we really attend to these movements, our labor discovers in the repetition of these gestures a constant productivity that sets up its own circuit of expression, operating outside any systems that would contain or explicate them. The "calls" of these gestures have to be met on their own terms. And this circuit of expression or gestural exchange is not produced through corporeal performance alone. The repetition of the shots that make up this scene and the constant fluidity within and between those shots play their part. It is through the various elements of the filmic performance that the gestural work of the film is carried out, moving these familiar gestures of engagement away from any obvious meaning.

From this example we can see that the originary gesture in dancefilm demands attention to its moves as it manifests and explores the new space-time it both enters and creates; it improvises its way into this space-time and challenges the respondent not to betray the spirit in which it occurs. I use the term *improvise* to indicate the type of labor required of the respondent by these films: We are asked to provide for

Figure 7.1 *Ritual in Transfigured Time* (1945–1946, d. Maya Deren). Courtesy of the Maya Deren Collection, Howard Gotlieb Archival Research Center, Boston University.

the occasion, or occurring of the actus, an unpremeditated, extemporaneous reaction that makes critical response a challenge. With nothing to hang onto but the *potential* of the gesture—as Lyotard describes it—we are left to our own resources, compelled by these strange, summoning gestures to find a way to meet them. Beyond succumbing and indulging, we are put to work by the gestural dancefilm to produce an appropriate returning gesture. This is the impetus of such films: to produce, yield, bring out something exterior, yet akin to itself. We are called upon to improvise our response as we follow a trace of movements that we will never quite master, a choreography that will elude us each time despite the replay option. I shall refer to this as the *improvisational tendency* of the dancefilm—an aspect closely associated with the performative nature of Lyotard's gesture of the work of art and coinciding with a fundamental compositional strategy in choreographic practice.

In Italian choreographer Anna de Manincor's film, *da nero a nero. Tempo per pensare*, a dancer warms up side stage in a tight space between wings (fig. 7.2, video 7.2▶). The shadows of others performing onstage flit across the wall behind her. The shaking, stretching, twisting, frenzied movements of the dancer both occupy *and* create a space characterized by an *in-between-ness*. Her movements can barely be contained by the mid-shot that frames them or the tight space that encloses the dancer so that these gestures, which have the apparent function of preparing her for the stage, fill up this space, test its limits, and become a discrete performance. The

Figure 7.2 *da nero a nero. Tempo per pensare* (1999, d. Anna de Manincor). Film still courtesy and copyright Anna de Manincor.

adrenalin of such a preparation, the repeated shots, and the accelerating montage all conspire toward a climax, but suddenly we know this is not a lead up to anything; it is one complex *actus* teasing out a moment that should *not* have an autonomous life, but that improvises its way into the limelight. The film works with a moment that is unformed, unresolved, throwing a focus on the unremarkable and putting us to work to find a means to respond.

The opening scene of *da nero a nero* operates in the same way as the scene just described, but this time it is the space between sleeping and waking that provides the starting point. Limbs shift and stretch; stirring movements are followed by the stillness of sleep. The gestures of waking up become an exploration of the place between repose and action. Again we are made to wait, and again the anticipated purpose of these gestures begins to shrink in significance as the physical articulations that improvise their way into being impress us with their progress.

Both these instances in the film involve a teasing out of a moment through extended duration and repetition. The progress of the space-time-matter event goes beyond any simple actuality (i.e., she warms up prior to a performance, she wakes up and leaves the house), and there is an unpremeditated quality in the physical gestures themselves. This produces something exterior to the film—our response—which is called into the originating gesture's improvisatory spirit and shares the qualities of duration, expectancy, hesitancy, spontaneity, and intensity. With nothing to grab onto but the "almost" gestures of the dancer and the way they explore and test the space of the film, our work too becomes exploratory—an exercise that itself has no known outcome.

There is a correspondence to be made here between this productive, improvisatory, and challenging aspect of Lyotard's gesture and a characteristic of Deleuze's second sign of the affection-image. The *spatio-temporal autonomy* attributed to the affection-image as "power-qualities" or affects is revisited by Deleuze in Chapter 7 of *Cinema 1: The Movement-Image*—this time not in relation to the face but in an oppositional relation to what he refers to as the "state of things" or "event." He describes the "state of things" as including "a determinate space-time, spatio-temporal co-ordinates, objects and people, real connections between all these givens."[19] In contrast to this, the affects that are characterized by spatio-temporal autonomy, "only refer back to themselves, and constitute the 'expressed' of the state of things," operating on an independent field. They are the event "in its eternal aspect," an aspect that the accomplishment of the event cannot realize (to paraphrase Maurice Blanchot).[20]

Through this distinction between the state of things and expressive operations in film, Deleuze develops the idea of a "begun-again present."[21] Quoting Charles Péguy, he describes this effect in relation to Carl Theodor Dreyer's *Passion of Joan of Arc* (1928):

> ...two presents which ceaselessly intersect, one of which is endlessly arriving and the other is already established...the first has long been embodied, but the second continues to express itself and is even still looking for an expression. It is the same event but one part is profoundly realised in a state of things, whilst the other is all the more irreducible to all realisation.[22]

In a neat summary, he writes of this "mystery of the present" as the extraction of the "inexhaustible and brilliant part which goes beyond its own actualisation."[23]

---

[19] Gilles Deleuze, *Cinema 1: The Movement-Image*, trans. Hugh Tomlinson and Barbara Habberjam, (Minneapolis: University of Minnesota Press, 1986), 97. In the state of things, the affect exists also, but as "actualised, embodied in states of things," and "becomes sensation, sentiment, emotion or even impulse [*pulsion*] in a person" (97). The affect in the expressive field can never be determined in this way, is never "actualised," but exists as an expression of the "possible" (98).

[20] Ibid, 102.
[21] Ibid, 108.
[22] Ibid, 106.
[23] Idem.

Applied to dancefilm, this description of the "begun-again present" coincides with the *improvisational tendency* I have detailed above. The autonomy of the gestural field in these dancefilms operates beyond any actualization that could contain the gestures, producing the sense that something is being presented anew, is "endlessly arriving," and that we must improvise a response particularly for the occasion. We cannot depend on habits of viewing or pre-programmed responses. And the "begun-again present" takes on an altogether new priority in the dancefilm where the "state-of-things" or "event" can have a flimsy quality: for example, the in-between moments of life in de Manincor's film that sneak into the limelight. These are not familiar events or actions with foreseeable conclusions. What many dancefilms offer is an indeterminate space-time, subverting the filmic elements listed by Deleuze above ("a determinate space-time, spatio-temporal co-ordinates, objects and people, real connections between all these givens"), and I have shown how in *da nero a nero* gestural operations can play a major role in conspiring to bring about such subversions. In some dancefilms, there may be a complete absence of "givens," and the demands on the respondent to follow the lead of the film and improvise an appropriate response becomes an even greater challenge.

An example of this type of dancefilm would be Mahalya Middlemist's film *Falling* (1991). In this film, a woman lying on her side and filling the width of the frame rolls slowly toward the camera until she rolls off an edge and out of frame. The inevitability of each progression in the roll and the final fall *could* be the state of things, but this is never established as the trajectory of the film and the beginning of the actual fall are impossible to pinpoint. Surrounding the figure is a blackness that places the action in an indeterminate space where anything could feasibly happen. We can only watch and wait with plenty of time to speculate as to how the action will unfold. The begun-again present describes a productivity that outstrips the content and overflows, drawing the spectator into a process they cannot assimilate or contain. In *Falling*, the prolonged duration of the slow roll (each frame is repeated twenty-eight times) and the intense focus of the static frame claims our attention and draws us toward another level of production; beyond any inevitability of action we are caught up in the production of another movement, a potentiality, an *actus* that seeps out of the grainy images, the sepia hues, the duration, creating an autonomous circuit of expression that refers only to itself and challenges the title's clue of a final fall. *Falling* thus "produces" our response and we enter into the gestural field to become another *actus*, movement, thrust within that field, taking on its determining properties.

The final gestural operation described by Lyotard is the merging of *actus* and *situs* in the gestural order. Lyotard states, "The gesture that is the art work is ... situated in and situates space-time."[24] In becoming a space-time-matter event, Lyotard's gesture "immediately re-organises" that very space-time, once again determining its rule over that which it comes into contact with. In relation to the work of art, *actus* refers to "the gesture of a matter in, with, and toward space-time," which it "immediately re-organizes" as *situs*. The two terms are two sides of one encounter:

---

24 Lyotard (1993), 40.

The philosopher's difficulty with the work of art is due to this *actus* which is immediately also a *situs*. The gesture that is the art work is a *situs* because in coming to space-time it immediately re-organizes it: it both is situated in and situates space-time.[25]

This can be translated into the terms of the cinematic apparatus and the dancefilm by considering the gestures as movements featured on screen. The gesture's coming to the space-time of the film both situates the gesture in, and re-situates, the cinematic field. This is the power of the gestural *actus* in dancefilm to draw the mise en scène around itself. The *actus* of the originary gestures become the *situs* of the film; the gestures call the mise en scène into being. Adding the call-and-response aspect of Lyotard's gesture here, we have a filmic process that does not merely make sense of or "acquire" the gesture through its cinematic treatment, but one that allows it to retain its non-assimilable nature through cinematic operations that bend themselves to the original gesture.[26]

The *actus/situs* merger does not happen every time there is a corporeal movement on screen. A gesture can occur within a mise en scène where it simply functions to complete the scenario that is unfolding, so that while it enters the space-time of the mise en scène, it has no power over it and falls into *its* order. Examples of this type of functional gesture would be those mentioned earlier: a slap across a face, a body cringing away from danger, and so on. What is it about a particular gesture that demands a certain level of "discourse" with the filmic scenario, transforming the *situs* it enters and becoming inextricably bound to other filmic elements?

Hands offers an example of the merging of *actus* and *situs* through attention to the gestural performance. In this film featuring Jonathan Burrows's hand dance, the filmic performance is constituted through an attention to the articulation of the hands, and the performance of the hands is "produced" by the mise en scène within which it unfolds. As pointed out previously, there is nothing beyond or behind this cine-choreography. The production of the filmic performance through component gestures—like Lyotard's gesture of the work of art—creates an *actus/situs* with no other reference, nothing pre-existing that we can draw on in formulating our response.

Another example of this powerful type of cooperation—this time not from a dancefilm but from the work of a director particularly enthralled with the power of bodily gesture—would be the odd movement and pose performed by Nadine Nortier/Mouchette in Robert Bresson's film of the same name.[27] In a mid- to long-shot, drunk, and possibly scared in the forest shelter of her rapist, Nortier/Mouchette's hand moves away from her body and out in front of her face, out into the space around her as if she is caressing the air, or as if she is experiencing her hand disassociated from her body. She breaks this gesture to answer a question but returns to it, and it is as if the entire mise en scène is sucked in to focus on this inexplicable but engrossing action. Here, the mise en scène does not so much "bend" or come under the command of the gesture, but it falls like a lover into the power of this gentle and tentative action.

---

[25] Idem.
[26] Ibid, 39–40.
[27] *Mouchette* (1967, d. Robert Bresson).

Perhaps the lack of any "state of things" discussed above has something to do with the special condition of these gestures that call the mise en scène into such intense cooperation that they relinquish any connection with the profilmic. In fact, with the films under discussion here and using methods of analysis drawn from Lyotard's work on aesthetic production and reception, I have moved away from issues relating to the profilmic that persist in most writing on dancefilm. The gestural articulations themselves have been shown to include all aspects of the filmic performance, including the originary gestures that set the terms for the exchange. Filmic performance in dancefilm corresponds with the most challenging aspects of Lyotard's model of the work of art, and this is directly related to the choreographic nature of the originary gestures and how this informs the film as a whole. The model of gestural exchange set out here is based on the autonomy of the gestural articulations in dancefilm—that is, their status beyond the realm of the language of knowledge—and helps in establishing the specific nature of dancefilm, not just in relation to other screen forms but art forms in general.

In the gesture of the work of art of the dancefilm as a whole, where the operations of the gestural field inform the entire work creating an actus that occurs in the space-time of the screening, the spectator becomes part of the situs, part of the actus/ situs merger. In the following, Lyotard's model of a mise en scène, in which the role of the spectator becomes central, provides a way for thinking through the spectatorial body of dancefilm via *reflection, affect, somatic intelligence,* and a *polyesthetic mise en scène.*

7.2 Somatography: A Corporeal Model of the Mise en Scène

> . . . *"mise-en-scène"* . . . *[t]his ensemble which beseiges our sensory body.*
> Jean-François Lyotard[28]

For Lyotard, the work of art as gesture challenges thought and happens to thought from somewhere beyond it. Elaborating on the demands that the work of art makes upon the philosopher in "Gesture and Commentary," Lyotard explains that, within the context of philosophy and the operations of logic, the gesture of the work of art does not produce a "given," but "gives to and gives rise to thought."[29] The work of art challenges thought that would "acquire" it as "experience," digesting it through "memory."[30] It encourages the philosopher to "think about thought itself as a work of art," drawing his/her gestures out of philosophical discourse and into its own realm.[31]

---

[28] Lyotard (1977), 87.
[29] Lyotard (1993), 39.
[30] Lyotard places the gesture and its *actus* in opposition to the theorization of "experience" in the writings of Plato, Immanuel Kant, and Georg Wilhelm Friedrich Hegel, which present ways "for the given to be laid out within a reasonable discourse" (ibid, 41).
[31] Ibid, 43. Lyotard refers to Friedrich Nietzsche, Valéry, and Stéphane Mallarmé as originating a type of gestural language that drew closer to the terms of the work of art, connecting Lyotard's ideas with the French Symbolists who were so central to my discussion of Loïe Fuller.

According to Lyotard, in the encounter with the work of art the viewer cannot make connections through recognition, cannot dwell on details of the encounter through recollection, and cannot build upon the event within the trajectory of life experience. If this is the case, then what kind of thought is involved? Surely this is not thought at all but something preceding or eluding thought. And Lyotard, in fact, does *not* stop with the production of "thought"—a thought that does not resemble any thought we are familiar with—but moves on to arrive at "feeling...thought as it is affected." He does this via Immanuel Kant's *Critique of Aesthetic Judgement*, which he credits with bringing to light "the extreme contortions that the categories of the understanding and the ideas of reason must undergo if reflection is to have access to what is at stake in works of art." I will quote Lyotard at some length here to help us follow him in this step:

> By considerably freeing what he called "reflection" from categorical rules and ideas in order to draw near to what is most proper to art and aesthetic feelings, Kant was also announcing the dissolution of the argumentative power of philosophical discourse in these matters. The only guide left for reflection to follow was that which belonged purely and exclusively to it, namely, *feeling*. In other words, not thought insofar as it knows and wills, but as it is *affected*—regardless of what it does—by its act and its site, *as it feels itself to be*...and this feeling or affect happens to thought immediately...[32]

Now "what is proper to art" for Lyotard is not only discourse that responds to the thrust or actus of the work of art in a manner that is appropriate to it (that is, what thought *does*), but "aesthetic feelings" that provide a guide to accessing thought "as it is affected." This is thought "as it feels itself to be" immediately upon contact with the actus/situs of the work of art.

Lyotard introduces the concept of *affect* to his discussion of gestural operations and the work of art at the point where he focuses on the pre-gestural moment when the thrust of the work has found its mark. This shift in Lyotard's essay can be followed by a corresponding shift in our discussion of dancefilm in this final section to the kind of impact these films make upon the spectator prior to a considered response—that is, what happens between perception and our attempts to meet the call of the originating gesture. This brings my discussion back to the central issue of moving bodies and the particular role of the spectator's body within the gestural economy of dancefilm.

What kinds of correspondences can be found between Lyotard's affect and the gestural exchange of dancefilm that might help us arrive at a model for dancefilm spectatorship? Correspondences include a suspension of the logic of thought and language and an inherent motility and autonomy. I will show how Lyotard retains "thought" within his consideration of affect and feeling due to the parameters of his exploration (the effect of the work of art on philosophical discourse), but how thought must ultimately surrender its centrality in relation to the affective dimension of dancefilm. I turn instead to a model of *somatic intelligence* as being more appropriate for addressing the affective element of my dancefilm examples. Somatic intel-

---

[32] Ibid, 45. My emphasis.

ligence is a model of corporeal experience that places the body at the site where the thrust of the actus meets it mark—where "feelings" are registered that "provide knowledge of the unnamed."[33] Somatic intelligence will lead on to my discussion of Lyotard's model of a corporeal mise en scène—*somatography*—as the locale where the affective gestural exchange of dancefilm takes place.

We have encountered the concept of affect previously in the form of Deleuze's cinematic affect. For Deleuze, the *affection-image* is the cinematic image that corresponds to a "processing" brought about by problematic perceptions or actions. It is a movement of expression that both precedes, and exists independently of, actions and feelings.[34] The independence of the affect from the action or gesture it is related to, and the autonomy of Lyotard's gesture, is just one of the correspondences between these two conceptualizations of affective aesthetic production. Here, however, I will be limiting my discussion of the affect to Lyotard's model due to the different contexts from which Deleuze and Lyotard's concepts are drawn. Lyotard is dealing with the operations of the work of art in general, whereas Deleuze concentrates mainly on the production of affective cinematic images and processes of expression.[35] If Deleuze offers a model of cinematic affect, touching only momentarily on the role of the spectator,[36] Lyotard focuses his attention not only on the production of the affect, but also on its reception and our attempts, or more specifically the attempts of philosophers like himself, to process the power of the affect. Lyotard's work thus offers us a way of thinking about spectatorship and dancefilm that brings this book to its conclusion.

Lyotard describes the moment when the philosopher is confronted with the actus of the work of art, making philosophy give up "its *own* power": "… feeling or affect happens to thought immediately."[37] Like a mutinous onslaught, the affect overwhelms thought before it can attempt a translation, creating an impact via its thrust, which has the effect of disarming thought. This links us back to the motility of the originary gesture: its occurrence in space and time, its "crossing." While this relates to the *productivity* specific to the affective work of art, it has significance regarding the point of reception in that the affect *arrives* as a movement, thus creating an impact. The power of the affect is inseparable from a gathering of force through motility, and this aspect of the affect has a most direct and profound relation to my subject, the dancefilm, which features and is dominated by various movement orders. Brian Massumi writes:

> Affect is autonomous to the degree to which it escapes confinement in the particular body whose vitality, or potential for interaction, it is. Formed, qualified, situated

---

[33] William McClure, "Beheaded," *The Performance Space Quarterly*, 14 (Winter 1997): 24.

[34] Deleuze (1986), Chapters 6 and 7. It should be noted that Lyotard links affect directly to "feeling," while Deleuze insists that the two terms refer to discrete phenomena. For instance: "Affects aren't feelings, they're becomings that spill over beyond whoever lives through them" (Gilles Deleuze, *Negotiations: 1972–1990* [New York: Columbia University Press, 1995], 137).

[35] For instance: the circulation of affective forces beyond "the state of things," outstripping realized events as an endlessly arriving present, (concepts outlined in Deleuze 1986, Chapter 9), and the production of these forces through the gestures of the body, in any-space-whatevers, and via affective cinematic operations (Chapter 7).

[36] Deleuze does this mainly in his description of the "manual" linking of affective singularities and the tactile nature of the second sign of the affection-image (Ibid, Chapter 7).

[37] Lyotard (1993), 45.

perceptions and cognitions fulfilling functions of actual connection or blockage, are the *capture* and closure of affect.[38]

The life of the affect depends upon its condition as "potential," and in this way it does not belong to any "particular body" but must continue on its way. The idea that the affect is only sustainable as a movement or transmission, that it loses its autonomy when it is actualized as a "closed" form, points to its affinity with both dance and dancefilm, which are characterized by movement. While the affective force of live dance has been much discussed, my project here is to determine the specific nature of affect in relation to dancefilm via the model of gestural exchange I have established. Following Lyotard's definition, motility and dimensionality are now associated with the affect that becomes another movement within the gestural circuit of the dancefilm.

Another characteristic of affect mentioned in the Massumi quote above and shared with Lyotard's gestural order is the autonomy of the affect. For Lyotard, this autonomy is apparent in that the affect is something that happens to thought, operating as an immediate effect that suspends comprehension. This characteristic makes clear the affect's position *between* the thrust and response—its independent life beyond thought and in the body of the recipient who is drawn closer to the work. So the affect of the gesture of the work of art is not *there*, pre-existing in the work, nor *here* as a familiar end result, a recognizable feeling. As Lyotard states:

> ...a given curve, chromatism, rhythm, tonality, or envelopment does not include its affect within it...in the way that a word includes its meaning.... Affect has no such credentialed representative in the world of what I have been calling gestures.[39]

The affect of the work of art only exists as an instantaneous impact that, as Massumi points out, "is not entirely containable in knowledge, but is analysable in effect, as effect."[40] Massumi suggests here a way out of the conundrum of bringing to light that which precedes discourse: an attention to the *effects* of the affect. What I am hoping to arrive at here is a corporeal model for the meeting of the actus and situs as an *effect* on the body of the spectator of dancefilm.

With systems of knowledge and language failing him, Lyotard himself turns to the *effect* of the affect in "Gesture and Commentary." Lyotard compares the effects of the work of art on the philosopher to the "stupor that [Roland] Barthes attributes to lovers," who are reduced to repeating the phrase "I love you."[41] Earlier, Lyotard writes that:

> ...the philosopher, like a desperate lover, attempts to give to the work something he does not possess, namely, the words to carry on this gesture.[42]

---

[38] Brian Massumi, "The Autonomy of Affect," in *Deleuze: A Critical Reader*, ed. Paul Patton (Oxford: Blackwell Publishers, 1996), 228.

[39] Lyotard (1993), 46.

[40] Massumi (1996), footnote 3, 237.

[41] Lyotard (1993), 46.

[42] Ibid, 38. There is more use of the analogy of lovers: "He (the philosopher) was indebted to the work by virtue of the fact that, in its mere existence as a way of being toward space, time, form etc., it had preceded him...it had been his mistress in these matters. He owed it thought, for he was in love with the work his mistress; he was thus going to give it what he himself did not possess" (37).

The gesture of the work of art is, for Lyotard, a movement or articulation that precedes thought and seduces it—calls it to respond in a manner that exceeds it. In an attempt to account for the affect of the gesture of the work of art, to "carry on" the work begun there, the philosopher is at risk of "lapsing into aphasia," being completely seduced into silence by the *activity* of the affect in its immediate impact.[43] He writes that the work of art's "encoding, encrypting, or its analytic":

> will not have been what makes the work, here and now, an unpolished sentimental event which provokes or fails to provoke our love. I repeat: there is no method by which to account . . . for this sort of stupor by which thought suspends all activity . . . comes to a halt before the event of the work in order to linger near it.[44]

It is in this silence, this stupor induced by the "here and now" of the affect, that we discover its real power, a power compared by Lyotard, in a startling move, to the power of love. This suspension of activity that he compares to a lover's swoon, the focus on proximity, and the active power of the impact of the affect all seem to indicate a physical response, although Lyotard never refers to anything this specific. Instead we have an "unpolished, sentimental event," like a coy lover approaching and attempting to win us over, and there we are loitering around its doorway, lingering in the hope of getting close once more. The scenario is easy to construct given the performative tone of Lyotard's writing here. But is this all there is? An awkward silence between the seducer and the gob-smacked lover?

Lyotard's ideas regarding the impact of the affect in "Gesture and Commentary" progress in loops that barely touch on the role of the body via thought and back to questions of language and idiom.[45] In returning always to *thought*, to affect as a feeling that happens to thought, Lyotard inevitably arrives at a dead end. It has already been well-established that affect is exactly that which cannot be accounted for from *within* thought. Lyotard finally throws his hands up with his last sentence: "But I cannot say what would be the idiom in which the philosopher—if indeed he even remains a philosopher—might bring to light such an anamnesis."[46] In order to overcome the aphasia that haunts Lyotard's discussion of the affect of the work of art in relation to philosophical discourse, I will mobilize terms found in dance writing—*somatic expression* and *somatic intelligence*—which provide a way forward in

---

[43] Ibid, 46.

[44] Idem.

[45] Massumi also refers to the problems of a language structure "derived from theories of signification" and the need for "an asignifying philosophy of affect," and the tendency to fall into accounting for affect in terms of emotion (Massumi [1996], 221).

[46] Lyotard (1993), 48. *Anamnesis* was a doctrine of Plato's that can be found in *Meno* (80–86), *Phaedo* (72–77), *Phaedrus* (247–50), and *The Republic* (Book VII). (These references are listed in I. M. Crombie, *An Examination of Plato's Doctrines, Volume 2* [London: Routledge, 1962], 136.) According to this doctrine, the soul has pre-existed and accumulated knowledge that can be accessed through the effort to seek out truth. *Anamnesis* is recollection from a previous existence—the recognition felt when a conclusion corresponds with a "necessary truth" we have already acquired (Crombie [1962], 138). Lyotard suggests that the philosopher must practice on a work of art "an anamnesis of the space-time-matter that the work paradoxically makes into act, site, and gesture" (Lyotard [1993], 48). This would require that the philosopher access something in the space-time-matter of the gesture that connects with universal or preexisting truths or knowledges—ideas that work beyond the processes of logic and rationale and belong to a world that predates our existence. Regarding affect, this idea promotes a generalization of the experience of its forces that seem to be in direct contradiction with its nature as that which confounds any kind of consensus and creates multiple potentialities that may not ever approach anything as concrete as a "truth" or a distinct "experience."

accounting for the affective component of dancefilm. This is not to reject the characteristics of Lyotard's affect that will remain relevant throughout the following discussion—in particular, the motility, kinetic force, and autonomy of the affect. These characteristics serve to reinforce the significant role of affect within the gestural order I am applying to dancefilm, leading to a model of kinaesthetic spectatorship particular to the form.

I introduced the term *somatic expression* earlier in my discussion of Loïe Fuller, who provided a new model of corporeal performance at the beginning of the twentieth century. In a chapter of *Mourning Sex: Performing Public Memories*, Peggy Phelan compares the understanding of the hysteric's body in the early work of Josef Breuer and Sigmund Freud to the work of the dancer. She writes, "Psychoanalysis suggests that the body's 'truth' does not organize itself narratologically or chronologically. The body does not experience the world in the way that consciousness does."[47] Such an idea corresponds with the notion that affect, which involves a physiological impact, belongs to a realm beyond the structures of knowledge and consciousness. But rather than ending in aphasia or speechlessness, Phelan suggests that there are other orders of knowledge and experience beyond such structures that the body can access.

Phelan's argument supports the idea that the dancer has a special potential to explore the body's capacity to experience and gather such information. She compares the physical condition of the hysteric to that of the dancer where the absence of inbuilt narratives or order is played out as the dancer "*consciously* performs the body's discovery of its temporal and spatial dimensions."[48] While the psychic symptom of the hysteric results from the unconscious repression of "material that consciousness cannot fully absorb," the dancer's "symptomatic act" (as Felicia McCarren describes it) works to advantage the body's ability to access and express things "that consciousness and its discursive formations cannot."[49] If the dancing body in dancefilm is accessing corporeal knowledge and forms of expression that elude thought, what impact do the resulting originary gestures have upon the gestural exchange between film and viewer?

The idea that the body's systems of organization diverge from those of consciousness, and that the hysteric and the dancer share a capacity to "play out" and explore the body's temporal and spatial dimensions directly, brings me to the notion of *somatic intelligence* as a meeting ground between dancefilm and its audiences. While this term has great currency across dance studies, I would like to look at the way the concept was addressed by both Jane Goodall and William McClure in papers presented at a Sydney dance forum in 1997 that go beyond the terms of choreographic process. Goodall describes "how bodies think and how movement might be a form of thinking" in her essay, "Knowing What You're Doing." For Goodall, somatic intelligence provides a term that overcomes the mind/body binary instituted by René Descartes and reiterated by Darwinian hierarchies. Goodall recounts

---

[47] Peggy Phelan, *Mourning Sex: Performing Public Memories* (London: Routledge, 1997), 52.
[48] Idem.
[49] Ibid, 54.

physiological forms of intelligence gathering such as the mimicry of action and spoken language practiced by children and the indigenous people encountered by Charles Darwin "in the field." She describes how these examples provide evidence of a type of intelligence grounded in the body that is of equal value to forms of intelligence associated with cerebral logic and discourse. Goodall suggests that somatic forms of intelligence gathering have been programmatically eliminated from modern life. She cites "a loss of exploratory movement in everyday life," suggesting that "sex is about the only place left for it," along with the type of dancing that embraces experimentation and exploration.[50]

For McClure, somatic intelligence is the place in both philosophical discourse and dance where one is "cast outside the familiar surroundings of given structures"; "it is only feelings and sensations which can be admitted into this strange place— the only intelligence which can be had of the unformed is a somatic intelligence." Like Lyotard's affect, McClure's somatic intelligence is "a matter of receptivity" prior to conceptualization, but, unlike Lyotard's concept, the means by which we traverse the passage toward the unknown "is in this body...which feels where thought fails."[51] McClure puts the body firmly in the position of reception of the actus, prior to response: "The body feels before knowing where and when and what it is feeling." He equates such a place to "the abyss which separates one phrase of movement from the next," recalling Godard's *gestural anacrusis*: the "source" of movement, the "pre-movement zone."[52] This again illustrates how the dancer in dancefilm—and thus the audience member—can occupy the very place where bodily knowledge demands attention but where discourse fails.

When confronted with dancefilm as a work of art, the spectator may well fall prey to aphasia, but this does not mark the end of the encounter. By altering the terms of the discussion to those informed by the body, one allows for the fact that there are *corporeal* knowledges and experiences that are both given and received in the aesthetic encounter, specifically in the case of dancefilm. This fact has been implicit in my discussion of dancefilm where I have described cinematic operations in corporeal terms (*micro-choreographies*, *gestural stylization*, *gestural anacrusis*, *idiogest*) and have often hinted at the affective impact of such work. With the originary gesture of the dancefilm founded in the operations of dance and choreography (whether corporeally realized or not), it is the moving body that sets the terms for the encounter and the entire circuit of gestural exchange. We meet the actus of the work of art with exploratory movements through a gestural exchange with the dancefilm. The following description of a somatic model of the mise en scène provides a site for the playing out of the gestural exchange, from the component gestures to the affect of the gestural thrust, to our gestures of response.

Lyotard's article, "The Unconscious As Mise-en-scène," contains a model of the mise en scène that returns us to the actus/situs merger of dancefilm. This article,

---

[50] Jane Goodall, "Knowing What You're Doing," *The Performance Space Quarterly*, 14 (Winter 1997): 23. In this essay, Goodall references a live performance, *Bug*, by Sue-ellen Kohler, which was the basis for the film *Vivarium* (1993, d. Mahalya Middlemist), discussed in Chapter 2.

[51] McClure (1997), 24–25.

[52] Ibid, 26.

written in 1977, also addresses the conditions of aesthetic production and previews some of the themes in "Gesture and Commentary" but draws on examples from live performance and film—Richard Strauss's opera, *Der Rosenkavalier* (1911), and Michael Snow's film, *La Région Centrale* (1970–71)—which brings his ideas closer to my subject than the plastic arts referenced in "Gesture and Commentary."[53]

In "The Unconscious As Mise-en-scène," *mise en scène* is defined by Lyotard as "to stage"—"to transmit signifiers from a 'primary' space to another space, which is the auditorium of a theater, cinema, or any related art."[54] For our purposes, and in relation to dancefilm, this would refer to the transmission of the profilmic performance, as well as the lighting, the use of the camera, editing, and so on, to make up the new "space" of the cinematic mise en scène.[55] Lyotard describes how a "single reference imposed on all the messages which make up the work" is utilized to avoid the potential disorder that could result from the "heterogeneity of the arts" that makes up the mise en scène.[56] In his example of a Strauss opera, this single reference is the story of *Der Rosenkavalier*. But his next point is that this reference is also the *product* of the mise en scène. The reference produces *and is produced by* the mise en scène just as the gesture in Lyotard's gestural model of aesthetic production "is situated in and situates space-time."

The differences between the example Lyotard uses here and dancefilm are significant. The story of *Der Rosenkavalier* is a determined single reference that is actualized in the staging or mise en scène of the performance of Strauss's late nineteenth-century Viennese opera. The gestures of dancefilm are not determined or actualized. They have more in common with the Snow example mentioned above, which Lyotard arrives at later in the essay: They tend to have unidentified objects/objectives, decentralized subjects, and they do not support one singular truth but a multiplicity of perspectives. But the above description of the central gesture or story of the film *being produced by the mise en scène that it also produces*, along with the concept of "somatography," runs across both classical and contemporary examples in Lyotard's essay.

Lyotard gives the mise en scène the power of bestowing *life*, and what it brings to life is bodies:

"Give life" means two things: 1) the mise-en-scéne turns written signifiers into speech, song, and movements executed by bodies capable of moving, singing and speaking; [2)] and this transcription is intended for other living bodies—the spectators—capable of

---

[53] *La Région Centrale* is discussed at the end of the article as an example of a "postmodern" cinematographic mise en scène, which is set in opposition to the classic model of the mise en scène informing Sigmund Freud's psychoanalytic methodology that Lyotard equates with the staging of a Richard Strauss opera. He writes: "My goal in choosing [Snow's work] is to make clear *a contrario* just how much the Freudian conception of the unconscious and even desire depends on a particular esthetic [sic], that of official late nineteenth century Viennese theater and opera" (Ibid, 95). I will not go into Lyotard's argument relating to Freud's unconscious as mise en scène here, as my interest is in his proposed model of mise en scène in relation to theater and film.

[54] Ibid, 87.

[55] James Monaco defines the *cinematic mise en scène* as: "The term usually used to denote that part of the cinematic process that takes place on the set, as opposed to montage, which takes place afterwards. Literally the 'putting-in-the-scene': the direction of actors, placement of cameras, choice of lenses et cetera" (James Monaco, *How to Read a Film* [New York: Oxford University Press, 1981], 441).

[56] Lyotard (1977), 87.

being moved by these songs, movements, and words. It is this transcribing on and for bodies, considered as multi-sensory personalities, which is the work characteristic of the mise-en-scéne.[57]

Lyotard describes this *transcription* as "a kind of somatography"—a writing on/of the body.[58] He then goes on to compare the mise en scène itself to those human bodies it brings to life and that it gathers into play. Lyotard writes of the mise en scène's "elementary unity" being "polyesthetic like the human body," and that "[t]he idea of performance" with which the mise en scène is associated "seems linked to the idea of inscription on the body."[59]

The term *somatography* offers a concept of cinematic production that, like somatic intelligence, grounds my discussion in terms of the body, providing the language to consider a gestural cinematic exchange dominated by originary gestures based on dance and choreography. In doing so, it also provides room for the inclusion of affect, spectators "capable of being moved," as yet another somatically grounded element in the gestural exchange of dancefilm. In such a situation, the idea of a corporeal(-like) mise en scène takes on special meaning and significance; the mise en scène becomes the site of the affective encounter where bodies collide with bodies rather than thought, where the transcription of signifiers into the component gestures of the work of art are met by the gestures of the "living bodies" who are capable of feeling. What Lyotard suggests is a mise en scène that acts as a kind of sensitive field, a "polyesthetic" site, that mimics the body's physical susceptibilities and its performative tendencies in order to carry out its duties of transmission between other performative bodies: *a corporeal mise en scène.*[60]

Revisiting Maya Deren's *Ritual in Transfigured Time* (1946), I can speculate on the kinds of effects that this gestural exchange might provoke. The insistent invitation found in this film, with the gestural language drawing us into the call-and-response relation, can be taken a step further with the physiological dimension of Lyotard's corporeal model of the mise en scène. The proximity found to be central to the film's movements can be re-read as an expression of the autonomy of the affect—the affect that we see moving between the figures on screen, the gestures they throw to each other and that seem to pass around the group without being absorbed and without actual contact being made, "contaminates" the mise en scène in the manner of Lyotard's polyesthetic model. The gestural exchange has begun and we are drawn into a circuit of transference where the polyesthetic entities involved resonate with the same potentialities, but realize none; our engagement sustains as a potential in the manner of the originary gestures on screen.

The terms for such a gestural exchange were already in place in the pre-cinematic performances of Loïe Fuller. The gestures of Fuller's art have been described as exemplifying two key characteristics of dancefilm: the fusion of a motile corporeality with

---

[57] Ibid, 88.
[58] Idem.
[59] Lyotard (1977), 88.
[60] *Aesthetics*, in its original meaning, refers to "things perceptible by the senses as opposed to things thinkable or immaterial," so the polyaesthetic body would be one susceptible to the multiple activities of the senses (Onions 1993).

technology to transform the figure's capacity for meaning production, and the figure's ability to influence the space-time configuration in which it exists. As a performance that "redefines the female body as a producer of images,"[61] Fuller's dancing prefigured the role of the moving body in dancefilm as that which can exceed language-based representation and deny the reduction of the body to a definable totality. Her performance was a work of art that had an undeniable impact on its recipients and a revolutionary effect on language. As Fuller herself stated, "I can express this force which is indefinable but certain in its impact. I have motion…motion and not language is truthful."[62] Through a fusion with the component gestures of technology, the performing body disappears into the mise en scène to the place of the unformed where the only constant is motion, creating the conditions for the responses of writers such as Stéphane Mallarmé and Paul Valéry who, more than willingly, acceded to the conditions of the originary gesture that remained unassimilable. The multiple, mobile subjectivity produced through the mise en scène also claimed the surrounding space in a perfect example of the merging of actus and situs, the whole encounter having a corporeal character prescribed by the originary gesture.

The cine-choreographic operations in films such as *Water Motor* (1978, d. Babette Mangolte) also begin with originary gestures that are challenging, this time to the extreme. Yvonne Rainer describes the movement of Trisha Brown featured in these films as "something that was truly new…. The pressure was clearly on me—on all of us in the audience—to 'see again,' to catch up with the spirit that was leading the way."[63] This movement, which I have called *anarchic phrasing*, calls for radical component gestures in the transmission to the mise en scène of the work of art, demanding an intense discourse between the heterogeneous elements. The dance is dissolved into the new cine-choreographic order that is founded on the *gestural anacrusis*, the pre-movement zone that I have compared to the pre-gestural site of the affect. In this dancefilm order, the pre-gestural—the exploration and discovery of the body's geography—dominates the terms of the exchange, so that the gestural circuit absorbs the affect. The originary gesture, which is itself described as *disarmed*, is so sympathetic to the terms of the affect that the entire circuit takes on a corporeal, affective quality.

In the case of *micro-choreographic* operations in dancefilm, the non-hierarchied, multiple sites of the performing body shot in close-up produce a polyesthetic mise en scène that can "draw our attention to movements, poses, and gestures of the body as sites of meaning and/or affect," to quote Jodi Brooks.[64] The staging of these originary, performative gestures that draw attention to their occurring in the space-time of the mise en scène create a decentralized, mutable, "constantly changing surface," a "sensory surface" that articulates through consistent motion.[65] The filmed subject is

[61] Felicia McCarren, "The 'Symptomatic' Act Circa 1900: Hysteria, Hypnosis, Electricity and Dance," *Critical Inquiry*, 21, 4 (1995a): 758.

[62] Loïe Fuller, *Fifteen Years of a Dancer's Life* (New York: Dance Horizons, 1913), 71–72.

[63] Yvonne Rainer, "Engineering Calamity: Trisha Brown," *Writings on Dance*, 18–19 (Winter 1999b): 177.

[64] Jodi Brooks, "Rituals of the Filmic Body," *Writings on Dance: Dance on Screen*, 17 (Summer 1997–1998): 17.

[65] Ibid, 19.

open to the action of the close-up upon it, merging the actus and situs into a mise en scène that constitutes a micro-choreography. The spectator enters into the "sensory" mise en scène, acceding to the affectivity of this gestural exchange. As Trevor Patrick describes, in the case of his film *Nine Cauldrons* (1997, d. Paul Hampton and Trevor Patrick), the activity of a somatic intelligence or corporeal intelligence gathering, a "dialogue between body and mind... offers the viewer a point of entry into the experience of the body" that can only be met by the body of the spectator *first*, prior to a more formulated response.[66]

What of the gestural order in those dancefilms where recognizable human bodies are absent, but a dancerly or choreographic quality dominates? In Lyotard's essay "Acinema," Michael Snow's *La Région Centrale* provides a kind of marker in relation to non-functional, nonfigurative-based movement coinciding as it does with Lyotard's description of a "simple *sterile difference* in an audio-visual field."[67] The same actus/situs merger exists but in a different configuration. Lyotard writes that "all the figures smash themselves on Snow's film," a very different description to the ordered mise en scène of *Der Rosenkavalier* with its commanding single reference that controls the heterogeneous elements.[68]

In *La Région Centrale*, the "figures" or individual "gestures" find their way into the mise en scène via the camera's movements, which are produced via a mechanical device that allows the camera a full range of movement around the point where it is fixed to a shaft that also rotates. Thus, "the accumulation of figures on the film succeeds in not constituting any identifiable geometric space, such as a stage," nor any ordered development through time.[69] Yet the "deframing" that this results in only intensifies the conflation of the actus and the situs, the two floating free of any determinations or actualities beyond the mechanical facts related to the shoot. This happens at both levels: The mise en scène is entirely bound to the random gestures of the filmic apparatus, and the spectator has nothing to do but become another floating gesture within the exchange, acceding to the actions of the originating gestures of the film.

There is a continuation of the idea of somatography across the two examples Lyotard provides. He writes in relation to Snow's film:

> Language is not made for telling the truth and film is not made to disguise truth on a fantasmatic stage. Both are inexhaustible means for experimenting.... They create their own reference, therefore their object is not identifiable; they create their own addressee, a disconcerted body, invited to stretch its sensory capacities beyond measure.[70]

The film's mise en scène creates a specific spectatorial body through experimentation with cinematic movement and ideas of referentiality and objectivity, and in complicating the single reference of the classic mise en scène throws up a challenge

---

[66] Trevor Patrick, "Subtle Bodies," MAP *Movement and Performance Symposium Papers*, ed. Erin Brannigan, 34 (Canberra: Ausdance Inc., 1999).
[67] Lyotard (1978), 53.
[68] Lyotard (1977), 96.
[69] Ibid, 97.
[70] Ibid, 96.

for the bodies it puts into discourse. The bodies involved in the transcription or somatography of this film's mise en scène are "stretched" to new limits.

The motion studies I have described such as *Emak Bakia* (1927, d. Man Ray) and the abstraction of the profilmic performance in films such as *Infected* (2001, d. Gina Czarnecki) and *Scrub Solo Series* (2000–2001, d. Antonin de Bemels) are affiliated with the extreme example of Snow's film described here by Lyotard. In *Emak Bakia*, an indulgence in close-ups unrelated to a narrative drive produces a "poetry of things" through the animation of objects. The small, unidentified moving parts produce independent, animated micro-choreographies that float free of any determination, constituting movement for movement's sake. The mechanical transformation at the site of the mise en scène produces abstract, dancerly motion that stretches the sensory capacity of the viewer who has no reference point for these manufactured motions.

The movements in *Infected* present a similar challenge to the "disconcerted body" of the spectator. The viewer enters into this somatography where the profilmic body is so transformed through special effects that it produces a cine-choreography of the order of the unformed. The stage of the mise en scène becomes a shifting foundation; the movements elude our ability to follow. Again the spectator is set adrift in a gestural circuit where the originary gesture provides little to hang onto. Our improvised, extemporaneous responses begin with an encounter with an unknown and uncanny mode of somatic expression.

This is a cinema where all of the tendencies of the gestural exchange I have developed through Lyotard's writings reach a limit of some sort. The call-and-response imperative of the autonomous gesture produces a "disconcerted" audience response, and the performative, improvisatory nature of the gestural sphere that calls us to work on the potential there presents a real challenge to our physical and mental capacity. The actus/situs merger and the role of the mise en scène as a polyesthestic field mimics the work of bodies both on and off screen that are stretched to new limits. This is a cinema where "the force used to stage something has no goal other than to make manifest its potentiality," its life as a space-time-matter event: a cinema of "heretofore unexperienced intensities" that "permit us to quarter sensibility and draw it out beyond this old body."[71]

In this conclusion to the book, I have offered a model for considering the operations of dancefilm that includes all aspects of this particular type of screen art form: from the profilmic, originary gestures, through the cinematic elements of the filmic performance that constitute the component gestures, to the somatography where the affective force on the body of the spectator meets the bodies brought to life by the mise en scène. Lyotard's ideas regarding the production and reception of the work of art and the general nature of the mise en scène across disciplinary distinctions, together with notions of somatic expression and intelligence drawn from writings on dance, provide terms for an analysis of dancefilm grounded in the body and gesture rather than language and logic. The corporeal profile of this model of gestural exchange has

---

[71] Ibid, 97–98.

been applied to the variety of examples from across the cine-choreographic orders represented in this book.

This chapter thus draws together the specific characteristics of cine-choreographic orders such as those dominated by depersonalization, micro-choreographies, and the gestural anacrusis, in a consideration of the more general terms of dancefilm. Those terms include the challenging nature of the originary gestures (referred to elsewhere in the book as the oppositional tendencies of dance), the influence of those gestures on the quality of the film as a whole, and the motile character of each component of the filmic performance. These "performative" characteristics, in turn, have an effect on the spectatorial encounter with dancefilm, highlighting the affinity of the form's operations with those of the affect. The autonomy that characterizes the gestural operations in dancefilm calls for the very process of analysis undertaken throughout this book. Critical discourse around dancefilm requires specific attention to the unique, radical, and divergent characteristics of its production and reception, calling for terms that take into account its multisensory and kinaesthetic nature.

This final chapter is also a call for considering the particularity of dancefilm not only within screen culture but within the arts in general, including the plastic and performing arts with which dancefilm has always connected. Lyotard's model of the reception of the work of art provides an opportunity for such a perspective. Being a deeply interdisciplinary form, I have addressed the historical confrontation of creative disciplines evidenced in the development of dancefilm across this book by bringing film theory, dance theory, and philosophy to the task of describing dominant aesthetic modes or operations in the form. This has produced interdisciplinary terminology that points to the new filmic and choreographic practices instituted by dancefilm.

Essential to this process has been the identification of a body of work that is international in scale and includes vastly divergent forms. Researching a broad range of examples in film and video archives around the world revealed a *cinema of movement* that is characterized by distinctive techniques, operations, and effects. Key examples have illustrated the specific types of cinematic movements produced by dancefilm: micromovements, deterritorialized movement, vertical movement, stylized movement, movement that transfers across people and things, continual and excessive movement. All of these cine-choreographies have been linked to dance practices and vice versa so that the radical quality of these movement orders—which can appear to challenge the limits of cinematic movement per se—have been traced to the nature of dance as an oppositional form of human action. This particular understanding of dance may appear to conflict with the postmodern charter that brought dance closer to the pedestrian body, but it reflects the condition of the choreographic when it enters cinematic terrain, whether film art or film industry.

Like the recurrence of *gesture* across this book, *dance* and *choreography* have been applied in both their most specific and broadly conceptual terms, indicating how ubiquitous, far-reaching, and productive all three concepts are, connecting dancefilm to so many other fields of creative production and critical inquiry. The films and videos of artists such as Maya Deren, Bob Fosse, Jean Renoir, Chris Cunningham, Babette Mangolte, and Man Ray are all extensive forms with connections to numerous aesthetic traditions and ideas (for example, ritual, abstraction, genre, experimentation, and advertising). But the examples I have chosen from each art-ist's body of work—which often involved collaborations with dancers and choreographers—can all be understood as participating in this cinema of movement through their demonstration of cine-choreographic operations. So while indicating how dispersive this cinema of movement can be, I have also detailed some aesthetic, and corresponding theoretical, parameters for dancefilm. These contributions are offered as gestures whose potential will only be realized, of course, through circulation and exchange.

Filmmography

Affair in Trinidad (1952, d. Vincent Sherman)
All Is Full of Love (1999, d. Chris Cunningham)
Amy Muller (1896, Edison Motion Pictures)
Annabelle Serpentine Dance (1897, d. Thomas A. Edison)
At Land (1944, d. Maya Deren)
The Bandwagon (1953, d. Vincente Minnelli)
Behaviour (1995, d. Margie Medlin)
Betsy Ross Dance (1903, American Mutoscope and Biograph Co.)
Betty Ford (2002, d. Oliver Husain, Michel Klöfkorn, and Anna Berger)
Black and Tan (1929, d. Dudley Murphy)
Black Spring (2002, d. Benoit Dervaux)
Blush (2005, d. Wim Vandekeybus)
boy (1995, d. Peter Anderson and Rosemary Lee)
Brigadoon (1954, d. Vincente Minnelli)
Broken Blossoms (1919, d. D. W. Griffith)
Bus Stop (1956, d. Joshua Logan)
Cabaret (1972, d. Bob Fosse)
Carefree (1938, d. Mark Sandrich)
Carmencita (1894, d. William K. L. Dickson)
Contrecoup (1997, d. Pascal Magnin)
Cover Girl (1944, Charles Vidor)
da nero a nero. Tempo per pensare (1999, d. Anna de Manincor)
A Dance of the Ages (1913, d. Thomas A. Edison)
Danse Serpentine (c.1900, d. Paul Nadar)
Dance Serpentine, No. 765 (1896, d. Louis Lumière)
Dancer in the Dark (2000, d. Lars von Trier)
Dancing Lady (1933, d. David O. Selznick)
The Dancing Pirate (1936, d. Lloyd Corrigan)
Dead Dreams of Monochrome Men (1990, d. David Hinton)
Divine Horsemen (1977, from Haitian Voudou footage shot by Maya Deren between 1947 and
    1954, posthumously assembled by Teiji and Cherel Ito)
Dust (1998, d. Anthony Atanasio)
Elba and Frederico (1993, d. Wim Vandekeybus)
Element (1973, d. Amy Greenfield)
Emak Bakia (1927, d. Man Ray)
Entr'Acte (1924, Francis Picabia and René Clair)
Falling (1991, d. Mahalya Middlemist)
Film about a Woman Who . . . (1974, d. Yvonne Rainer)
Fisticuffs (2004, d. Miranda Pennell)
Flying Down to Rio (1933, d. Thornton Freeland)

Follow the Fleet (1936, d. Mark Sandrich)
The Gay Divorcee (1934, d. Mark Sandrich)
Gentlemen Prefer Blondes (1953, d. Howard Hawks)
Gilda (1946, d. Charles Vidor)
Gold Diggers of 1933 (1933, d. Mervyn LeRoy)
Hand Movie (1968, d. Yvonne Rainer)
Hands (1995, d. Adam Roberts)
Human Radio (2002, d. Miranda Pennell)
Immersion (1998, d. Jodi Kaplan)
Infected (2001, Gina Czarnecki)
In Person (1935, d. William A. Seiter)
In the Mirror of Maya Deren (2001, d. Martina Kudláček)
Intolerance (1916, D. W. Griffiths)
Jeanne d'Arc (1928, d. Carl Theodor Dreyer)
Jeanne Dielman, 23 Quai du Commerce, 1080 Bruxelles (1975, d. Chantal Akerman)
Kangaroo (1998, d. Pierre Yves Clouin)
Karina (1902, American Mutoscope and Biograph Co.)
Kitty Foyle (1940, d. Sam Wood)
La Création de la Danse Serpentine (1908, Segundo de Chomon)
La Marche des Machines (1928, d. Eugene Deslaw)
La Région Centrale (1970–1971, d. Michael Snow)
Ladies of the Chorus (1949, d. Phil Karlson)
La féerie des ballets fantastiques de Loïe Fuller (1934, d. Gab Sorère and George Busby)
The Lament of the Empress (1989, d. Pina Bausch)
Le Lys (1934, d. George R. Busby)
Le Lys de la Vie (1921, d. Loïe Fuller)
Let's Make Love (1960, d. George Cukor)
The Little Big (1999, d. Pierre Yves Clouin)
Little Lillian Toe Dancer (1903, American Mutoscope and Biograph Co.)
Lives of Performers (1972, d. Yvonne Rainer)
Loïe Fuller et ses imitatrices (1994, d. Giovanni Lista)
Lucky (2001, d. Clara van Gool)
Magnetic North (2003, d. Miranda Pennell)
The Man Who Envied Women (1985, d. Yvonne Rainer)
Meditation on Violence (1948, d. Maya Deren)
Meshes of the Afternoon (1943, d. Maya Deren)
The Moebius Strip (2002, d. Vincent Pluss)
Monoloog van Fumiyo Ikeda op het einde van Ottone, Ottone, (1989, d. Anne Teresa De
    Keersmaeker and Walter Verdin)
Mouchette (1967, d. Robert Bresson)
Movement from the Soul (1990, d. Dayna Goldfine and Daniel Geller)
News from Home (1976, d. Chantal Akerman)
Niagara (1953, d. Henry Hathaway)
Nine Cauldrons (1997, d. Paul Hampton and Trevor Patrick)
Nussin (1998, d. Clara van Gool)
Oklahoma (1955, d. Fred Zinnemann)
On the Town (1949, d. Stanley Donen and Gene Kelly)
Orphans of the Storm (1921, d. D. W. Griffith)
Our Dancing Daughters (1928, d. Harry Beaumont)
The Pajama Game (1957, d. Stanley Donen and George Abbott)

The Prince and the Showgirl (1957, d. Lawrence Olivier)
Princess Ali (1895, Edison Motion Pictures)
Princess Rajah Dance (1904, American Mutoscope and Biograph Co.)
Reines d'un Jour (1996, d. Pascal Magnin)
Resonance (1991, d. Stephen Cummins and Simon Hunt)
Ritual in Transfigured Time (1945–1946, d. Maya Deren)
River of No Return (1954, d. Otto Preminger)
Ruth Dennis, Skirt Dancer (1894, Edison Co.)
Scrub Solo Series (1999–2001, d. Antonin De Bemels)
Serpentine Dance (performed by Ameta, 1903, American Mutoscope and Biograph Co.)
Serpentine Dance (performed by Crissie Sheridan, 1897, d. Thomas A. Edison)
Seven Brides for Seven Brothers (1954, d. Stanley Donen)
Shall We Dance (1937, d. Mark Sandrich)
Silk Stockings (1957, d. Rouben Mamoulian)
Singin' in the Rain (1952, d. Stanley Donen and Gene Kelly)
Some Like It Hot (1959, d. Billy Wilder)
So This Is Paris (1926, d. Ernst Lubitsch)
The Sound of Music (1965, d. Robert Wise)
South Pacific (1958, d. Joshua Logan)
A Star Is Born (1954, d. Sidney Luft)
The Story of Vernon and Irene Castle (1939, d. H. C. Potter)
The Strawberry Blonde (1941, d. Raoul Walsh)
Stroboscopic Trilogy (2003–2005, d. Antonin De Bemels)
A Study in Choreography for Camera (1945, d. Maya Deren)
Sur un air de Charleston (1926, d. Jean Renoir)
Sweet Charity (1969, d. Bob Fosse)
Swing Time (1936, d. George Stevens)
Tattoo (2001, d. Miranda Pennell)
There's No Business Like Show Business (1954, d. Walter Lang)
Three Satie Spoons (1961, d. Yvonne Rainer)
Ticket to Tomahawk (1950, d. Richard Sale)
Top Hat (1935, d. Mark Sandrich)
Torres Strait Islanders (1898, d. Alfred Cort Haddon)
Touched (1994, d. David Hinton)
Transport (1971, d. Amy Greenfield)
Trio A (1978, d. Yvonne Rainer)
Undercurrent (2000, d. Catherine Greenhalgh)
The Very Eye of Night (1959, d. Maya Deren)
Vivarium (1993, d. Mahalya Middlemist)
Volleyball (1967, d. Yvonne Rainer)
Water Motor (1978, d. Babette Mangolte)
Watermotor for Dancer and Camera (1980, d. Peter Campus)
Waterproof (1986, d. Jean-Louis Le Tacon)
The Whirl of Life (1915, d. Oliver D. Bailey)
Workman (1998, d. Pierre Yves Clouin)
Yankee Doodle Dandy (1942, d. Hal B. Wallis and William Cagney)
You Made Me Love You (2005, d. Miranda Pennell)
You'll Never Get Rich (1941, d. Sidney Lanfield)
Young Man of Manhattan (1930, d. Monta Bell)

Bibliography

Acocella, J., and Garafola, L. editors. *André Levinson on Dance: Writings from Paris in the Twenties*. Anover and London: Wesleyan University Press, 1991.

Agamben, Giorgio. *Means without End: Notes on Politics*, trans. Vincenzo Binetti and Cesare Casarino. Minneapolis: University of Minnesota Press, 2000.

Albright, Ann Cooper. *Traces of Light: Absence and Presence in the Work of Loïe Fuller*. Middletown, Connecticut: Wesleyan University Press, 2007.

Albright, Rick editor, *Genre, the Musical: A Reader*. London: Routledge, 1981.

Altman, Rick. *The American Film Musical*. Indianapolis: Indiana University Press, 1987.

Arroyo, José. "How Do You Solve a Problem Like von Trier?" *Sight and Sound* 10, no. 9 (2000): 14–16.

Asman, Carrie. "Return of the Sign to the Body: Benjamin and Gesture in the Age of Retheatricalization." *Discourse* 16, no. 3 (1993): 46–64.

Auerbach, Jonathan. *Body Shots: Early Cinema's Incarnations*. Berkeley: University of California Press, 2007.

Aumont, Jacques. *Du Visage au cinéma*. Paris: Éditions de l'Etoile/*Cahiers du cinéma*, 1992.

Auslander, Philip. *Liveness: Performance in a Mediatized Culture*. London: Routledge, 1999.

Balázs, Béla. *Theory of the Film: Character and Growth of a New Art*, trans. Edith Bone. New York: Arno Press, 1972.

———. "Visible Man, or the Culture of Film (1924)." Intro. Erica Carter, trans. Rodney Livingstone. *Screen* 48, no. 1 (Spring 2007): 91–108.

Banes, Sally. *Dancing Women: Female Bodies on Stage*. London: Routledge, 1998.

———. "An Open Field: Yvonne Rainer As Dance Theorist." In Sachs (2003), 21–39.

Bargues, M., and A. Coutinot editors. *Impressions Danse Catalogue*. Paris: Georges Pompidou Centre, 1988.

Barthes, Roland. *Mythologies*, ed. and trans. Annette Lavers. London: Granada, 1973.

Bazin, André. *What Is Cinema? Volume 1*, ed. and trans. Hugh Gray. Berkeley: University of California Press, 1967.

Bean, Jennifer M. "Technologies of Early Stardom and the Extraordinary Body." *Camera Obscura* 48, 16, no. 3 (2001): 8–57.

Benjamin, Walter. *Illuminations*, ed. Hannah Arendt, trans. Harry Zohn. London: Fontana Press, 1982.

Bergson, Henri. *Creative Evolution*, trans. Arthur Mitchell. New York: Dover Publications, 1998.

Berman, Marshall. *All That Is Solid Melts Into Air: The Experience of Modernity*. New York: Viking Penguin, 1988.

Bozzini, Annie. "They Film As They Dance." *Ballett International* no. 1 (1991): 37–39.

Bramley, Ian. "Return of the Narrative." *Dance Theatre Journal* 14, no. 4 (1999): 26–29.

Brannigan, Erin. "Maya Deren, Dance, and Gestural Encounters in *Ritual in Transfigured Time*." *Senses of Cinema* no. 22, (Sept-Oct 2002). Online, Available: http://archive.sensesofcinema.com/contents/02/22/deren.html. December 30, 2008.

———. "'La Loïe' As Pre-Cinematic Performance—Descriptive Continuity of Movement." *Senses of Cinema* no. 28 (Sept–Oct 2003). Online. Available: www.sensesofcinema.com/contents/03/28/la_loie.html. December 30, 2008.

———. "Great Directors: Yvonne Rainer." *Senses of Cinema* no. 27, (July-Aug 2003). Online. Available: http://archive.sensesofcinema.com/contents/directors/03/rainer.html. December 30, 2008.

Braudy, Leo. *The World in a Frame: What We See in Films.* New York: Anchor Press/Doubleday, 1977.

Brooks, Jodi. "Rituals of the Filmic Body." *Writings on Dance: Dance on Screen*, no. 17 (Summer 1997–1998): 15–20.

———. "Crisis and the Everyday: Some Thoughts on Gesture and Crisis in Cassavetes and Benjamin." In Stern and Kouvaros (1999), 73–104.

———. "Ghosting the Machine: the Sounds of Tap and the Sounds of Film." *Screen* 44, no. 4 (2003): 355–78.

Brooks, Virginia. "Dance and Film." *Ballett International* no. 2 (1993a): 23–25.

———. "Movement in Fixed Space and Time." *Ballett International*, no. 3 (1993b): 25–27.

Brown, Trisha. "Locus, 1975." In Teicher (2002), 87.

Bukatman, Scott. *Matters of Gravity: Special Effects and Supermen in the 20th Century.* Durham: Duke University Press, 2003.

Burt, Ramsay. *Alien Bodies: Representations of Modernity, "Race" and Nation in Early Modern Dance.* London: Routledge, 1998.

———. *Judson Dance Theatre: Performative Traces.* New York: Routledge, 2006.

Butler, Alison. "'Motor-driven Metaphysics': Movement, Time and Action in the Films of Maya Deren." *Screen*, 48, no. 1 (2007): 1–23.

Cage, John. "Grace and Clarity." In Kostelanetz (1992), 21–24.

Carroll, Noël. "Toward a Definition of Moving-Picture Dance." *Dance Research Journal* 33, no. 1 (2001): 46–61.

Carter, Alexandra editor. *The Routledge Dance Studies Reader.* London: Routledge, 1998.

Charney, L., and Schwartz, V. R. editors. *Cinema and the Invention of Modern Life.* Berkeley: University of California Press, 1995.

Clark, V. A., Hodson, M., and Neiman, C. editors. *The Legend of Maya Deren: A Documentary Biography and Collected Works. Volume 1 Part One: Signatures (1917–42).* New York: Anthology Film Archives, 1984.

———. *The Legend of Maya Deren: A Documentary Biography and Collected Works. Volume 1 Part Two: Chambers (1942–47).* New York: Anthology Film Archives, 1988.

Climenhaga, Royd. *Pina Bausch.* London: Routledge, 2009.

Cohan, Steven. "'Feminizing' the Song-and-Dance Man: Fred Astaire and the Spectacle of Masculinity in the Hollywood Musical." In Cohan and Hark (1993), 46–69.

Cohan, Steven, and Hark, Ina Rae. *Screening the Male: Exploring Masculinities in Hollywood Cinema.* London: Routledge, 1993.

Collins, Jim. "Toward Defining a Matrix of the Musical Comedy: The Place of the Spectator Within the Textual Mechanisms." In Altman (1981), 134–46.

Cook, Pam. *The Cinema Book.* London: BFI, 1985.

Copeland, R., and Cohen, M. editors. *What Is Dance?* Oxford: Oxford University Press, 1983.

Copeland, R. "The Limitations of Cine-dance." In *Filmdance Festival* program. New York: The Experimental Intermedia Foundation, 1983, 7–11.

Cowan, Michael. "The Heart Machine: 'Rhythm' and Body in Weimer Film and Fritz Lang's Metropolis." *Modernism/Modernity* 14, no. 2 (2007): 225–48.

Cowie, B., and Aggiss, L. with Bramley, I. editors. *Anarchic Dance.* London: Routledge, 2006.

Crisp, Clement. "Past Glories Recaptured," *Financial Times*, December 16, 1989.

Cunningham, M., and Lesschaeve, J. *The Dancer and the Dance*. New York: Marion Boyars, 1991.

Current, R. N., and Current, M. E. *Loie Fuller: Goddess of Light*. Boston: Northeastern University Press, 1997.

Daly, Ann. *Critical Gestures: Writings on Dance and Culture*. Middletown, Connecticut: Wesleyan University Press, 2002.

———. *Done into Dance: Isadora Duncan in America*. Bloomington: Indiana University Press, 1995.

DeFrantz, Thomas F. "Due Unto Dunham." *Village Voice*, June 6, 2006.

Delamater, Jerome. *Dance in the Hollywood Musical*. Michigan: UMI Research Press, 1981.

Deleuze, Gilles. *Cinema 1: The Movement-Image*, trans. Hugh Tomlinson and Barbara Habberjam. Minneapolis: University of Minnesota Press, 1986.

———. *Cinema 2: The Time-Image*, trans. Hugh Tomlinson and Robert Galeta. Minneapolis: University of Minnesota Press, 1989.

———. *Negotiations: 1972–1990*. New York: Columbia University Press, 1995.

Deleuze, G., and Guattari, F. *A Thousand Plateaus: Capitalism and Schizophrenia*, trans. Brian Massumi. London: The Athlone Press, 1988.

Delsarte, François. *Delsarte System of Oratory*. New York: Edgar S. Werner, 1893.

De Morinni, Clare. "Loie Fuller: The Fairy of Light." *Dance Index* 1, no. 3 (1942): 40–51.

Dempster, Elizabeth. "Women Writing the Body: Let's Watch a Little How She Dances." In Carter (1998), 223–29.

Deren, Maya. "Chamber Films." *Filmwise* no. 2 (1961): 38–39.

———. "Notes, Essays, Letters." *Film Culture* no. 39 (1965): 1–56.

———. "Cine-Dance." *Dance Perspectives* no. 30 (1967): 10–13.

———. "An Anagram of Ideas on Art, Form and Film." In Nichols (2001), 267–322.

Deren, M., Miller, A., Thomas, D., Tyler, P., and Mass, W. "Poetry and the Film: A Symposium." In Sitney (1971), 171–86.

Desmond, Jane. "Dancing out the Difference: Cultural Imperialism and Ruth St. Denis's 'Radha' of 1906." *signs* 17, no. 1 (1991): 28–49.

Doane, Mary Ann. "The Close-Up: Scale and Detail in the Cinema." *Differences: A Journal of Feminist Cultural Studies* 14, no. 3 (2003), 89–97.

Dobbels, D., and Rabant, C. "The Missing Gesture: An Interview with Hubert Godard." *Writings on Dance: The French Issue* no. 15 (Winter 1996): 38–47.

Dodds, Sherril. "Televisualised." *Dance Theatre Journal* 13, no. 4 (1997): 44–47.

———. *Dance On Screen: Genres and Media from Hollywood to Experimental Art*. Houndmills, Basingstoke, Hampshire: Palgrave, 2001.

Donald, James. "Jazz Modernism and Film Art: Dudley Murphy and *Ballet mécanique*." *MODERNISM/Modernity* 16, no. 1 (2009): 25–49.

Dulac, Germaine. "Aesthetics, Obstacles, Integral *Cinégraphie*." In *French Film Theory and Criticism Vol.1 1907–1929*, trans. Stuart Liebman, ed. Richard Abel, 389–97. Princeton: Princeton University Press, 1988.

Duncan, Isadora. *My Life*. London: Victor Gollancz, 1928.

Dyer, Richard. "Entertainment and Utopia." In Nichols (1985), 220–32.

———. *Heavenly Bodies*. London: BFI and Macmillan, 1986.

———. "*A Star is Born* and the Construction of Authenticity." In *Stardom: Industry of Desire*, ed. Christine Gledhill, 132–40. London: Routledge, 1991.

Dyer, R., and Mueller, J. "Two Analyses of 'Dancing in the Dark' (*The Bandwagon*, 1953)." In Carter (1998), 288–93.

Eisele, Harro. "Recorded and Yet Moving Pictures." *Ballett International*, no. 8 (1990): 15–16.

Eisenstein, Sergei. *Film Form: Essays in Film Theory*, ed. and trans. Jay Leyda. San Diego: Harcourt, 1949.

Epstein, Jean. "Magnification and Other Writings," trans. Stuart Liebman. *October* no. 3 (Spring, 1977): 9–25.

Fernandes, Ciane. *Bausch and the Wuppertal Dance Theater: The Aesthetics of Repetition and Transformation.* New York: Peter Lang, 2005.

Fetterman, William. "Merce Cunningham and John Cage: Choreographic Cross-currents." *Choreography and Dance* 4, no. 3 (1997): 59–78.

Feuer, Jane. *The Hollywood Musical*, 2nd Ed. Bloomington: Indiana University Press, 1993.

Fildes, S., and McPherson, K. editors. *Opensource [Videodance] Symposium* (Nairnshire, Scotland: Goat Media, 2007).

———. *Opensource [Videodance] Symposium 2007* (Nairnshire, Scotland: Goat Media, 2009).

Filmdance Festival program (New York: The Experimental Intermedia Foundation, 1983).

Fischer, Lucy. *Shot/Countershot: Film Tradition and Women's Cinema.* Princeton: Princeton University Press, 1989.

Foster, Susan Leigh. *Reading Dancing: Bodies and Subjects in Contemporary American Dance.* Berkeley: University of California Press, 1986.

——— editor. *Corporealities.* London: Routledge, 1996a.

———. *Choreography and Narrative: Ballet's Staging of Story and Desire.* Bloomington: Indiana University Press, 1996b.

———. "Choreographing Empathy." *Topoi* 24 (2005): 81–89.

———. "Dance Theory?" In *Teaching Dance Studies*, ed. Judith Chazin-Bennahum, 19–33. New York: Routledge, 2005.

Franko, Mark. *Dancing Modernism/Performing Politics.* Indianapolis: Indiana University Press, 1995.

———. "Aesthetic Agencies in Flux: Talley Beatty, Maya Deren and the Modern Dance Tradition in *Study in Choreography for Camera*." In Nichols (2001), 131–49.

Frisby, David. *Fragments of Modernity: Theories of Modernity in the Work of Simmel, Kracauer and Benjamin.* Cambridge: MIT Press, 1986.

Fuller, Loïe. *Fifteen Years of a Dancer's Life.* New York: Dance Horizons, 1913.

Garafola, Lynn. "Dance, Film, and the Ballets Russes." *Dance Research* 16, no. 1 (1998): 3–25.

Garelick, Rhonda K. "Electric Salome: The Mechanical Dances of Loie Fuller." In *Rising Star: Dandyism, Gender, and Performance in the Fin de Siècle.* Princeton: Princeton University Press, 1998.

———. *Electric Salome: Loie Fuller's Performance of Modernism.* Princeton: Princeton University Press, 2007.

Geller, Theresa L. "The Personal Cinema of Maya Deren: *Meshes of the Afternoon* and its Critical Reception in the History of the Avant-garde." *Biography* 29, no.1 (2006): 140–58.

Genné, Beth. "Dancin' in the Rain: Gene Kelly's Musical Films." In Mitoma (2002), 71–77.

Gish, L., and Pinchot, A. *The Movies, Mr Griffith, and Me.* New Jersey: Prentice-Hall, 1969.

Godard, Hubert. "Gesture and Its Perception," trans. Sally Gardner. *Writings on Dance* 22 (Summer 2003–2004): 57–61.

Goldberg, Marianne. "Trisha Brown, U.S. Dance, and the Visual Arts: Composing Structure." In Teicher (2002), 29–45.

Goodall, Jane. "Knowing What You're Doing." *The Performance Space Quarterly*, no. 14 (Winter 1997): 20–23.

———. *Performance and Evolution in the Age of Darwin: Out of the Natural Order.* London: Routledge, 2002.

Goodeve, Thryza Nichols. "Rainer Talking Pictures." *Art in America* 85, no. 7 (1997): 56–65.

Graham, Martha. *Blood Memory*. London: Macmillan, 1991.

Greenfield, Amy. "Filmdance: Space, Time and Energy." In *Filmdance Festival* program, 1–6. New York: The Experimental Intermedia Foundation, 1983.

Guido, Laurent. "Rhythmic Bodies/Movies: Dance As Attraction in Early Film Culture." In *The Cinema of Attractions Reloaded*, ed. Wanda Strauven, 140–56. Amsterdam: Amsterdam University Press, 2007.

Gunning, Tom. "The Cinema of Attractions." In *Early Cinema: Space, Frame, Narrative*, eds. T. Elsaesser with A. Barker, 54–60. London: BFI, 1990.

———. *D. W. Griffith and the Origins of American Narrative Cinema: The Early Years at Biograph*. Urbana: University of Illinois Press, 1991.

———. "Tracing the Individual Body: Photography, Detectives and Early Cinema." In Charney and Schwartz (1995), 15–45.

———. "Loïe Fuller and the Art of Motion." In *Camera Obscura, Camera Lucida*, eds. R. Allen and M. Turvey, 75–89. Amsterdam: Amsterdam University Press, 2003.

———. "Light, Motion, Cinema! The Heritage of Loie Fuller and Germaine Dulac." *Framework* 46, no. 1 (2005): 107–29.

Haller, Robert. "Amy Greenfield: Film, Dynamic Movement, and Transformation." In *Women's Experimental Cinema: Critical Frameworks*, ed. Robin Blaetz, 152–66. Durham: Duke University Press, 2007.

Hansen, Miriam. "Benjamin, Cinema and Experience: 'The Blue Flower in the Land of Technology'." *New German Critique*, no. 40 (Winter 1987): 179–224.

———. *Babel and Babylon: Spectatorship in American Silent Film*. Cambridge: Harvard University Press, 1991.

Hansen, Miriam Bratu. "Introduction." In Kracauer (1997), vii–xiv.

Haslam, Wendy. "Maya Deren: The High Priestess of Experimental Cinema." Online. Available: www.sensesofcinema.com/contents/directors/02/deren.html. December 30, 2008.

Heath, Stephen. *Questions of Cinema*. London: Macmillan Press, 1981.

Hewitt, Andrew. *Social Choreography*. Durham: Duke University Press, 2005.

Hoghe, Raimund. "The Theatre of Pina Bausch," trans. Stephen Tree. *The Drama Review: TDR* 24, no. 1 (1980): 63–74.

Houstoun, Wendy. Unpublished interview with the author, February, 1999.

Jackson, Renata. "The Modernist Poetics of Maya Deren." In Nichols (2001), 47–76.

———. *The Modernist Aesthetics and Experimental Film Practice of Maya Deren (1917–1961)*. Lewiston, New York: The Edwin Meller Press, 2002.

Jaques-Dalcroze, Emile. *Rhythm, Music and Education*, trans. Harold F. Rubenstein. London: The Dalcroze Society, 1973.

Jeong, Ok Hee. "Reflections on Maya Deren's Forgotten Film, *The Very Eye of Night*." *Dance Chronicle*, 32, no. 3 (2009): 412–441.

Jordan, S., and Allen, D. editors. *Parallel Lines*. London: John Libbey and Co., 1993.

Jowitt, Deborah. *Time and the Dancing Image*. Berkeley: University of California Press, 1988.

Judovitz, Dalia. "Dada Cinema: At the Limits of Modernity." *Art & Text*, no. 34 (Spring 1989): 46–63.

Kendall, Elizabeth. *Where She Danced*. New York: Alfred A. Knopf, 1979.

Kendrick, Walter. "Dancing in the Dark." *Salmagundi*, no. 118–19 (Spring–Summer 1998): 16–28.

Kermode, Frank. "Poet and Dancer before Diaghilev." In Copeland and Cohen (1983), 145–60.

Kern, Stephen. *The Culture of Time and Space, 1880–1918*. Boston: Harvard University Press, 1983.

Koch, Gertrud. "Béla Balázs: The Physiognomy of Things." *New German Critique*, no. 40 (Winter 1987): 167–78.

———. "Face and Mass: Towards an Aesthetic of the Cross-Cut in Film." *New German Critique* no. 95 (Spring/Summer 2005): 139–48.

Koritz, Amy. *Gendering Bodies/Performing Art: Dance and Literature in Early Twentieth-Century British Culture*. Ann Arbor: The University of Michigan Press, 1995.

Kostelanetz, Richard. *Merce Cunningham: Dancing in Space and Time*. Chicago: A Cappella Books, 1992.

Kouvaros, George. "Where Does It Happen? The Place of Performance in the Work of John Cassavetes." *Screen* 39, no. 3 (1998): 244–58.

Kracauer, Siegfried. *Theory of Film: The Redemption of Physical Reality*. Princeton: Princeton University Press, 1997.

Lambert, Carrie. "'Moving Still' Mediating Yvonne Rainer's *Trio A*." *October*, no. 89 (1999): 87–112.

———. "On Being Moved: Rainer and the Aesthetics of Empathy." In Sachs (2003), 41–63.

Lambert-Beatty, Carrie. *Being Watched: Yvonne Rainer and the 1960s*. Cambridge: The MIT Press, 2008.

Lehmann, A. G. *The Symbolist Aesthetic in France 1885–1895*. Oxford: Basil Blackwell, 1950.

Lepecki, A., and Banes, S. *The Senses in Performance*. New York: Routledge, 2007.

Levinas, Emmanuel. *Totality and Infinity: An Essay on Exteriority*, trans. Alphonso Lingis. Netherlands: Kluwer Academic Publishers, 1991.

Lista, Giovanni. *Loïe Fuller: Danseuse de la Belle Époque*. Paris: Hermann Danse, 2007.

Louppe, Laurence. "Corporeal Sources: A Journey through the Work of Trisha Brown." *Writings on Dance: The French Issue* no. 15 (Winter 1996a): 6–11.

———. "Singular, Moving Geographies: An Interview with Hubert Godard." *Writings on Dance: The French Issue*, no. 15 (Winter 1996b): 12–21.

Lyotard, Jean-François. "The Unconscious As Mise-en-Scène." In *Performance in Post-Modern Culture*, eds. M. Benamou and C. Caramello, 87–98. Madison: Coda Press, 1977.

———. "Acinema." *Wide Angle* 2, no. 3 (1978): 53–59.

———. "Gesture and Commentary." *Iyyun, The Jerusalem Philosophical Quarterly* 42, no. 1 (1993): 37–48.

McCarthur, Benjamin. *Actors and American Culture, 1880–1920*. Philadelphia: Temple University Press, 1984.

McCarren, Felicia. "The 'Symptomatic Act' Circa 1900: Hysteria, Hypnosis, Electricity, Dance." *Critical Inquiry* no. 21 (Summer 1995a): 748–74.

———. "Stéphane Mallarmé, Loïe Fuller, and the Theater of Femininity." In *Bodies of the Text*, eds. E. W. Goellner and J. S. Murphy, 217–30. New Brunswick: Rutgers University Press, 1995b.

———. *Dance Pathologies: Performance, Poetics, Medicine*. California: Stanford University Press, 1998.

———. *Dancing Machines: Choreographies of the Age of Mechanical Reproduction*. California: Stanford University Press, 2003.

McClure, William. "Beheaded." *The Performance Space Quarterly*, no. 14 (Winter 1997): 24–26.

McLean, Adrienne. "Feeling and the Filmed Body: Judy Garland and the Kinesics of Suffering." *Film Quarterly* 55, no. 3 (2002): 2–15.

———. *Being Rita Hayworth: Labor, Identity, and Hollywood Stardom*. New Brunswick, New Jersey: Rutgers University Press, 2004.

———. *Dying Swans and Madmen: Ballet, the Body and Narrative Cinema*. New Brunswick, New Jersey: Rutgers University Press, 2008.

McPherson, Katrina. *Making Video Dance*. London: Routledge, 2006.

MacDonald, Scott. "Nathanial Dorsky and Larry Jordan on Stan Brakhage, Maya Deren, Joseph Cornell, and Bruce Conner." *Quarterly Review of Film and Video* 24, no.1 (2007): 1–10.

Macey, David. "Obituary: Jean-François Lyotard 1924–1998." *Radical Philosophy: A Journal of Socialist and Feminist Philosophy*, September/October (1990): 53–55.

Maletic, Vera. "Videodance—Technology—Attitude Shift." *Dance Research Journal* 19, no. 2 (1987/88): 3–7.

Mallarmé, Stéphane. *Selected Prose Poems, Essays and Letters*, trans. Bradford Cook. Baltimore: John Hopkins University Press, 1956.

———. *Mallarmé in Prose*, ed. Mary Ann Caws, trans. Rosemary Lloyd. New York: New Directions Books, 2001.

Mangolte, Babette. "My History (The Intractable)." *October*, no. 86 (1998): 83–106.

———. "On the Making of *Water Motor*, a Dance by Trisha Brown Filmed by Babette Mangolte." Unpublished paper, September 2003.

Manning, Erin. *Politics of Touch: Sense, Movement, Sovereignty*. Minneapolis: University of Minnesota Press, 2007.

——— *Relationscapes: Movement, Art, Philosophy*. Cambridge, Massachusetts: The MIT Press, 2009.

Marks, Laura. *The Skin of the Film: Intercultural Cinema, Embodiment and the Senses*. Durham: Duke University Press, 2000.

———. *Touch: Sensuous Theory and Multisensory Media*. Minneapolis: University of Minnesota Press, 2002.

Martin, John. *The Modern Dance*. New York: Dance Horizons, 1972.

———. "Dance As a Means of Communication." In Copeland and Cohen (1983), 22–23.

Massumi, Brian. "The Autonomy of Affect." In *Deleuze: A Critical Reader*, ed. Paul Patton, 217–39. Oxford: Blackwell Publishers, 1996.

Maynard, Olga. *American Modern Dancer: The Pioneers*. Boston, Toronto: Little, Brown and Company, 1965.

Mekas, Jonas. "A Few Notes on Maya Deren." In *Inverted Odysseys: Claude Cahun, Maya Deren and Cindy Sherman*, ed. Shelley Rice, 127–32. Boston: MIT Press, 1999.

Merwin, Ted. "Loïe Fuller's Influence on F. T. Marinetti's Futurist Dance." *Dance Chronicle* 21 no. 1 (1998): 73–92.

Mester, Terri A. *Movement and Modernism: Yeats, Eliot, Lawrence, Williams and Early-Twentieth Century Dance*. Fayetteville: The University of Arkansas Press, 1997.

Michelson, Annette. "Film and Radical Aspiration." In *Film Theory and Criticism*, eds. G. Mast and M. Cohen, 617–35. New York: Oxford University Press, 1979.

———. "Poetics and Savage Thought." In Nichols (2001), 21–45.

Mitoma, Judy editor. *Envisioning Dance on Film and Video*. New York: Routledge, 2002.

Monaco, James. *How to Read a Film*. New York: Oxford University Press, 1981.

Mordden, Ethan. *The Hollywood Musical*. New York: St. Martin's Press, 1981.

———. *Movie Star: A Look at the Women Who Made Hollywood*. New York: St. Martin's Press, 1983.

Morris, Bob. "35mm Motions." *Film Comment* 25, no. 2 (1989): 47–49.

Mueller, John. "Fred Astaire and the Integrated Musical." *Cinema Journal* 24, no. 1 (1984): 28–40.

Nagrin, Daniel. "Nine Points on Making Your Own Dance Video." *Dance Theatre Journal* 6, no. 1 (1988): 33–36.

Naremore, James. *Acting in the Cinema*. Berkeley: University of California Press, 1988.

Nichols, Bill editor. *Movies and Methods Volume II*. Berkeley: University of California Press, 1985.

————— editor. *Maya Deren and the American Avant-Garde*. Berkeley: University of California Press, 2001.

Noland, C., and Ness, S. editors. *Migrations of Gesture*. Minneapolis: University of Minnesota Press, 2008.

Noys, Benjamin. "Gestural Cinema?: Giorgio Agamben on Film." Online. Available: http://www.film-philosophy.com/vol8-2004/n22noys. December 20, 2008.

Parkinson, David. "Dancing in the Streets." *Sight and Sound* 3, no. 1 (1993): 31–33.

Patrick, Trevor. "Subtle Bodies." In *MAP Movement and Performance Symposium Papers*, ed. Erin Brannigan, 31–34. Canberra: Ausdance Inc., 1999.

Pattullo, Lauren. "Narrative and Spectacle in the Hollywood Musical: Contrasting the Choreography of Busby Berkely and Gene Kelly." *Research in Dance Education* 8, no. 1 (2007): 73–85.

Pearlman, Karen. *Cutting Rhythms: Shaping the Film Edit*. Amsterdam: Focal Press, 2009.

Pearson, Roberta E. *Eloquent Gestures: The Transformation of Performance Style in the Griffith Biograph Films*. Berkeley: University of California Press, 1992.

Phelan, Peggy. *Mourning Sex: Performing Public Memories*. London: Routledge, 1997.

—————. "'I Never See You As You Are': Invitations and Displacements in Dance Writing." In *Dancing Desires: Choreographing Sexualities on and off the Stage*, ed. Jane C. Desmond, 415–22. Madison: The University of Wisconsin Press, 2001.

Portanova, Stamatia, and Antonin De Bemels. "Stroboscopic Trilogy." *Inflexions* no. 2 (2008). Online. Available: www.inflexions.org. July 9, 2009.

Pramaggiore, Maria. "Performance and Persona in the US Avant-Garde: The Case of Maya Deren." *Cinema Journal* 36, no. 2 (1997): 17–40.

Preston-Dunlop, Valerie editor. *Dance Words*. Switzerland: Harwood Academic Publishers, 1995.

Pridden, Deirdre. *The Art of Dance in French Literature*. London: Adam & Charles Black, 1952.

Pritchard, Jane. "Movement on the Silent Screen." *Dance Theatre Journal* 12, no. 3 (1996): 26–30.

Rabinbach, Anson. *The Human Motor: Energy, Fatigue, and the Origins of Modernity*. Berkeley: University of California Press, 1990.

Rabinovitz, Lauren. *Point of Resistance: Women, Power and Politics in the New York Avant-Garde Cinema, 1943–71*. Urbana: University of Illinois Press, 1991.

Rainer, Yvonne. "A Quasi Survey of Some 'Minimalist' Tendencies in the Quantitatively Minimal Dance Activity Amidst the Plethora, or an Analysis of *Trio A*." In Copeland and Cohen (1983), 325–32.

—————. "'No' to Spectacle...." In Carter (1998), 35.

—————. "Engineering Calamity: Trisha Brown." *Writings on Dance: Constellations of Things*, no. 18–19 (Winter 1999a): 166–79.

————— editor. *A Woman Who...Essays, Interviews, Scripts*. Baltimore: The Johns Hopkins University Press, 1999b.

—————. "A Fond Memoir of Sundry Reflections on a Friend and Her Art." In Teicher 2002, 47–53.

—————. *Feelings Are Facts: A Life*. Cambridge: MIT Press, 2006.

Rajchman, John. "Jean-François Lyotard's Underground Aesthetics." *October* 86 (1998): 3–18.

Ray, Man. "Emak Bakia." In *Close Up 1927–1933: Cinema and Modernism*, eds. J. Donald, A. Friedberg, and L. Marcus, 43–48. Princeton: Princeton University Press, 1998.

Reynolds, Dee. "The Dancer As Woman: Loïe Fuller and Stéphane Mallarmé." In *Impressions of French Modernity*, ed. Richard Hobbs, 155–72. Manchester: Manchester University Press, 1998.

————. *Rhythmic Subjects*. Alton, Hampshire: Dance Books, 2007.

Rogers, Ginger. *Ginger: My Story*. London: Headline, 1991.

Rosenberg, Douglas. "Video Space: A Site for Choreography." *Leonardo* 33, no. 4 (2000): 275–80.

Rosenblatt, Nina Lara. "Photogenic Neurasthenia: On Mass and Medium in the 1920s." *October* 86 (1998): 47–62.

Rosiny, Claudia. "Film Review: The Lament of the Empress." *Ballett International*, no. 6–7 (1990): 74.

————. *Videotanz: Panorama einer intermedialen Kunstforum*. Zurich: Chronos Verlag, 1999.

Rothfield, Philipa. "Performing Sexuality, The Scintillations of Movement." In *Performing Sexualities*, ed. Michelle Boulous Walker, 57–66. Brisbane: Institute of Modern Art, 1994.

Rubidge, Sarah. "Dancelines 2." *Dance Theatre Journal* 6, no. 1 (1988): 6–9.

Russell, Catherine. "Ecstatic Ethnography: Maya Deren and the Filming of Possession Rituals." In *Rites of Realism: Essays on Corporeal Cinema*, ed. Ivone Margulies, 270–93. Durham: Duke University Press, 2003.

Ruyter, Nancy Lee Chalfa. *Reformers and Visionaries: The Americanization of the Art of Dance*. New York: Dance Horizons, 1979.

————. *The Cultivation of Mind and Body in Nineteenth Century American Delsartism*. Connecticut: Greenwood Press, 1999.

Sachs, Sid editor. *Yvonne Rainer: Radical Juxtapositions 1961–2002*. Philadelphia: The University of the Arts, 2003.

Sagolla, Lisa Jo. "The Influence of Modern Dance on American Musical Theatre Choreography of the 1940s." In Overby and Humphrey 1989, 47–68.

Sanchez-Colberg, Ana. "Reflections on Meaning and Making in Pina Bausch's *The Lament of the Empress*." In Jordan and Allen (1993), 217–34.

Satin, Lesley. "Movement and the Body in Maya Deren's Meshes of the Afternoon." *Women and Performance* 6, no. 2 (1993): 41–56.

Schmidt, Jochen. "Exploitation or Symbiosis." *Ballett International*, no. 1 (1991): 97–99.

Schwartz, Hillel. "Torque: The New Kinaesthetic of the Twentieth Century." In *Incorporations*, eds. J. Crary and S. Kwinter, 71–127. New York: Zone, 1992.

Servos, Norbert. *Pina Bausch Dance Theatre*. Munich: K. Keiser, 2008.

Sharp, W., and Bear, L. "The Performer As Persona: An Interview with Yvonne Rainer." *Avalanche* no. 5 (Summer 1972): 46–59.

Shaviro, Steven. *The Cinematic Body*. Minneapolis: University of Minnesota Press, 1993.

Shawn, Ted. *Every Little Movement*. New York: Dance Horizons, 1974.

————. *One Thousand and One Night Stands*, with Gray Poole. New York: Da Capo Press, 1979.

————. *Ruth St. Denis—Pioneer & Prophet, Being A History of Her Cycle of Oriental Dances. Volume I—The Text*. Marton Press, 2009.

Simondson, Helen. "Stranger in a Strange Land." In *Is Technology the Future for Dance?* ed. Hilary Trotter, 146–49. Canberra: Ausdance, 1996.

Singer, Ben. "Modernity, Hyperstimulus, and the Rise of Pop Sensationalism." In Charney and Shwartz (1995), 72–99.

————. "Manhattan Nickelodeons: New Data on Audiences and Exhibitors." In *The Silent Cinema Reader*, eds. Lee Grieveson and Peter Krämer, 119–34. London: Routledge, 2004.

Sitney, P. Adams editor. *The Film Culture Reader*. New York: Prager Publishers Inc., 1971.

————. *Visionary Film: The American Avant-Garde*. New York: Oxford University Press, 1979.

Smyth, Mary M. "Kinaesthetic Communication in Dance." *Dance Research Journal* 16, no. 2 (1984): 19–22.

Sobchack, Vivian. *Carnal Thought: Embodiment and Moving Image Culture*. Berkeley: University of California Press, 2004.

————— "What My Fingers Knew: The Cinesthetic Subject. Or Vision in the Flesh." Online. Available: www.sensesofcinema.com/contents/00/5/fingers.html. December 30, 2008.

Sommer, Sally. "Loïe Fuller." *The Drama Review* 19, no. 1 (1975): 53–67.

Sorell, Walter. *The Dance Through the Ages*. London: Thames and Hudson, 1967.

Sparshott, Francis. *A Measured Pace: Toward a Philosophical Understanding of the Arts of Dance*. Toronto: University of Toronto Press, 1995.

Starr, Frances. *Changes: Notes on Choreography*. New York: Something Else Press, 1969.

Stearns, M., and Stearns J. *Jazz Dance: The Story of American Vernacular Dance*. New York: Da Capo Press, 1994.

Stern, Lesley. "As Long As This Life Lasts," *Photofile* (Winter 1987): 15–19.

—————. "Acting out of Character: *The King of Comedy* As Histrionic Text." In Stern and Kouvaros 1995, 277–305.

—————. "Paths that Wind through the Thicket of Things." *Critical Inquiry* 28, no. 1 (2001): 317–54.

—————. "Putting on a Show, or the Ghostliness of Gesture." Online. Available: http://www.sensesofcinema.com/contents/02/21/sd_stern.html. October 1, 2005.

Stern, L., and Kouvaros, G. editors. *Falling for You: Essays on Cinema and Performance*. Sydney: Power Publications, 1999.

Studlar, Gaylan. "Valentino, 'Optic Intoxication,' and Dance Madness." In Cohan and Hark 1993, 23–45.

—————. "Out Salomeing Salome: Dance, the New Woman, and Fan Magazine Orientalism." In *Visions of the East*, ed. Matthew Berstein and Gaylan Studlar, 99–129. New Brunswick, New Jersey: Rutgers University Press, 1997.

Sulcas, Roslyn. "Forsythe and Film: Habits of Seeing." In Mitoma 2002, 95–101.

Swender, Rebecca. "The Problem of the Divo: New Models for Analyzing Silent-Film Performance." *Journal of Film and Video* 58, no. 1–2 (2006): 7–20.

Teicher, Hendel. *Trisha Brown: Dance and Art in Dialogue, 1961–2001*. Cambridge: MIT Press, 2002.

Terry, Walter. *Miss Ruth: The "More Living Life" of Ruth St. Denis*. New York: Dodd, Mead & Co., 1969.

—————. *Ted Shawn: Father of American Dance*. New York: The Dial Press, 1976.

Thomas, Helen. *Dance Modernity and Culture*. London: Routledge, 1995.

Todd, Arthur. "From Chaplin to Kelly: The Dance on Film." *Theatre Arts* XXXV no. 8 (1951): 50–91.

Turim, Maureen. "Gentlemen Consume Blondes." In *Issues in Feminist Film Criticism*, ed. Patricia Erens, 101–11. Bloomington: Indiana University Press, 1993.

—————. "The Ethics of Form: Structure and Gender in Maya Deren's Challenge to the Cinema." In Nichols (2001), 77–102.

—————. "The Violence of Desire in Avant-Garde Film." In *Women and Experimental Filmmaking*, eds. J. Petrolle and V. Wright Wexman, 71–90. Urbana: University of Illinois Press, 2005.

Vaccarino, Elisa. *La Musa dello schermo freddo*. Genova: Kosta and Nolan, 1996.

—————. "Dance and Video." *Ballett International* no. 8–9 (1997): 59.

Valéry, Paul. "Philosophy of the Dance." In *The Collected Works of Paul Valéry, Volume 13*, ed. Jackson Mathews, trans. Ralph Manheim, 197–211. London: Routledge and Kegan Paul, 1964.

—————. "Dance and the Soul." In *Selected Writings*, 184–98. New York: New Directions, 1950.

Valis Hill, Constance. *Brotherhood in Rhythm: The Jazz Tap Dancing of the Nicholas Brothers*. New York: Oxford University Press, 2000.

Walker, Julia A. "'In the Grip of an Obsession': Delsarte and the Quest for Self-Possession in *The Cabinet of Dr. Caligari*." *Theatre Journal* 58 (2006): 617–31.

———. *Expressionism and Modernism in American Theatre: Bodies, Voices, Words*. New York: Cambridge University Press, 2005.

Wilcox, Emily. "Dance as L'intervention: Health and Aesthetics of Experience in French Contemporary Dance." *Body & Society* 11, no. 4 (2005): 109–39.

Wollen, P., and Allan, Vicky. "A–Z of Cinema: D-Dance." *Sight and Sound* 6, no. 9 (1996): 28–31.

Wollen, Peter. *Singin' in the Rain*. London: BFI, 1992.

———. "Brooks and the Bob." *Sight and Sound* 4, no. 2 (1994): 22–25.

Wood, Catherine. *Yvonne Rainer: The Mind Is a Muscle*. London: Afterfall Books, 2007.

Yampolsky, Mikhail. "Mask Face and Machine Face." *The Drama Review* 38, no. 3 (1994): 60–74.

Index

Lightning Source UK Ltd.
Milton Keynes UK
UKOW02f2041061114

241193UK00002B/163/P